The Power of

Legitimacy

Among Nations

THE POWER OF
LEGITIMACY
AMONG NATIONS

Thomas M. Franck

New York   Oxford
OXFORD UNIVERSITY PRESS
1990

Oxford University Press

Oxford   New York   Toronto
Delhi   Bombay   Calcutta   Madras   Karachi
Petaling Jaya   Singapore   Hong Kong   Tokyo
Nairobi   Dar es Salaam   Cape Town
Melbourne   Auckland

and associated companies in
Berlin   Ibadan

Copyright © 1990 by Thomas M. Franck

Published by Oxford University Press, Inc.,
200 Madison Avenue, New York, New York 10016

Oxford is a registered trademark of Oxford University Press

Library of Congress Cataloging-in-Publication Data
Franck, Thomas M.
The power of legitimacy among nations / Thomas M. Franck.
p.   cm.   Includes biobliographical references.
ISBN 0-19-506178-0
1. Recognition (International law)   2. Legitimacy of governments.
3. International relations.   I. Title.
JX4044.F68   1990
341.26—dc20   89-70908

2 4 6 8 9 7 5 3 1
Printed in the United States of America
on acid-free paper

In profound admiration and enduring friendship this study is dedicated to *Judge Manfred Lachs*. His life and work demonstrate that the never-ending search for enlightenment can neither be diminished nor contained by the temporal metes and bounds of political fashion.

Acknowledgments

"I am so far from being ashamed of having looted any other old and new writers that I even avow that the great part of [this work] is either the result of my reading or of my relations with friends, excluding some . . . examples which have come within my own experience."

E. Nys*

It has been truly wondrous: three years in another place on the landscape of the mind, far from the madding headnotes and hoppers brimming with draft bills mewling to become laws. Three years to forage through the granary of our intellectual tradition, yahooing down the temple of reason's vistaed nave.

Such respite is a blessed necessity for scholars of international law, as also, I am told, for members of other contemplative orders in which professional self-doubt is an occupational hazard. For a time, those embers can be banked. But extinguished? Never.

Twenty years ago, when a teaching novice, I published *The Structure of Impartiality*. That done, I stopped worrying, let alone writing, about matters of teleology, preferring to concentrate on repairing the machine, tightening a bolt here and there. But the Big Questions will be put off only for a time, then their clamor rises above denial. Unattended things on the back burner have a tendency to scorch. The unpaid debt compounds. The account must be met.

* "Introduction" to A. Gentili, *De Legationibus Libri Tres* (G. Laing trans., quoting Jean Hotman (1552–1639)); *reprinted in* 2 *Classics of International Law* 22a (1924).

This, then, is my accounting, a highly personal search for meaning in my chosen field. Of necessity, the search has been solitary. But wonderful companions have provided nourishment along the way. The Filomen D'Agostino and Max E. Greenberg Research Fund of New York University School of Law facilitated two productive summers largely free of distraction. My colleagues, David Richards and Irene Brown, joined me in teaching an experimental seminar—Legitimacy and Justice in the International System—which served the invaluable function that well-positioned out-of-town tryouts afford the lucky playwright. The helpful comments of Professors Brown and Richards, as also the many ideas and sources to which they awakened me, immeasurably deepened my own understanding. So, too, did the dialogue with that extraordinary group of students.

Several other persons read all or parts of the manuscript at various stages of its gestation and helped, encouraged, provoked, and sustained my oft-flagging faith. Among them were Judge Manfred Lachs, Michael Sharpston, Professors Paul Chevigny, Ronald Dworkin, David Kennedy, Theodor Meron, Thomas Nagel, Alfred Rubin, Oscar Schachter, and Detlev Vagts. To each I am truly grateful, as I am, also, to my superb and devoted research assistants: Steven Hawkins, Lisa Landau, Michael Nelson, Laurie Oberembt, William Richter, and Scott Senecal. The final chapter of this book is based on an article, published elsewhere, which Mr. Hawkins and I wrote jointly. That experience of co-authorship with a particularly gifted student was another of the unqualified rewards of the teaching enterprise.

Finally—and this has become joyously trite in twenty-five years of collaboration—I celebrate the work of Rochelle Fenchel, my administrative assistant, who guided innumerable drafts through the computer maze, rounding up stray footnotes, questioning wayward form and substance and, generally, cheering me up and on at every season. To be constantly buoyed by her wisdom and spirit is, itself, fully worth the voyage.

T. M. F.

New York
February 1990

Contents

The Power of

Legitimacy

Among Nations

1

Prelude: Why a Quest

for Legitimacy?

the absence of any patent and obvious source of obligation . . .
deprives the international jurist of any manifest point at which
he can rest, and which he can regard as a satisfactory terminal
point beyond which there is no practical necessity to go.

Sir G. G. Fitzmaurice*

. . . fidelity is no natural virtue, and . . . promises have no
force, antecedent to human conventions.

D. Hume**

In the international system, rules usually are not enforced yet they
are mostly obeyed. Lacking support from a coercive power comparable to that which provides backing for the laws of a nation,
the rules of the international community nevertheless elicit much
compliance on the part of sovereign states. Why do powerful nations obey powerless rules? That is the subject of this excursion
into power: more precisely, the power which rules exert on states,
both the weak and, more remarkably, the strong.

A series of events connected with the role of the U.S. Navy in
protecting vessels in the Persian Gulf brings this question to life.
Early in 1988, the U.S. Defense Department became aware of a

---

* "The Foundations of the Authority of International Law and the Problem
of Enforcement," 19 *Mod. L. Rev.* 1, 10 (1956).

** "Of the Obligation of Promises," in *A Treatise of Human Nature* (bk. III,
sec. V), 568–78 (E. C. Mossner, ed., 1969).

ship approaching the Gulf with a load of Chinese-made Silkworm missiles en route to Iran. The Navy believed the delivery of these potent weapons would increase materially the danger to both protected and protecting U.S. ships and the Defense Department therefore, quite cogently, argued for permission to interdict the delivery. The State Department, however, countered that such a seizure on the high seas, under the universally recognized rules of war and neutrality, would constitute aggressive blockade tantamount to an act of war against Iran. The U.S., if it enforced a naval blockade, would lose its purchase on brokering peace as a neutral. In the event, the delivery ship with its cargo of missiles was allowed to pass. Deference to systemic rules had won out over tactical advantage in the internal struggle for control of U.S. policy.

Why should this have been so? In the minds of those who pride themselves on their hard-nosed realism—and they seem at all times and in all places to comprise a formidable group of advocates—this should not have happened. Obedience to rules, in the minds of these persons, is a sign of weakness. It is an unworthy abdication of the prerogatives and responsibilities of national power. A hard nose goes with a hard fist. Speaking of this "realist" form of advocacy, Hugo Grotius observed with despair some 350 years ago that there is "no lack of men" who make light of the international rule system "as if it were nothing but an empty name. On most men's lips are the words of Euphemus, quoted by Thucydides, that for a kind or a free city nothing is wrong that is to their advantage."[1]

Yet, in this Persian Gulf encounter, Washington chose to play by the rules. In microcosm, this focuses our subject, the puzzle we have begun to explore. In the absence of a world government and a global coercive power to enforce its laws, why did the U.S. leadership, despite its evident power to do as it wished, opt to forgo the obvious short-term strategic benefits of seizing the Silkworms? Why did pre-eminent American power defer to the rules of the sanctionless system? What was it about the rules of neutrality and belligerency which exerted so strong a compliance pull on policymakers?

This is a different question from a more familiar one which

asks why *citizens* obey the law. Yet the line of inquiry that ener-
gizes the legal philosophers in their speculations about societies of
natural persons, as opposed to states, is not so different as to justify
the alienation of the two branches—the national and international—of legal philosophy. There are differences between law's
place in national society and the place of rules in the society of
nations, but those differences do not justify the closing of the
international rule system to philosophical inquiry aided by the
insights developed by the study of national and sub-national communities. On the contrary, the differences create a tantalizing intellectual symbiosis.

Apparently, however, it has not been tantalizing enough. Teleology—the study of ends or ultimate causes—is a major preoccupa-
tion of scholars of national legal systems, and social scientists
working in such fields as sociology, labor relations, politics, and
anthropology. Treating law as a phenomenon worthy of study,
they seek to understand the root causes of patterned behavior.
Why—literally: to what end?—are laws obeyed? Why is governance (dominion) accepted? "Do existing conventions deserve our
allegiance? If not, what set of conventions does?"[2] These questions
are asked both by "value-free" inquirers seeking only to test their
latest hypothesis of social organization, and, also, by many others,
with various agendas, including ideologues of right or left, the
first perhaps trying to buttress sacred and secular institutions of
governance, the second possibly preparing the conceptual path to
revolution by studying the mythological and class-based origins of
social stasis.

Yet, oddly, almost no one, nowadays, seems to ask this sort
of fundamental teleological question of the *international* system.
Typically, philosophers of law, with a few notable exceptions such
as H. L. A. Hart and Oscar Schachter, treat international law as a
"no go" area.[3] While there is a literature on the formal sources of
international law—treaties, custom, etc.—this is not the same as
an examination into the *reasons* why rules do, or do not, obligate.
The latter question is largely shunned. Yet, this has not always
been the case. When both the national and international systems
of dominance, governance, or order were based on similar divine

or natural-order rationales, such questions were addressed to both national and international systems, if only because, in the two fields of inquiry, the respective phenomena of social behavior could not be separated neatly. The same "natural" or divine validation which was believed to authorize national governance also validated the rules of interstate behavior. God's writ, or the natural order of things, was no respecter of the puny lines drawn by men on maps.

That unity between the laws of God and of man, of the international system and of nations, ended with the advent of legal positivism; indeed, with the late writings of Hugo Grotius in the seventeenth century. Since the mid-nineteenth century—and certainly since the advent of the twentieth—legal philosophy has focused almost exclusively on national legal systems. The teleological question, while ever more a subject of inquiry and discourse among students of British, French, or American jurisprudence, has seemed to fade into irrelevance in the international arena. In the words of W. Michael Reisman, one of the few internationalists to have persisted in the teleological quest, for "almost a century now, theoretical interest has been sporadic and slight."[4] This, quite simply, may be because international laws are thought *not* to be obeyed and the governance of international institutions and their norms *not* to be accepted. It is fashionable now, as in Thucydides' time, to see these as mere paper-fictions and they seem no more formidable for being embossed in such grand but unrealistic documents as the Charter of the United Nations, not to mention the self-serving books by professors of international law attempting to justify their salaries and prerogatives at law schools. International "law" is thus exposed as a quirky modern consequence of the disparity in salary scales between the law school and departments of political science or philosophy. Many modern social scientists, moreover, quite simply do not even see any international system, let alone an international pattern of deference to systemic norms, worth bothering about. Who would bother to inquire as to *why* a system of rules is obeyed when there is little evidence either of a system or of obedience? It may strike some as odd, but it is probably demonstrable that there is even more of a fashion for "hard-nosed realism" among academics, and especially among those specializing in the international rule system, than in the foreign ministries.

Such expression of cynicism by the theorists, twenty-four hundred years after Thucydides, should not be altogether surprising. Yet its periodic recurrence is unfortunate at several levels. At the level of the intellectual agenda, nowadays, when these sorts of teleologically based questions are asked of national legal systems, they have produced important speculative insights and social hypotheses which, in turn, help to generate grand socio-political and jurisprudential philosophy or, at least, useful insights into the workings of a social order. If the questions are not answered once and for all, the quest nevertheless produces important spin-offs, rather like a full-throttled space program. Even its unsatisfying discoveries, in due course, can give rise to passionate, or, in any event, intellectually engaging controversy in which the social "is" and the social "ought" (actual present, and alternative contingent, realities) interact to set minds thinking about how and why things are, and how they might or ought to be. Sociological jurisprudence, for example, by focusing on the decisions of judges as *the* "source" of law, has not quieted the doubters, but it has helped spotlight and de-mystify the role of judges and made the process of judicial selection more consciously and politically alert. In sharp contrast, international law—because such "how" and "why" questions are rarely asked—tends instead to generate dull, rather absurdly defensive, rule description and even more plodding prescription, as if the grand issues of domination, communication, obedience, and transformation lie forever beyond the attention span of serious international scholars. The rules are recited, new rules are proposed, but few ask why these, or any other rules are, or are not, or should or should not be, obeyed. Perhaps this is because the scholars assume the questions redundant: since even the traditional international rules are not enforced, alternative new norms similarly would be ignored. This, after all, is *international* law. Disobedience is thought—albeit wrongly—to be the prevalent practice, and, thus, the study of norms—either the is *or* the ought of a normative prescription—is irrelevant. States do as states do. That, to paraphrase

Keats, is all we know and all we need to know. The subject is dismissed as unproductive.

Any contemporary philosophy of international normativity therefore tends to appear in print as, at most, the scraggly tail on elegant, fully developed theories intended to explain the dynamics of *national* legal phenomena. This is not only unfortunate but quite unnecessary because the jurisprudential inquests directed to the role of law in national communities provide ready tools for fruitful inquiry into the international system. With little adumbration and adaption, these mature philosophical inquiries could do much more to further an examination of the international arena than has been asked of them. Some of the basic notions, in particular, seem applicable to an understanding of the nature, purposes, and workings of the international arena. For example, in the search for a teleology of organized authority, political and social philosophers from Aristotle[5] to Ronald Dworkin[6] have advanced sophisticated concepts of *polis*, the civil society or community, in which the citizen's affiliation, as a matter of status, engenders reciprocal rights and duties which, in turn, endow governance with what amounts to an architectural construct of socially pooled power. Surely that says something to which the student of the international system might profitably pay heed. Teleologically speaking, one might hypothesize that nations obey rules of the community of states because they thereby manifest their membership in that community, which, in turn, validates their statehood. This is not a hypothesis, however, which much engages the attention of international legal scholars in the last years of the twentieth century. Nor is there much current interest in trying to apply the insights of Hobbes, who advanced a comparable concept of pooled, or delegated, power but did so by means of the formalized fiction of the *social compact*: an imagined contract between persons in the state of nature intends to provide the parties with such benefits as security of person and property.[7] John Locke, John Rawls, and Paul Ricoeur[8] have characterized the phenomenon of social assent to law primarily in various illustrative or imaginative quasi-contractarian and bargaining metaphors which also might be of more than passing interest if applied to relations between states.

This philosophical transference could be assayed without first having to satisfy the inquirer that the international system of law is like national legal systems. It could be done without empirical evidence that the rules of the international system are usually obeyed, or that there is a community of states. Instead, it is only necessary to posit *some* instances of state behavior that accord with normative behavioral constraints and ask why those constraints should weigh in the policy decisions of governments in the absence of an effective global sovereign. Such a modest and easily found fragmentary data base—the Persian Gulf encounter is one instance—is the only requisite for speculative inquiry as to why states obey rules. It is not necessary to the inquiry that all, or even most, rules be obeyed.

Sometimes these great teleological issues are actually stumbled upon by those who traverse the world stage. Yet, usually, they evince no awareness that there are signposts of theory available to help mark and illumine the way, so the road is not taken. For example, at a speech at Dartmouth College on May 10, 1988, U.N. Secretary-General Perez de Cuellar characterized as an unfortunate "difficulty" in U.S.-U.N. relations the tendency of Americans to "see their country's membership in an international organization, as a limitation of the full exercise of its sovereignty." This would be less a problem, he suggested, if these Americans could see the U.N. through the eyes of other member states. For the great majority of members, he said, "joining the United Nations was the final confirmation of independence, nationhood, and sovereignty."[9] Implicit in this is the thought that Americans were misunderstanding the meaning of membership in the Organization, which enhances, rather than diminishes, each member's status. The misunderstanding, however, may also be that of the Secretary-General in equating three very different teleological concepts: independence, nationhood, and sovereignty. Membership in the U.N., if taken seriously, *is* a limitation on a nation's sovereignty—that is what membership is *for*: to limit unilateralism—although it may also sometimes enhance the member's independence and it certainly confirms its statehood. What makes this confusion serious is that it only encourages the illusion, shared by Americans and many others, that it is possible to have the benefits of membership in the community without also accepting the limitations imposed by the social compact establishing it. The U.N. compact, while it does indeed confirm states' statehood, their entitlement to equal rights as members—including a degree of independence—also simultaneously limits their sovereignty, their right to behave as if in a state of nature. To get the problem analyzed correctly, however, would require a grounding in sociologically and anthropologically based contractarian jurisprudence, or the use of some other teleologically honed analytical tools. Unfortunately, such a jurisprudential teleology is not, nowadays, prominent in the study of international rules and organizations.

The internationalist's options for conceptual borrowing, moreover, certainly are not limited to the various brands of *polis* theory, or contractarianism. For one, there is the quite formidable line of analysis which eschews the *polis*, emphasizing, instead, an empirically demonstrable *power hierarchy*. Some tribal status mythology and the concept of divine right of rulers starts here.[10] Jeremy Bentham led the stripping away of law's mysticism and its pretension to divine or "natural" origins, substituting the majesty of the state's law-making and adjudicating institutions.[11] This accorded with the rise of nationalism and suggested a positivistic "law of nations" made and enforced by sovereign states. John Austin, writing at the height of an era of de-mystifying positivism, defined law as the enforced command of a sovereign to a subject,[12] a perspective on social organization not unrelated to that adopted by Marx, at least for purposes of describing the capitalist *status quo:* law as the enforced will of a ruling class.[13] Holmes saw the law as an emanation of judicial power.[14] Power-hierarchy analysis, mingled with interpersonal and intergroup dynamic concepts derived from psychology and sociology, also marks the work of some scholars loosely pinned to the critical legal studies designation.[15] Surely power-disparity as a way of seeing and examining the phenomena of normativity, authority, and obedience speaks in tones of almost voluptuous suggestiveness to the student and scientist examining the world order in this era of resilient superpower hegemony. Yet Bentham was almost alone in seeing these possibilities,[16] and Austin rejected them out of hand[17] because the international system could adduce no recognizable sovereign.

More than the *tools* of analysis may be borrowed. The *differences* between modes of teleological analysis developed to account for obedience to national legal systems ought also to be illuminating to scholars studying world order. In part, such differences of analytical mode are attributable to differences in quest. Although they may not say so specifically, Aristotle and the contractarians are really developing an idealized theory of the origin of rights, while Austin, Marx and the "Crits" are trying to describe how elites, in *fact*, govern or manipulate, perhaps, but not necessarily, as part of the observers' predilection for achieving radical change. The debates between such perspectives, and the differences in definition that are their penumbra, continue to enliven the study of obedience to national authority, but, except in very recent work by David W. Kennedy, there are few echoes in the field of international law.[18]

Let us take another example of insights observed by jurisprudence but not developed in the international context. What do international lawyers make of *disobedience*? Writing in 1971, John Rawls, despite his contractarian tendencies, defended the right to some civil disobedience, which might be seen as a breach of the social contract, at least in a democracy. He upheld such actions by citizens against the state, finding them not merely socially desirable but also valid manifestations of the protester's morally compelled adherence to a higher—but not necessarily divine—scheme of order, one which assuredly is not contractarian, but the validity of which (to go to the other end of the spectrum) Austin emphatically would not recognize.[19] Rawls's theory of rights, which rejects as unsatisfactory the mere empirical observation of how elites in fact govern, has freed itself to approve, however conditionally, the refusal of a citizen to do as the elite commands. Any theory of rights in which *justice* plays a validating role is loosening—not necessarily cutting—both the contractarian and the Austinian bonds and thereby encouraging a belief that whatever is, need not be. It suggests that the end which law serves, good order, may sometimes be advanced by disobeying the law, and establishes a bridge—albeit a bridge of sighs—between *right* and *might*. Indeed, with even more recent legal-philosophical writings, there has emerged a coherent, more radical theory which may be roughly characterized as presuming that whatever is (at least what power and role allocation there is) ought *not* to be, that good order requires a measure of perpetual regenerative antinormativity.[20] In this conflict, therefore, the terms "law" and "right" take on strategic significance, with Austinians emphasizing law, contractarians emphasizing process, and liberatarians preferring to emphasize rights in explaining why persons do or do not—or may not, or should not—obey.

What is rarely noted in all this systematic inquiry, however, is that obedience to national authority is currently most often challenged in connection with the dissenting citizen's sense of an *international* or supranational obligation, and in connection with some sense of an "ought" which has its roots in a perceived *international* order. Anti-war, pro-environmental, pro-human rights campaigns throughout the world nowadays pose some of the most salient challenges to national governance and raise the most searching questions about why authority is, or is not, obeyed. These campaigns brandish an international normative order against those empowered by the state. The international war crimes trials which followed the demise of Hitler's Evil Empire gave powerful impetus to the notion that there is a global-system-based duty to disobey positive law when it serves demonic ends. This episode briefly succeeded in focusing attention on an international rule system which is the repository of inalienable rights, rights that may even have the capacity to invalidate the duty to obey national laws. The campaign of the Third World for a New International Economic Order, more recently, once again has challenged present power-driven command structures called "law" in the name of "rights" derived from notions of justice. Yet little of this excitement has translated into systematic current research into teleological theory by the scholarly community working on world order. There is some norm prescription. There are even inquiries, from time to time, into sources of the rules. But there is almost no critical examination of the phenomenon commonly called international law, what it is for and why it is (or is not) compelling.

On the contrary, international studies seem paralyzed, rather than inspired by jurisprudence, perhaps because most observers of national legal systems—Austinians, contractarians, even libertarians—seem to agree that domination or governance requires *some* exercise of power by an elite in authority. If such dominance cannot be located in the global arena, where is one to begin? Little comfort has been derived by internationalists from the minority of social philosophers who reject every authoritarian basis for a theory rationalizing, let alone justifying, obedience. Such utopians as Foucault, who suspect and reject all prescriptive notions of dominance[21] and visualize a truly cooperative society in which norms operate on the basis of shared interest and non-coerced social conditioning, themselves have no internationalist bent, nor have they spawned internationally oriented counterparts. Moreover, their rather elastic notion of "social conditioning" cannot altogether escape the suspicion that it, too, employs a disguised, if gentler, form of conventional power-based "authority."

Nonexistent, also, is some internationalist counterpart to the "minimal state" libertarian philosophers, from John Locke (both a contractarian and libertarian) to Robert Nozik,[22] who suffer the notion of governance by constituted political authority but accept as justified only a very short-leashed state with sharply circumscribed powers. Yet such minimalist concepts of what is justifiable governance ought to be highly suggestive to students of the international system, if only because they make rather a virtue of the necessity compelled by a world of jealous national sovereigns. One would expect some philosophical inquiry into the proper limits of an international system of obligation. For example, the potent Western critique of the third world's campaign for a New International Information Order (NIIO) would be more persuasive if, instead of merely decrying its aspect of "censorship"—specifically, the proposed "licensing" of journalists—it put forward a theory of the limits of global regulatory authority over transnational communications based on broader teleological precepts. All the more odd to find the complete absence of any transference from nation-based to globally based systematic libertarian theory. If the NIIO is attacked on teleological grounds, this is invariably derived from the attacker's national jurisprudential views; for example, on an American's unexamined assumption that everyone ought—indeed, would *want*—to be responsive to the philosophical underpinnings of the U.S. Bill of Rights. And where is the critique, from a global philosophical perspective, of the heavy-handed anti-libertarian provision in the International Convention on the Elimination of All Forms of Racial Discrimination which requires states to criminalize "all dissemination of ideas based on racial superiority or hatred. . . ."[23] Who thinks methodically about such cacophony between human rights and freedom? Where is the John Stuart Mill of international libertarian theory? International lawyers are so busy making—or making up—what they are pleased to call international "law" and defending its authority that there appears to be too little time or inclination left for thinking systematically about areas of international activity which ought forever to be free from regulation.

Certainly, notions of basic human rights, limits on authority, distributive justice, and so forth developed in one society or culture, may have global application, but the transfer must be justified and its rationale cannot simply be assumed. What appears to American journalists as the "right" to publish may appear in India as incitement to the sort of religious strife which has killed hundreds of thousands of Muslims and Hindus in the past fifty years. Without teleological justification, transfer will fail. With it, transfer is often, hearteningly possible. Societies may disagree about the extent of pamphleteers' entitlement to freedom of the pen, but there is not much disagreement about freedom to torture.[24] Should we not inquire why there is agreement on some liberties and not on others? The remarkable thing about philosophical inquiry into basic notions of global "rights," however, is not that it is done badly but that it is scarcely done at all. The debates preceding the adoption of the Universal Human Rights Covenants[25] are lawyers' and politicians', but assuredly not philosophers', discourses.

The non-transference of theory from national to international thinking is the more striking when one's focus shifts from concepts of rights and norms to the role of coercion in securing obedience. Here, again, philosophers studying the nation-*polis* have launched propositions of extraordinary importance. In utopian philosophy, for example, coercive dominance looms as the central evil, and much effort is devoted to demonstrating that it is not only undesirable but unnecessary to an orderly, just society. Among the majority who reject the utopian-libertarian analyses, on the other hand, there is vigorous, often scintillating disagreement on the importance of coercion in the matrix of factors that induce obedience and facilitate the decent *polis*. Marxist and Austinian observers of national systems argue as to whether power to enforce is only a necessary or also a sufficient condition of habitual obedience and effective governance. Why is there no parallel debate among students of the international system?

Neither Marxists nor Austinians, admittedly, give much comfort to those concerned with visualizing an international "community" in which rules are obeyed and obligations taken seriously. They appear to agree with Machiavelli that the requisites for order are "good laws and good arms . . . [but] there cannot be good laws where there are not good arms."[26]

That would seem to slam the door on the internationalists. Yet it does nothing of the kind. Most contemporary legal philosophers deem coercive power necessary but insufficient to secure habitual social assent to governance. They posit that stable governance and habitual obedience can be secured (perhaps can *only* be secured except in the short-run) if the quality of governance by the "dominant elite" exhibits other characteristics besides dominant power. In chapter 6 of *Law's Empire*, Dworkin identifies three such characteristics: *fairness, justice,* and *integrity* (the last being a principled, more textured variant of consistency, which we will discuss under the designation *coherence*). Others focus on authority as process, identifying its necessary or desirable characteristics, such as consent, openness, and participation. A leading exponent of this view, Jurgen Habermas, emphasizes the role of discursive validation,[27] somewhat in the tradition of Aeschylus and Aristotle, who may have been the first in the Western tradition to have identified reasoned communication as an essential factor in securing social assent to elites' exercise of power.[28]

Thus, although coercive power is rarely absent altogether from these explanations of obedience to law in the national community, the line of inquiry represented by Dworkin and Habermas can surely be read as an invitation to the internationalist, an opening to consider non-coercive factors in understanding the phenomenon of global obligation and rule conformity. This the internationalist can do by borrowing and adapting both theory and terminology. Those who claim to have identified one or more non-coercive factors in the engendering of obedience generally use the term *legitimacy* and its variant, *legitimation*, to enclose some or all of the additional or alternative (non-coercive) requisites of obedience. Legitimacy thus ought to be, and, as it happens, *is* a term with which students of the international system have considerable familiarity. But familiarity has not led to much creative thinking about that notion, either. The tendency is simply to make superficial declamations about a government's, an initiative's, or a rule's legitimacy without serious examination of what is meant. Deployed by students of national legal systems, the concept of legitimacy is often used to postulate and explain what, other than a command and its enforcement, is required to create a propensity among the citizens generally to obey the rulers and the rules. The internationalist ought to feel both comfortable with, and stimulated by, this notion of legitimacy as the non-coercive factor, or bundle of factors, predisposing toward voluntary obedience.

A partial definition of legitimacy adapted to the international system could be formulated thus: *a property of a rule or rule-making institution which itself exerts a pull towards compliance on those addressed normatively.* "Those addressed" might include nations, international organizations, leadership elites, and, on occasion, multinational corporations and the global populace.

It becomes more apparent on closer inspection that the concept of legitimacy profitably can be adapted in some such fashion to illuminate basic philosophical questions about the international rule-system. The philosophers of the national community who champion legitimacy teleology fall, more or less, into three categories, although some adhere to each. All three address issues both familiar and important to internationalists. The first group, led by Max Weber,[29] defines the legitimacy factor in terms of a rather narrowly specific *process*. A process, in this sense, is usually set out in a superior framework of reference, rules about how laws are made, how governors are chosen and how public participation is achieved. In this view, a sovereign's command, when applied, acquires the additional legitimacy necessary to promote habitual obedience without encountering serious resistance *only* when the rule's subject is aware that the rule, and the ruler, both have a legitimate validity. By this is meant, for example, that the legislature which enacted the law was honestly elected, that the legislation was duly passed by a majority with a quorum present, and, perhaps, that the law is not *ad hominem* or, in Dworkin's phrase, a "checkerboard" approach to social regulation which applies frivolously, or mendaciously, unequal distinctions to its subjects. To say the least, that ought to interest, and have resonance for, the student of the international system.

The second group defines legitimacy in more complex *procedural-substantive* terms. It is interested not only in how a ruler and a rule were chosen, but also in whether the rules made, and commands given, were considered in the light of all relevant data, both objective and attitudinal. Habermas speaks of a discursive validation which is rooted in scientific empiricist reasoning that produces a rational result.[30] In his view, the "procedures and presuppositions of justification are themselves now the legitimating grounds on which the validity of legitimation is based. The idea of an agreement that comes to pass among all parties, as free and equal, determines the procedural type of legitimacy in modern times."[31] He distinguishes this from "a contingent or forced consensus" and "domination . . . accepted *without reason* by the bulk of the population. . . ."[32] The latter is inherently unstable or, to put it empirically, has low value in predicting whether the public will obey. Surely that, too, is relevant and highly suggestive to those seeking to understand (and reform) the international system.

The third group, composed particularly, but by no means exclusively, of neo-Marxist philosophers and related students of radical social restructuring, prefers to focus entirely, or principally, on *outcomes*. In this view, a system seeking to validate itself—and its commands—must be defensible in terms of the equality, fairness, justice, and freedom which are realized by those commands.[33] How could that fail to be relevant to anyone seeking to understand the effect of the global north-south chasm on the prospects, processes, and outcomes of the international rule system and its institutions?

Naturally, these three arbitrary categories of legitimation theory do not fully accommodate all the nuanced positions of every jurisprudential thinker. Dworkin's approach, for example, integrates parts of all three categories. For the most part, however, the problem is not so much over-categorization as under-estimation of the differences between the categories, a problem inadvertently made more serious by a misleading sharing of vocabulary among scholars who mean different things.

Of course, there is confusion. All three of these teleological camps may use the same label, *legitimacy*, to explain why something beyond a coercively enforced sovereign command is needed to create a system in which law is habitually obeyed. But the concept of legitimacy, or the validation of rules and rule-making, is really a bracketing of many integral factors, which are related but different and which must be investigated by reference to different social data. In the national context, this matrix of data encompasses the procedures by which power is delegated to governing elites; the procedures by which elites inform themselves before making rules or deciding specific controversies between citizens; the procedures by which legislative decisions are taken, explicated, and ventilated; the probity and "integrity" of a specific law or decision, that is, how it fits into the coherent principles underlying a network of specific commands; its social utility, that is, its distributive fairness and instrumental effectiveness; the equality with which the same rule is applied to various situations; the validation of specific rules by secondary rules about rules; the validation of a community by its members' acceptance of ultimate rules of recognition that are not otherwise validated but which define the essence of the community. Much of this, too, can be adapted for use in understanding legitimacy in the international community. At a minimum, it suggests that, in the international context, another part of the definition of legitimacy is: *the perception of those addressed by a rule or a rule-making institution that the rule or institution has come into being and operates in accordance with generally accepted principles of right process.*

So legitimacy theory has many mansions. If this be muddle, it is muddle of a very high order, and it should merely heighten the interest of the internationalist. Not surprisingly, the deconstructability of the commonly deployed concept of legitimacy has raised questions about its scientific utility. Alan Hyde, in a searching analysis of legitimacy theory as a disciplined approach to the understanding of power and obedience in the state, has suggested that the concept either means too little or too much to be useful in understanding or predicting systemic obedience behavior. In particular, Hyde has argued that no one has ever demonstrated empirically that a subject obeys the sovereign's command, solely or even in part, because of a belief in the legitimacy of the process (he uses the term in the Weberian sense) since one cannot be expected to isolate that factor in one's motivation from such other strands as fear of punishment for disobedience, or a self-interested expectation of benefits to be derived by obedience.[34] The same criticism could be made of efforts to study other, non-Weberian concepts of the legitimacy factor in the national community. These concepts, too, cannot be isolated in the individual's motivation. Thus, the critics say, the legitimacy factor's existence is unprovable.

This line of criticism might seem, at first, extraordinarily disheartening to those seeking to borrow concepts taken from the rich mass of obedience theory developed by students of national communities and to apply or adapt these to the international scene. Here is a window of opportunity, the work done on noncoercive factors, being shut because it cannot be studied in a controlled environment, disentangled from other contributing factors, its very existence only hypothesized but essentially unprovable. If legitimacy is beyond the reach of discrete inquiry in the highly developed national community, how is one to justify the pursuit of it in an international "community" of states the existential validity of which, to say the least, is open to serious challenge? If legitimacy is an elusive factor in studying rule-conformity in the national context, it is surely much more of a wild goose chase to attempt to study it in the international arena, where rule-conformity itself is such a "sometime thing."

It is at this point that the observant reader will spot a pregnant paradox. It is this: the international system's weakness (in the Austinian sense) is its peculiar strength as a laboratory for those seeking to isolate and study the legitimacy factor. In international governance there is no sovereign, certainly not one regularly capable of coercively enforcing its commands. Empirically, the Austinian critique of international law as non-law is beyond reproach if one accepts that coercion is a necessary component of law and order. Yet it is also empirically verifiable that some, indeed *many*, international rules of conduct are habitually obeyed by states. Otherwise, for example, no mail would go from one state to another, no currency or commercial transactions could take place, and passenger flights over foreign territory or the high seas would routinely encounter the reception of Korean Airlines flight 007 which was shot down over Kamchatka on September 1, 1983, killing all 269 passengers, or of Iran's civilian flight 655, shot down over the Persian Gulf by a U.S. warship in 1988. Yet, this sort of violence, fortunately, is a one-in-a-million deviance from the pacific norm. Thus, to whatever extent any rules are obeyed in the international system, they *must* be obeyed due to some factor, or mix of factors, other than the Austinian one. It appears that we have, in the world of nations, what cannot be reproduced even experimentally in the domestic order: a "system" of rules which permits the observation of one or more manifestly non-Austinian factors operating to secure behavioral conformity with its noncoercive commands.

In sum: there is at least the hypothetical possibility that, if one could show that there are rules which are *habitually* obeyed in international relations, then one may be able—indeed, may *only* be able—to account for that phenomenon by postulating an instrumental non-Austinian factor; one which is *not* a sovereign command, *not* enforced coercively, *not*, even, obeyed solely by reason of short-term self-interest gratification, since gratification cannot explain consistent deference to rules that are unlikely always to benefit equally all parties to interactions. It turns out that the concept of legitimacy developed in the national context is not only adaptable to international usage but that, in applying to the compliance behavior of states the theory developed to explain individual compliance behavior, it may prove possible to learn things about the nature and role of legitimacy which could not be garnered from studying its effect on the behavior of persons.

That is the *descriptive* justification for putting legitimacy theory to the test in international life. If one is ever to demonstrate the existence of the legitimacy factor in securing obedience to norms, the global *polis* is where that elusive factor may be found, isolated, and studied by the social scientist. Such a verification of the role of legitimacy in inducing rule compliance would surely be of significance far beyond the precincts of the international system, but the international system is the only place where legitimacy may be observed "on the hoof" and where the theory of legitimacy's validating function might actually be tested on a grand scale.

But there is also a *prescriptive* justification for studying legitimacy in the global arena. If a legitimacy factor—actually, a legitimacy syndrome of several factors—can be observed affecting state behavior in the direction of rule-conformity, then the international system's failure to perfect its rudimentary system of rules of conduct—the widely regretted fact that there is not more obedience to more norms—may not be attributable solely to the usual Austinian culprit: the absence of a global sovereign with worldwide coercive enforcement power. Also, or even *instead*, the black holes in the normative fabric may be due to a lack of legitimacy in the rules and the institutional processes by which they are made, interpreted and applied.

To put it perhaps a bit too baldly: a person arriving on earth from Mars would be seriously misled if the visitor were to try to understand how nations behave by reading the U.N. Charter or

an international law textbook, even one by so eminent and inde-
fatigable a scholar as, say, Sir Hersch Lauterpacht.[35] Nations simply
do not behave—in many instances—as reported in these texts. But
what if this dissonance were not explicable, either solely or primarily, in terms of the missing global monarch with a supranational police force? What if, more modestly, it turned out that
texts which are rarely obeyed are obeyed rarely because—or *in part*
because—they, or the institutions which generated them, do not
appear legitimate to most, or to many states some, or most, of the
time?

It surely would be useful to know if that were an (or the)
operative explanation of the rule texts' shortcomings as a factor in
international relations. It would be cause, too, for optimism. Almost everyone, today, concedes that the world is not about to elect
a global sovereign endowed with overriding enforcement power.
Kant's observation remains correct: "the state is still to be preferred to an amalgamation of the separate nations under a single
power which has overruled the rest and created a universal mon-
archy. For the laws progressively lose their impact as the government increases its range, and a soulless despotism, after crushing
the germs of goodness, will finally lapse into anarchy."[36] If a new
global sovereign were the essential prerequisite for a system of substantive and procedural norms commanding general obedience,
then any such system is surely not worth bothering about; it would
be doomed for the foreseeable future. But what if the coercive
sovereign were not the only factor—or even a *necessary* factor—in
creating a system of habitually obeyed norms? What if it were
possible to demonstrate that, even in the absence of an Austinian,
Marxist, tribal or divine law-enforcer, many international rules, nevertheless, are widely obeyed? And what if it were hypothetically
feasible to identify one or more non-Austinian factors which, in
the international setting are necessary and, perhaps, even sufficient
to create patterns of adherence to rules which, much of the time,
seem to operate and survive without the help of sovereigns and
police? What if the evolution of a system of rules ordinarily obeyed
by states were possible without a coercive infrastructure? What if
the perfection of that system by the creation of a global sovereign

could reasonably be thought of as only the final culmination of a process in the perfection of the community, rather than its *sine qua non?*

Some thinking along these lines guided James Madison in his writing of the American Constitution. Discussing federal police power and its potential use against a state of the federation, he observed at the Convention of 1787 that "the more he reflected on the use of force, the more he doubted the practicability, the justice and the efficacy of it when applied to people collectively and not individually. . . . The use of force against a State, would look more like a declaration of war, than an infliction of punishment. . . . He hoped that such a system would be framed as might render this recourse unnecessary."[37] That is why he and Jefferson took the position that the new Constitution could be trusted to pull towards *voluntary* compliance those to whom it is addressed, relying exclusively on the "cumulative respect of a patriotic citizenry" for the validity of its ideas.[38] They saw the Constitution, uniquely, as embodying "government based on consent,"[39] a consent earned by the text's embodiment of the legitimate aspirations of the people.

This was still the guiding idea forty years later, when John Taylor, that astute political commentator of Caroline, Virginia, wrote that the federal government "is not a national government; it is a league between nations. By this league, a limited power only over persons and property was given to the representatives of the united nations. This power cannot be further extended, under the pretext of *national* good, because the league does not create a national government." It is most obviously in his use of terms—united nations, league—that Taylor reminds us of the parallels between the origins of the United States and the present voluntarist international community. More profoundly, however, this parallel emerges from his description of the limits on federal enforcement power. "A federal government," he observed, was created "to provide for the interests of states as separate nations." That "federal league creates a government for exercising specified powers, as to those cases only, wherein the united nations have a common interest; and contains no clause for investing it with the greater power of acting upon persons and property."[40] In other words, the federal system, in 1820, closely resembled the one nowadays operating in the community of nations. Legitimacy was relied upon to ensure popular compliance. Not until the civil war did the coercive supremacy of the federal authority fully emerge. Before that watershed was reached, however, the federal government had not been paralyzed vis-à-vis the states but functioned consensually, for the most part, by virtue of its perceived legitimacy, precisely as Madison had intended.

Both the early history of the United States and, today, the operation of the international community inspire the hypothesis that legitimacy has the power to pull toward compliance those who cannot be compelled. Beyond suggesting this hypothesis, the international community presents a venue where the hypothesis may be studied in a socio-political setting. If it could be demonstrated that legitimacy validates the international normative order, and that it exerts a pull on states in the direction of uncoerced rule compliance, then we would have found a tool necessary for the construction of a world order which—to take the most extreme hypothesis—could safely postpone, or skip, the "coercive sovereign" stage in social development. It could proceed, instead, directly from the disordered state of nature to a system of law operating on non-coerced legitimacy-induced consent.

However tantalizing these prospects are, they are far beyond the reach of this study. Obviously, it would be extraordinarily difficult to demonstrate empirically legitimacy's properties as an independent variable, determining rules' compliance pull in a non-Austinian rule community. Our more modest objective is to develop not proof but to reinforce the hypothesis by adding some credible evidence and positing logical deduction. To begin our quest, we now have a working definition of legitimacy as it applies to the rules applicable among states. *Legitimacy is a property of a rule or rule-making institution which itself exerts a pull toward compliance on those addressed normatively because those addressed believe that the rule or institution has come into being and operates in accordance with generally accepted principles of right process.*

The benefits to be anticipated from our quest should not be

overstated. As we shall see, legitimacy is not merely a matter of assembling readily available ingredients and mixing them in the right proportions. For example, the legitimacy of a rule may depend in part on its accompaniment of rituals and symbols; but, to be effective validators of the rule, these validators must necessarily have developed naturally over protracted periods of time. They cannot be purchased on demand. Similarly, we will observe that a rule's legitimacy depends in part on whether it is buttressed by a hierarchy of rules about how rules are to be made which, themselves, are a manifestation of community. Such a socio-political community, in theory, could be invented by a global constitutional conference, but it is unlikely to happen in such a sudden, deliberate move. Like ritual, community mostly happens gradually. Thus, while one benefit to be derived from studying the properties of legitimacy may be to enable the social engineer to shore up the rules' degree of legitimation, another is to help the social conservationist develop appreciation of the extent to which existing rules already have been legitimated by historical and social forces which need to be cherished and nourished precisely because they cannot be replicated on demand. The legal philosopher's role as conservator, in sum, is to help society understand not merely what to do, but how to appreciate what has already happened and what is happening.

To begin to develop a taxonomy of legitimacy's properties, we have posed an operational question: *Why do nations obey rules?* And we have adduced a hypothetical answer to this question: *Because they perceive the rule and its institutional penumbra to have a high degree of legitimacy.* In this hypothesis, legitimacy is assigned the role of an independent variable, one which controls the extent to which a rule is perceived to exert a powerful pull toward compliance on those to whom it is addressed. That hypothesis is no new insight. It comes to us from those colleagues who have taken journeys to the outer reaches of the national *polis* but no further. It purports to tell us what legitimacy *does*. Legal philosophy also tells us what law—the law of the national *polis*—is: what are its properties in a rule-community of natural persons. It remains to be seen whether these insights will be a reliable guide for a global expedition into a community of states; but there is intuitive reason to be optimistic. As we traverse the global *polis* in search of "legitimacy," we already have three insights to guide us, derived from the work of these others, each of which fits our own observations of international behavior. *First*, if there is such a variable as legitimacy, it is most likely to be found in its unalloyed state exactly where we are looking, that is, in the international arena. *Second*, legitimacy exerts a pull to compliance which is powered by the quality of the rule or of the rule-making institution and not by coercive authority. It exerts a claim to compliance in the voluntarist mode. *Third*, since the compliance pull of various rules and institutions varies widely, it follows that if legitimacy is a determinant of the strength of a rule's compliance pull, then legitimacy, too, must be a matter of degree. With that, we can begin.

2

The Irrelevance of
Law and Non-Law

Authority is a word on everybody's lips today. The young attack it and the old demand respect for it. Parents have lost it and policemen enforce it. Experts claim it and artists spurn it, while scholars seek it and lawyers cite it. Philosophers reconcile it with liberty and theologians demonstrate its compatibility with conscience. Bureaucrats pretend they have it and politicians wish they did. Everyone agrees that there is less of it than there used to be.

John H. Schaar*

In their external relations, sovereigns are bound by no law; they are like our ancestors before the recognition or imposition of the social contract. A prerequisite of law is a superior authority whether delegated from below or imposed from above—where there is no recognized authority, there is no law.

Occidental of Umm al Qaywayn v. A Certain Cargo, etc.,
577 F.2d 1196, 1204 (1978).

The three observations about legitimacy which conclude Chapter 1 are theoretically deduced from what we know about the international system: that many of its rules display authority *in themselves,* which is to say that they are obeyed despite the fact that the system has no sovereign and no gendarmes. The third observation— that legitimacy must be a matter of degree—is also theoretically deducible from the readily observed fact that in the international

* "Legitimacy in the Modern State," in *Legitimacy and the State* (W. E. Connolly ed., 1984).

27

arena some rules are usually obeyed, while others are never, or only rarely, translated into state practice. Yet, none of the rules is backed by the sort of coercive force that is used to enforce nations' domestic legal systems. This makes it significant that the capacity of rule texts to describe, and conform, state behavior varies from rule to rule and time to time. Different rules of the international community appear to have differing strength to exert compliance pull. This being so, it follows, if there is such a factor as legitimacy militating toward rule-conforming state behavior, that the legitimacy of each rule, similarly, must vary by degrees.

That rules do, indeed, vary in their ability to predict and to induce conforming behavior is commonplace. This unexceptional proposition nevertheless tends to become the source of controversy when the discourse substitutes the word "law" for "rules." It is a controversy that ought to be addressed before going forward.

Almost everyone agrees that adherence to a system of rules is likely to be imperfect; but change the operative term to "legal system" and the proposition may generate vigorous controversy. If an entire system of laws is only obeyed here and there, now and then, and is not effectively enforced, or not universally thought to impose binding obligations, is it really a legal system at all? And if it is not a *legal system* we are examining, why should we concern ourselves with the study of the factors which conduce to obedience behavior? These questions, it will immediately be apparent to the reader, while also relevant to any nation's domestic legal system, most often are directed to *international* law. While some of the laws of every community are broken by some of the public some of the time, the national communities usually have the *means* to enforce their laws and this may be thought to make such laws impervious to occasional lapses of obedience. They remain law; chipped, perhaps, but still law. Not so the international system. Brierly, although he disagrees with the proposition, quotes the widely held view that international law is only "an attorney's mantle artfully displayed on the shoulders of arbitrary power" and "a decorous name for a convenience of the chancelleries."[41] It is a seductive epigram, which captures widespread cynicism toward the claim that the rules of the international system are *laws*.

As it happens, the cynic's abrasive observation should be embraced by students of the international system because it establishes the correct starting point for any discussion of the remarkable phenomenon of rule compliance in that non-Austinian context which is the community of states. If international law were *law* like any other, there would be nothing remarkable about states' conformity to legal mandates. It is precisely because international "law" is not like the laws with which citizens of states are familiar that the tendency of states to obey its commands is so extraordinary and invites an examination of the legitimacy factor. Moreover, it is because the rules of the international system are dynamically different from national laws that it is possible to speak of a rule's capacity to obligate as a matter of degree. In international legal writing, this is sometimes described by reference to Professor Richard Baxter's concepts of *hard* law and *soft* law—terms which would surely be thought to fit most uncomfortably into any theory of law in *national* communities, where all laws, obeyed or not and however inefficiently enforced, are thought of as *hard*.

The cynic's (or Austinian's) critique of international "law"— that it is not law because it is not enforced by a sovereign with superior power—is useful and ought to be welcomed by students of world order. Instead, most of the few philosophers and writers who set out to analyze the teleology of international law—that is, who search for the ultimate direction of the stream of international normative behavior—struggle mightily to prove Austin wrong and to demonstrate that international "law" *is law*. We find, for example, the distinguished scholar, Professor Anthony D'Amato, beginning a study published in 1986, *International Law: Process and Prospect*, with an entire chapter devoted to this very cause.[42]

D'Amato argues: 1) that international "law" is like national law because the latter actually operates independently of sovereign coercion, and, anyway, 2) that there really does exist in the global system a sort of enforcement of international "law"—analogous to the state sovereign's police power—which is the moral and diplomatic pressure states exert on each other to induce obedience to the "laws." D'Amato's point is that international "law" is not really as different from domestic law as Austin thought, since the former is neither as unenforced nor the latter as enforced—or as dependent on police enforcement—as Austinian analysis might lead us to expect.

This compels D'Amato to argue that the international legal system is quite similar, in its essentials, to the more familiar domestic legal systems. His admirable purpose is to ensure that international "law" is taken seriously, the way one ordinarily takes national and local law. But to secure this objective, D'Amato is forced to some rather disputable descriptive assertions. For example, he asks his readers to accept that the "fact that some states disobey periodically some rules of international law does not, itself, mean that those rules are not rules of law because even in domestic societies some people (e.g. criminals) break the law from time to time." We might rejoin, however, that such a similarity is outweighed by striking dissimilarities. For one, domestic criminals have a reasonable prospect of being caught by the police, and, it is generally believed, this inhibits some prospective law breakers from pursuing their perceived self-interest, whereas no such inhibitions operate at the global level because there are no police and because the "law" breakers have the advantage of private armies to a degree undreamed of by the most expansive gangland *capos*. The state contemplating a breach of the rules is much more likely to conclude that it has a better prospect of "getting away with it" than the criminal in even the most lawless of our cities. This leads to a different proportion of occasional (and habitual) scofflaws in domestic and international systems. It also makes it more remarkable that so many states obey so many rules, which is the phenomenon which is the central starting point of our investigation. It is *not* similarly remarkable that most Americans obey most laws, because—among other reasons—of the presence of a police-enforcement factor.

D'Amato next admits that "the fact that most states obey most rules of international law most of the time is not enough to call those rules 'legal' because we are especially concerned with 'important' cases where states may get away with violating rules of international law."[43] But, he explains, while this would seem to argue against the identity of international and national law, that conundrum can be overcome, at least in part, if we analogize international "law" to the sort of domestic law which pits a citizen against the *state*. In such important citizen-versus-government conflicts, domestic law, too, cannot really be said to be enforced by the system except to the extent a losing government party agrees to "enforce" against itself, which, he concludes, cannot be called enforcement at all because it is actually voluntary compliance. Moreover, states do not always agree to such self-enforcement, just as states in the international community do not always restrain themselves. In this way, D'Amato seeks to convince us, national law is not nearly so Austinian, nor so *hard*, as is claimed by the critics of the "pretensions" of international "law."

The skeptic, however, will respond that almost *all* international legal disputes, by definition, are "important" in this sense (involving states as one, or both, parties and thus dependent on self-enforcement) whereas, domestically, the mix is quite different, most disputes being either between citizens which end in state-enforced judgments, or else cases between citizen and state in which the state wins and enforces against the losing citizen. Thus, domestically, most law does not depend on self-enforcement, whereas international "law" is almost wholly dependent on voluntary compliance.

D'Amato's argument—that the international and domestic legal systems are really twins—is elegant, but, ultimately, it rings false. The reader reaches into subjective experiential impressions, and the propositions *feel* wrong. The conduct of states in international relations is *not* like, not even *quite a bit* like, the way persons (or institutions) interact in a nation. A government which refuses to obey its own domestic law is subject to a broad range of remedies: impeachment, writs of mandamus, Congressional hearings, remedial legislation, defeat at the polls, or revolt in the streets. Nothing comparable comes into play at the level of the global system when a state disobeys international "law." True, nations might rally, as some did during the 1950 invasion of South Korea by North Korea, to defend the victim and repel the transgressor. In many instances, however, rule violation engenders nothing more from the international community than a desultory debate in a

U.N. organ like the General Assembly perhaps culminating in a censorious resolution. Most of the time there is not even that. To understate the point: the probable, predictable, direct, imposed costs of disobedience are higher in every mature domestic system than in its international counterpart. That, surely, is why the Hitlers and Stalins of the world preferred to carry out even their most draconian domestic actions by manipulating the contents of the law, rather than by outright confrontation with it, even while giving hardly a second thought to the boldest violations of international "law."[44]

Those international lawyers who insist on the proposition that "international law is law" take on a far heavier burden of justification than is necessary to validate their professional existence, and, besides, far more than one can reasonably be sustained either empirically or intuitively. If "international law is law" in the same sense as nations' codexes, then the U.N. Charter, a solemn multilateral treaty with more than 150 state parties, would serve as a reasonably accurate guide to the ways of the world when read by a Martian on a first flight to earth, in the same way that the Constitution of the United States, the Internal Revenue Code, the anti-trust laws, or even the criminal code would give that Martian a general approximation of how things really are in America. But we know this is not so. Most national law—American, Romanian, even, lately, Chinese—paints a relatively accurate picture of actual community behavior for the extra-terrestial visitor. But the extensive body of international "law," oft restated in solemn texts, which forbids direct or indirect intervention by one state in the domestic affairs of another,[45] precludes the aggressive use of force by one state against another,[46] and requires adherence to human rights standards[47] simply, if sadly, is not predictive of the ways of the world. With foreknowledge of national law, the Martian visitor could probably operate fairly safely and effectively in each of the countries whose legal systems had been studied. There are exceptions, it is true. A reading of the New York City property tax assessment rolls would lead the Martian to believe that most one-, two-, and three-family homes in that city are eminently affordable. New Yorkers know, while Martians possibly do not, that those rolls have long been notoriously, if fairly uniformly, undervalued at about 10 percent of market value. In domestic law, however, such lie-telling laws are quite unusual and the target of recurrent bouts of reform. International "law," on the other hand, paints a picture which, while perhaps roughly accurate in part, is incomplete and sometimes misleading. The visitor to our planet guided solely by reliance on the reading of treaties and international "law" texts, Candide-like, would probably endure such unpleasant surprises as being arbitrarily murdered, jailed, tortured, expropriated, polluted, hijacked, or drafted into foreign-supported insurrections.

This does not deny that there is nobility in the fight being waged by D'Amato and others against the prevalent Austinian contempt for "international law as law." One way to badger publics and governments to play by the rules, even when it is inconvenient for them to do so, is to keep insisting that the various texts *are* law and that not playing by them is *illegal*. But what D'Amato wants to call international law is not law as in "The U.S. Code annotated." To insist otherwise is to be led on a wild goose chase inside an intellectual cul-de-sac which might have been designed by a malevolent John Austin to divert and trap the unwary idealist into trying to prove the unprovable.

The point would be of little but academic interest, here, were it not for the fact that a serious study of the role of rules in interstate relations must start precisely from the assumption that international "law" is *not* law in the sense in which that word is used in the national context: because the international legal *system* is not like its national counterpart, despite significant similarities, and despite the fact—a truly remarkable one—that it *is* a system of obligations for an emerging global community: as we shall soon attempt to demonstrate. That is why it is necessary to begin with an ungracious but conceptually essential rejection of the benevolent impulse toward international "law" which motivates D'Amato and others. Those who see international "law" as just another legal system severely discount one of the most extraordinary things about the international system—the central subject of this study—which is the occurrence of a not inconsequential amount of habitual state obedience to rules and acceptance of obligations *despite* the underdeveloped condition of the system's structures, processes, and, of course, enforcement mechanisms. Nothwithstanding these shortcomings, most states much of the time act in conformity with a quite sophisticated set of international rules—rules, moreover, made and interpreted by processes which, in turn, are validated by procedural rules about rules. Surely it is more useful to examine why these unenforced rules, which are not sovereign commands, are so often obeyed (and, by contrast, why some are not obeyed) than to deploy fictions in an effort to make reality out of what, at most, is a disfunctional, or misleading, metaphor.

Whether a government's particular action in relation to other governments is "illegal" or merely reprehensible—for example, because a regime has broken its promise not to do what it is doing—at first seems to turn only on an essentially sterile definitional fiat. To the extent this is so, everyone is free to use the term of personal choice. However, that choice—like the one between "laws" and "rights" mooted in Chapter 1—affects more than the hortatory aspect of communication. It is a strategic choice. If the conduct is "illegal" then it is possible to say "state A has broken the law," which is perhaps a weightier shell to fire at A than, "A has broken its promise." But suppose A has kept its promise, even under circumstances that would have made it advantageous not to do so. Then the statement "A has acted to its own disadvantage because it feels obliged to obey the *law*" is simply misleading, since the ordinary listener would conjure up a sovereign enforcing the law against the backdrop of a compelling enforcement mechanism ready to be summoned if necessary to secure compliance. On the other hand, the descriptive statement which sets our teleological inquiry on the right track is quite different: "State A has acted to its own disadvantage because it feels obliged to do so by its *promise*." This opens up quite another direction of inquiry. Why does A take its promise seriously even in circumstances when it would appear advantageous not to do so? Why is an unenforceable commitment treated as an obligation capable of affecting conduct? If I agree to meet you at noon under the clock in front of our city's courthouse and I fail to appear because a more enticing opportunity has presented itself, I have done something which is

1) morally reprehensible (wasted your time and effort), 2) anti-systemic (you are not likely again to enter into those kinds of arrangements with me and, perhaps, not with others either), and 3) socially corrosive (you will have learned to distrust not only me but, perhaps, all persons). Yet I will have done nothing illegal, and little is gained by arguing that my promise to meet you is like a contract, or that it is illegal to miss an appointment. My promise and your reliance on it would constitute a law—a contract—only if the promise could be enforced by your summoning the help of powerful societal institutions: a legislature to make such promises legally binding, a court to rule in your favor and a sheriff to force me to appear on time or to pay damages. It may well be true that most citizens, too, obey laws for reasons that have nothing to do with fear of enforcement, but a law's capacity to elicit compliance is grounded in its special status as a *state-sanctioned* commitment. This makes national law no twin of international "law."

In endorsing the definitional distinction between a commitment enforceable at law and one which is not, it is not necessary also to embrace the Austinian concept of a coercive command as defining both the necessary *and sufficient* components of law. Our endorsement merely seeks to reserve the term *law* for describing a system of commands which, among its other obedience-inducing components, enjoys the contingent support of superior coercive power. It is not necessary to be an Austinian to see a large difference between the U.S. Internal Revenue Code and the Treaty on the Peaceful Uses of Outer Space. To admit this difference, moreover, emphatically is not tantamount to an admission that the Outer Space Treaty has no effect on conduct, creates no obligations, or need not be taken seriously. Such an admission would be demonstrably false. It does acknowledge, however, that if nations carry out the strictures of the space treaty it is not due to fear of the enforcement power of some force or forces that are the functional equivalent of a global sovereign. That is not the sole, or even *a* reason for their compliance.[48] Once that is acknowledged, the obedience phenomenon becomes far more theoretically interesting precisely because it occurs *outside* the context of enforced sovereign commands and sanctions and thus must be based on some other well-spring of obligation: which brings us back on the track to legitimacy.

It also releases us from law's binary bind. The question "Is international law, *law?*" really asks whether the norms of the international system do, or do not, impose an absolute obligation on its subjects. *Law* is the sort of norm which does *absolutely oblige*, albeit perhaps occasionally subject to defeasance by some posited "higher" obligation—to "justice," perhaps. This property of law as a normally ineluctable obligation—one, moreover, which is usually enforced—permits the observer to say to a scofflaw that his law-defying behavior is "illegal," whether or not that illegal conduct actually has led, or is likely to lead, to such normal consequences of illegality as arrest, or a civil suit for damages. In a mature national legal system the observation that "crossing the street against the light is illegal" also carries the useful message that, to cross against the light means violating a law which has been duly enacted by a constitutionally authorized legislature, is consistently enforced by the legislatively authorized police and is applied by legally constituted courts dispensing the laws fairly and honestly. Of course, it is also possible for law to exist in less ideal circumstances. In a different context the statement "crossing the street against the light is illegal" might merely mean that a dictator, acting with the backing of an armed junta, has decreed whimsically that anyone crossing a street against the traffic light may be shot. In such primitive circumstances, it might further be accurate to predict that a pedestrian may cross against the light if he or she is willing to pay a sufficient bribe to an arresting officer or a corrupt trial judge. Such a law and legal system has no element of legitimacy to support it, yet it has ample coercive back-up. New York City, for example, has hundreds of laws which, to the extent they are enforced, appear to serve primarily as the vehicles for the corrupt practices of bureaucrats who extort bribes—rather than compliance—from violators. Such a primitive system is one of *law*—in the sense that it is coercively enforced— but utterly lacks legitimacy. It is regarded by the citizenry with widespread cynicism, yet also with a high degree of coerced respect. It is law of a particularly primitive, convoluted kind. In both sophisticated and primitive conditions, however, an observer can readily detect a clear public notion that there is a rule which is "the law" and that, while its enforcement may vary, its existence is demonstrable by reference to the law-making process—whether democratic or corrupt, legitimate or illegitimate—currently operating in the community. Citizens of both primitive and sophisticated national communities would understand that the law exposes to penalty costs those who violate its rulers' commands. Indeed, in national legal systems an illegitimate regime may compensate, at least in the short-run, for its laws' illegitimacy by an increased emphasis on enforcement. The illegitimate law is thereby reprieved; it remains the law until the revolution.

That one ought to keep one's appointments with friends, by contrast, is a social convention, not a law. Although the convention may be obeyed, that does not make it a *legal* norm. This is not merely a matter of semantics but also of a fundamental difference. The legality of a law (as distinct from its *legitimacy*) is not a matter of degree, even if the laws' enforcement may at times be lax or corrupt. The pedestrian street-crossing rules are absolute obligations. The social rule about keeping appointments is not a law and its ability to achieve compliance is not an *either/or* proposition but a matter of degree, which, in turn, depends on whether, and how much, the subjects of the rule *believe themselves obliged—despite their countervailing self-interest*—to act in accordance with the rule. This, in turn, it will be argued in this study, may depend on the *legitimacy* of the rule at a given moment and in a particular situational context.

The rule that appointments should be kept is not a law, but, rather, a secular rule supported by the perceived needs of society for an orderly, peaceful community. It is this perceived need, not in any part the coercive power of the state and its enforcement bureaucracy, which keeps people keeping appointments. It is this same perception which keeps states, most of the time, complying with most of the rules of the international system.

It should be noted in passing, since we will revert to the subject in Chapter 13, that the sense of voluntarist social obligation which is here under discussion—the feeling that one, or, rather, that *everyone, should* keep appointments—may be supported by two separate, if sometimes coinciding dynamics. The *first* is the belief that the rule is *legitimate* because it has come into being in accordance with the prescription for right rule-making in a secular community (of persons or of states) which needs rules to function. Legitimacy, therefore, is about right process and about community. A *second* dynamic pulling toward voluntary rule compliance is the belief that a rule is *just*, because it incorporates principles of *fairness* as these are understood by a moral community (which may, or may not, be coextant with the secular community to which the rule is addressed). This point is made, here, merely to indicate that, in our discourse on the legitimacy of rules it is useful to bear in mind those two other forces capable of pulling towards rule compliance: the threat of *coercion* and the moral suasion of a shared sense of *justice*.

At the end of this volume, we shall try to distinguish and also relate legitimacy and justice. For the present, the task is to locate legitimacy in relation to law. Laws can be legitimate or illegitimate, just as they can be just or unjust. The distinction between laws and legitimate rules that are not laws (such as those operating in the community of states) derives from the way in which each secures compliance. Law obligates at least in part because of its location within an infrastructure of government, constitution, courts, and police. The rules of the international system obligate—to the extent they do—primarily because they are like the house rules of a club. Membership in the club confers a desirable status, with socially recognized privileges and duties and *it is the desire to be a member of the club, to benefit by the status of membership, that is the ultimate motivator of conformist behavior: that and the clarity with which the rules communicate, the integrity of the process by which the rules were made and are applied, their venerable pedigree and conceptual coherence. In short, it is the legitimacy of the rules which conduces to their being respected.* These facets of legitimacy also undoubtedly influence citizens' compliance with the law, but the law has additional means at its disposal when these legitimacy-factors fail to suffice. It is in order to make this point, so crucial to the identification of legitimacy, that so much has been made of the difference between laws and rules obeyed in a voluntarist mode from which centralized coercion is absent. This must not, however, obscure the point that the two have much in common.

Evidently, obligations of states in the global community much more closely approximate the house rules of a club, or the social rule about keeping appointments, than they resemble the duty of citizens to cross intersections only on the green light. There may be an element of obligation in both kinds of rules, but the significant question is: What kind of an obligation? If the obligation is a *legal* one, it is theoretically absolute and objective. If a rule is not subject to this binary test, then the obligation, depending on the perception of its legitimacy, is relative and situational. Obedience to law is a recognition of the power of the organized state; obedience to international rules is a recognition of the existence of an organized international community, but one that only loosely resembles the modern state and does not issue or enforce sovereign commands. Rather, the function of this community is to legitimate, or withhold legitimacy, from its members, institutions, rules and modes of conduct, thereby affecting both the rights and duties of members and institutions, as well as the rules' capacity to obligate and secure the community's compliant behavior.

International "law" thus is not of a *legal* order of obligation, despite the important resemblances. If law is to any degree attributable to the activities of courts, legislatures, executive departments and police forces, then international "law," still underdeveloped in respect of all four of these, is not law, not in *that* sense. In that definitional context, much international "law" is, at best, an admirable aspiration and a filching of some word pictures from the gallery of national legal terminology. It is, rather, in Reisman's words, the fruit of communications "between elites and politically relevant groups which shapes wide expectations about appropriate future behavior."[49] Reisman prefers to adhere to the term "functional lawmaking" in describing this process,[50] but it only vaguely resembles the legislative process normally associated with mature legal systems. Someday, perhaps, the international system will come to have law and legal institutions that resemble their domestic counterparts, although a world of five billion persons could (and should) never have a centralized legal system mirroring that of the nations. In any event, that is not the condition of the global rule system now, and it is not likely to be in the foreseeable future. H.L.A. Hart puts it more gently: "though it is consistent with the usage of the last 150 years to use the expression 'law' here, the absence of an international legislature, courts with compulsory jurisdiction, and centrally organized sanctions have inspired misgivings, at any rate in the breasts of legal theorists."[51]

The misgivings, however, are not a cause for despair, nor should they be the end of the road of theoretical inquiry. On the contrary, the misgivings are the right starting point for any realistic and intellectually stimulating hunt for those elements which conduce to the growth of an orderly international community. In the domestic community, the coercive power of the governing elite, no doubt often augmented by the perception that its orders are legitimate, induces the citizenry to obey the law's commands. In the international community, the legitimacy of the rules—and of the process by which they are made and applied—conduces to compliant state behavior. For those interested in the theory of social organization it is much more exciting to study a system of rules which conduces to a fairly high level of perceived obligation among members of a voluntarist community than to search for the causes of obedience in a hierarchically structured society with an empowered elite.

3

Legitimacy:

A Matter of Degree

. . . words are wise men's counters, they do but reckon by them:
but they are the money of fools.

T. Hobbes*

If one concedes that "international law is not law" in any sense
that uses the national legal systems as its standard, one does not
thereby admit that the Martian who wishes to learn about international relations as practiced by states on earth would be completely without normative guidance. International relations are
not one damn thing after another, nor is the world system, in
Matthew Arnold's phrase, only "a darkling plain where ignorant
armies clash by night."[52] Most people do keep their appointments
and most states adhere to many international rules of conduct.
Certainly, there are texts that predict with some accuracy to relations between states, as also between states and citizens or
entities of other states (transnational corporations, for example)
and between persons or entities of one state and those of another.
These texts often read very much like the laws which are enacted
by national governments, but because they are not like those laws
we will use the neutral terms "rules" and "rule texts."

Some of these rules can be found in treaties, some in resolutions of international organizations, some in the judgments of

* *Leviathan*, 106 (C. B. Macpherson, ed., 1968).

international courts and arbitral tribunals, and still others in the "customary practice" of states as observed, reported, classified, and quantified by scholars and foreign offices. Some rules formally call themselves "law," while others (U.N. General Assembly resolutions, for example) do not. This body of rules is all set out in a mass of paper. Sensibly, our benevolent Martian, in a spaceship headed for earth, wants to know how seriously to take all these texts. Given the limited amount of reading time afforded by the journey, he asks whether some texts are more important than others. Which texts are most likely to be accurate descriptions and predictions of the reality into which the Martian is soon to be plunged?

It is notable that these operational questions can be asked by the Martian without ever having to get into a scholastic quibble about whether these rules—some of which more accurately than others predict state conduct—really are "law" in the same sense that term is employed to describe the U.S. Internal Revelue Code. The Martian ought not to care whether the texts we have given him meet Austin's—or anyone else's—test for being designated "law." If the Martian were even to ask the question, that would betray a dangerous misconception of the awaiting earthly reality. Instead, our space voyager needs to know which texts to take seriously, and which to take with a grain of salt. This, to recapitulate, is a matter of *degree*, as can readily be demonstrated by looking at how things actually work on earth. The international rules, in practice, vary in the extent they are able to exert a compliance pull on those to whom they are addressed.

In preparing a short list of readings for the Martian, evidently it would be useful to select those texts which most accurately portray how the world really is. The Martian should concentrate on rules with a strong compliance pull. The U.N. Charter, for example, would have to be cut up. The section on the Security Council's never-applied military enforcement powers (Chapter 7) could well be set aside. So could the section on the Trusteeship Council which has now virtually completed its mission. The Charter's articles bearing on the powers and procedures of the General Assembly and on the Secretariat and the Secretary-General might be included, but with an explanatory memorandum bringing the Martian up to date on the ways in which those rules have been expanded, contracted, and bent by the repeated practice of the parties. This is the sort of thing our space traveler wants to know. To the Martian, the definitional debate over whether international law is law, while perhaps an engaging introduction to speculative hermeneutics, would seem practically irrelevant. With the space-craft landing in two years, our Martian wants to know, in Professor Louis Henkin's felicitous phrase, "how nations behave,"[53] which is quite a different, more operational question.

Perhaps even more important for us earthlings, even if not for the Martian, is that Henkin's formulation of the question leads to quite a different line of theoretical inquiry from D'Amato's. If we stay on teleological track, without wandering into the Austin-ian cul-de-sac, we will soon reach the next, the *worldly*, question. It is this: *Why* do nations usually obey some rules and others less? Or, more accurately, Why do some rules exert a powerful compliance pull on states?

Unfortunately, the reduction of the Martian's reading—by eliminating texts that exert little compliance pull—is not as simple as it may sound. For one thing, actual compliance, which may be empirically demonstrable, is not quite the same as compliance pull. A state may violate a rule because the perception of national advantage to be gained by rule disobedience in a particular instance is so powerful as to overwhelm the most powerful compliance pull. Moreover, to the extent actual compliance by states does demonstrate a rule's compliance pull (that is, its legitimacy), it tends to do so in shades of gray. No rule text—not even a law, for that matter—depicts and predicts social behavior with complete accuracy. Compliance with rules is a matter of degree, i.e. to what *degree* is the text of a purported rule an accurate depiction and prediction of state conduct *and of the pressure to comply felt by the state, even when it fails to comply?*

That obedience to rules in the international system is imperfect does not distinguish rules from laws; but the consequences of imperfect obedience *on* international rules is significantly different from the impact on laws. If laws are imperfectly obeyed, they do not thereby necessarily suffer diminished legality. They do not, thereby, *ipso facto* become less binding. There is a binary quality here: a text either is or isn't a law. Even if a law is disobeyed, that does not terminate its ability to obligate and does not license disobedience. With a few arguable exceptions[54] the failure of states to obey an international rule, however, does affect its "rule-ness." It becomes more acceptable for others also to ignore the rule, until, eventually, habitual disobedience may lead to the rule's demise.[55] Thus the degree to which a rule is obeyed affects the *degree* to which it is cognizable as a valid obligation. Reciprocally, the extent to which a rule is cognizable as a legitimate obligation affects the extent to which it is obeyed. This is true even though, as we have observed, mere disobedience does not necessarily negate compliance pull. A sophisticated measure of the strength of a rule's compliance pull would have to take into account the psychic cost paid by a violator as well as the rule's overall compliance record. Obviously, however, a rule which is generally obeyed exerts a higher psychic toll on a violator than one habitually violated. We are dealing not only with a matter of degree, but one measurable by a multi-dimensional formula. International normativity, in other words, is not subject to the straightforward binary test applicable to law, and this liberates us to think about rules and obligations in the community of states without having to prod and distort reality to make the rules fit evidently ill-suited categories borrowed from a quite different system of order. While something either is or is not a law, a rule's degree of beingness is infinitely variable, depending on the degree to which those to whom it is addressed believe themselves obligated by it. Our inquiry aims to discover what objective factors influence that belief.

Freed from the binary constraints of "law," international rule texts, at least in theory, can be sorted hierarchically: in a descending order beginning with those which are highly descriptive and predictive, through others which are somewhat so, to ones which have little to do with "how nations behave." The trouble is that, even at the theoretical level, because we are dealing with a question of degree, we will find it quite difficult to decide where to cut off the Martian's reading list. The Load Line Convention[56] would clearly be high on our list, as would the U.S.-Mexico Agreement on Exchange of Prisoners.[57] The Kellog-Briand Pact,[58] obviously, would be out, as would be, probably, the treaty establishing the Permanent Court of International Arbitration, even though its members still have the procedural authority to nominate the judges of quite another institution, the International Court of Justice.[59] But where in the hierarchy do we put the treaty on the Peaceful Uses of Outer Space,[60] which may or may not turn out to predict accurately what states will do—or feel they ought to do—when they have the technological capability— and the urge—to violate it? And what about the European Convention for the suppression of terrorism,[61] which hasn't been much tested either? Or the norms of the Geneva Convention[62] and customary rules[63] applicable to civil strife, which have had some— but not much—effect on behavior in the real world? What of a statement by country A's foreign office that it will impose a countervailing tariff on textile imports from country B in pursuance of A's understanding of a provision of a bilateral trade agreement: does that understanding" become part of the agreement; and is B later entitled to take reciprocal advantage of the "understanding" in obverse circumstances?

There are even more formidable practical obstacles that block the way to a definitive hierarchical ordering of international rules according to how effective they are in evoking a sense of obligation and securing voluntary state compliance. The difficulties in verification of data relevant to compliance make it risky to boast that we can measure and rank accurately the descriptive (and, *ipso facto*, the predictive) accuracy of any particular rule text. It would be necessary to measure empirically the actual degree of confluence between a textual statement (for example: "nations may not place communications space satellites in an orbit position reserved to another state") and the actual compliance pull the rule exerts on the behavior of states. That, in turn, requires measuring the degree to which each rule text has been implemented in actual past instances of state conduct, comparing that total against the number of instances in which the rule text has been ignored or deliberately not applied. The ratio thereby obtained, the compliance ratio, might be somewhat suggestive as to whether the rule text will be applied or disregarded in future contingencies and also as to the compliance pull which it exerts on states (which, as we have noted, is not demonstrable solely by whether they obey it in a specific instance or not). It will go some way toward telling us how "rule-like" it really is. But only *some* way: the compliance factor is but one indicator of a rule's perceived legitimacy. The rule against genocide, for example, has been but little put to the test (fortunately!) and, at that, its compliance record is not outstanding. Yet it can probably be said to enjoy a prevalent perception of high legitimacy due to other factors besides its record of compliance, factors we shall be examining in subsequent chapters. Were compliance the only standard, we would have what appears to be a tautology: legitimacy is determined by legitimacy (or compliance determines compliance). We shall see that the seeming tautology actually has greater value than, and is not as tautological as, at first appears. But on its face, the insight is not a particularly helpful one to persons attempting to understand the operational causality which accounts for a rule's compliance pull. We must try to get behind the seeming tautology.

The reader should remember our real reason for wanting such a listing of rule texts in descending order of the rules' capacity to affix a sense of obligation on states. We are not Martians on a spacecraft approaching earth but students of the international system approaching the concept of legitimacy in an effort to understand what influences states—in the absence of Austinian factors—to comply (usually, sometimes, never) with a rule of the voluntarist international system. Clearly, a systematic attempt to understand legitimacy as the, or a, factor in inducing compliance behavior would benefit from such a hierarchic sorting out of the rules which are the external manifestations of the phenomenon we are studying. If legitimacy conduces to uncoerced compliance, the study of high-compliance rules and, for contrast, low-compliance rules, might help us to identify properties of that which, depending on the degree to which it is to be found in a rule, affects the rule's capacity to induce compliance. Indeed, we have already deduced theoretically a particularly important identifying property of legitimacy: that it, like the "rule-ness" of the texts that manifest it, is a *matter of degree*, with some rules manifesting a higher legitimacy ratio or index than others. By ranking rules by their compliance pull we might, in theory, be able to detect the ubiquitous elements that seem to cause, or, more accurately, correlate with compliance pull.

Unfortunately, as a practical matter, it is not feasible to attempt a sort of atomic chart of international rule texts. While such an empirical approach might be technically feasible, it would also be fraught with conceptual and practical difficulties, not to mention huge costs in collecting and processing data. How would we categorize what was gathered? Was Tanzania, when it invaded Uganda and overthrew Idi Amin's dictatorship, violating the text prohibiting the use of force or upholding the texts pertaining to human rights and self-defense? Thousands of disputed cases could cloud the credibility of our statistical results.

A more modest alternative is to begin inductively: to examine *some* clusters of rules to see whether a series of hypotheses can be developed about correlations between qualities of the rules themselves and their comparative success or failure in pulling states to comply. Those might then be put forward as hypothetical properties of legitimacy, the controlling variable in rules' capacity to obligate. However, such a project, while it commends itself because of its realistic scale, could not do two things. It could only *hypothesize* (not *prove*) correlations. And it could only hypothesize *correlations*; it could not prove *causality*. In other words, an observation that ten texts written in black bold-faced type, on high quality white paper, were invariably applied in state practice, would be interesting. If we also observed ten other texts as to which the degree of compliance consistently fell as the type became smaller and the paper got thinner and grayer, then we might have a rational theoretical basis for hypothesizing that the quality of type and paper used in a rule text correlates with the rule's compliance pull on states and describes a property of legitimacy. The Martian might then feel justified in reading only the largest-face texts printed on the best bond, and we might likewise feel justified in proposing the hypothesis that a rule's legitimacy varies in relation to the kind of paper and print used in its text. We would not, however, have proven the validity of these hypothesized correlations. We certainly would not have demonstrated that rules are obeyed *because* of the size of the type and quality of the paper. Still, the Martian, for one, might find our hypotheses useful, at least in suggesting a grand empirical project designed around our workable set of hypotheses.

Having acknowledged what our present study cannot hope to accomplish, let us review its realistic aspiration. We want to know the extent to which behavior in international relations—both what states do and what they believe they ought to do—can be understood (predicted) by reference to rule texts and the principles that underlie and connect them, and any rule-making and rule-implementing institutions to which the rule is connected. We have deduced from actual state behavior that the descriptive and predictive value of a norm in interstate relations is a matter of degree. And we have hypothesized that this degree correlates with an "X" factor or factors which inhere in the rule or rule-making institution itself, there being no sovereign, no police, to compel compliance. We call this "X" factor the rule's, or institution's, *legitimacy*. In arriving at this hypothesis about the legitimacy factor, we have discarded the label "law," not because it is inherently unreasonable to apply it, for example, to the Vienna Convention on Treaties[64]—to which almost every nation adheres both formally and in practice—but for reasons central to our quest. We have observed that some international rules are more regularly obeyed than others. This interests us because we wish to know more about *why* unenforced rules seem to have the capacity to obligate. In the international system, unlike the national legal systems, if rules are obeyed it cannot be because the subject fears the coercive power of the sovereign. There is no global sovereign, no global sheriff. Consequently, conformity of state behavior to predictive texts must be due to something else. Our aim is to offer some credible hypotheses as to the properties of a rule and a rule-making process which are plausible indicators of the rule's ability to induce voluntary state compliance with its non-coercive command. What is it that causes states to feel obligated by rules? What accounts for their feeling more obligated by some rules than by others?

Specifically, four indicators of a rule's and a rule-making process' legitimacy will be hypothesized in the ensuing chapters. These indicators of rule-legitimacy in the community of states are: *determinacy, symbolic validation, coherence,* and *adherence.* Each of these terms will be examined and defined hereafter. The hypothesis asserts that, to the extent a rule, or rule process, exhibits these four properties it will exert a strong pull on states to comply. To the extent these properties are not present, the institution will be easier to ignore and the rule easier to avoid by a state tempted to pursue its short-term self-interest.

Admittedly, this focus on indicators—these four properties of rules—does not yield a self-sufficient account of the process by which nations are socialized into a rule-compliant community. How rules are made, interpreted, and applied is part of a dynamic, expansive, and complex set of social phenomena. As the anthropologist Sally Falk Moore has pointed out, "if one is dealing with *partial* order and *partial* control of social life by rules, then any analysis which focuses entirely on the orderly and rule-bound is limited indeed, and does not place the normative in the context of the whole complex of action, which certainly includes much more than conformity to or deviance from normative rules."[65] That complexity can be approached, however, by beginning with the rules themselves. Those seemingly inert artifacts are shaped by other, more dynamic forces and, like tree trunks and sea shells, tell their own story about the passionate winds and tides that determine experientially their varied shapes and textures.

4

Determinacy

. . . this common measure, some way, is right reason: with whom I should consent if there were any such thing to be found or known *in rerum natura*. But commonly they that call for right reason to decide any controversy, do mean their own.

T. Hobbes[*]

If the factor which determines the compliance pull of rule texts is a matter of degree, what determines the degree to which it is present in any given instance? Or, to ask the same question another way: What observable characteristics of a norm or rule of conduct increase or decrease its legitimacy?

It is the pursuit of answers to this question which motivates the rest of this book. One could have approached the social phenomenon of non-coerced obedience directly, through such openings as are afforded by study of myths, game theory, or contractarian notions of social compact. Indeed, each of these lines of inquiry will be pursued, but indirectly, through a unifying concept of *rule legitimacy:* that is, by approaching dynamic social forces through examination of rules, and rule-making or rule-applying processes. It should be kept in mind, however, that the norm-centered pursuit of our quest—the discovery of what it is about rules and the rule process that conduces to uncoerced compliance—is merely the story as told by lawyers, their native approach to a broader sociological, anthropological, and political

[*] *Elements of Law, Natural and Politic* (pt. II), ch. 10, para. 8 (F. Toennies, ed., 1969).

question: What promotes the formation of communities and what imbues members of a community with the will to live by rules?

In particular, we will be studying the formation of a *voluntarist secular community* and the compliance pull of rules in that specific context. The terms *secular* and *community* introduce new elements into our analysis which are by no means self-defining. By *secular* is meant the community in which rules are deployed to achieve order and promote such societal goals as trade, environmental protection, health, economic development, communications, and the peaceful enjoyment of the fruits of labor. The term is used, both here and elsewhere in this work, to distinguish such secular rules from rules which serve a moral community and seek to implement principles of justice. An example of a moral principle is the notion that all persons throughout the world are entitled to roughly equivalent life-chances. Such a principle is capable of generating more specific rules to govern behavior in a *moral* community. In Chapter 13 we will see that such moral rules sometimes pull toward compliance with secular rules and sometimes contradict them; or, put conversely, we will see that notions of justice may be adopted or adapted by a secular rule system. We will also see that the justice of rules—their morality as perceived by a moral community—exercises a compliance pull on those addressed which is similar to, but independent of, the compliance pull exerted by legitimacy. More of that, later. Those who cannot wait to examine the relation of justice to legitimacy could leap forward to Chapter 13 before reading on, but at some risk to orderly expositional development.

By *community* is meant a permanent system of multilateral, reciprocal interaction which is capable of validating its members, its institutions, and its rules. Such validation is associational, in the sense that members' rights and duties derive from belonging to the community. If one is tempted to stop, here, to examine the relation of legitimacy to justice, it is also tempting to attempt at this juncture to define the relationship between community and legitimacy. But this, too, has been postponed (to Chapter 12) for the sake of clarity. The role of community in validating rules is at the very core of the notion of legitimacy. Before getting there, however, it is logical to begin with the more formal, surface aspects of legitimacy, by examining the structure of rule texts themselves for evidence of *literary* properties which appear to exert a pull in the direction of voluntary compliance.

The pre-eminent literary property affecting legitimacy is the rule text's *determinacy*: that which makes its message clear. The same quality may also be termed its "transparency." Logical deduction suggests, even without recourse to anecdotal evidence, that rules which are perceived to have a high degree of determinacy—that is, readily ascertainable normative content—would seem to have a better chance of actually regulating conduct in the real world than those which are less determinate. For one thing, states or persons to whose conduct the rule is directed will know more precisely what is expected of them, which is a necessary first step toward compliance. As a U.S. citizen born abroad, the author knows from the text of the Constitution that he cannot aspire to the Presidency. This may be unfair and even inconsistent with other parts of the same instrument, but clear it surely is. The same Constitution's text, however, also sends quite opaque messages. If local environmental laws prohibit the building of bulkheads to protect eroding beachfront property, is the law "taking" that property without the requisite compensation? The text of the applicable "due process" clause of the Constitution is not nearly as transparent as the one requiring the President to be native-born.

In these examples, determinacy is more or less synonymous with *clarity*. In due course, we will see that this is an oversimplification. For the present, however, we may note that determinacy is most often achieved by textual clarity.

Clarity, in turn, may reflect the degree of agreement among a rule's authors. When there is consensus among legislators on how many copies of judicial decisions should be filed with the court registrar, the law will specify that number. However, when lawmakers paper over unresolved disagreements or uncertainties, they often put ambiguity into the text, leaving room for later fine-tuning. It is for this reason that a 1958 treaty on the underwater continental shelf was worded so as to allow off-shore mining to a depth of 200 meters, "or, beyond that limit, to where the depth of the superjacent waters admits of the exploitation of the natural resources of the said areas. . . ."[66] The limit set by that rule, in a sense, is no limit at all. The parties to the treaty simply disguised their differences, using a word-formula that left the matter in abeyance pending further work by courts, administrators, and by the evolution of customary state practice. The resultant vagueness permitted a rule to evolve flexibly, in response to advances in technology which the drafters could not foresee.

The U.S. Constitution is full of such deliberate lacunae. If the authors had been in agreement on whether the Congress, the President, or both, should have the authority to extend diplomatic recognition to foreign governments, the document they wrote would probably have said so. Instead, it is silent on recognition, only stipulating, in Article II, section 3, that the President "shall receive Ambassadors and other public Ministers." This hides a basic disagreement among the drafters, who deliberately resorted to creative indeterminacy. Jefferson thought that the clause should be interpreted as signifying that the "transaction of business with foreign nations is Executive altogether"[67] while Madison argued in the Federalist 44 that the clause meant only what it said, that "it would be highly improper to magnify the function into an important prerogative. . . ." In drafting the text, the Founding Fathers evidently decided not to decide, leaving the issue to future resolution. It was still unresolved as late as 1898, the year Congress "recognized" the independence of Cuba as an appendage to its declaration of war against Spain.[68] Since then, however, the recognition power appears in practice to have been captured by the Presidency.[69]

Some degree of indeterminacy is inevitable in any body of rules and, as noted, it may even have its uses in promoting agreement and achieving flexibility. But indeterminacy also has its costs, which are paid in the coin of legitimacy. Not only do indeterminate normative standards make it harder to know what is expected—perhaps because the authorities responsible for the rule text were themselves uncertain, or could not agree, or wished to preserve flexibility for the future, or just did not see the issue—but indeterminacy also makes it easier to justify non-compliance. To put it conversely, the more determinate a standard, the more difficult it is to justify non-compliance. Since few persons or states wish to be perceived as acting in flagrant violation of a generally recognized rule of conduct, they may try to resolve a conflict between the demands of the rule and their desire for interest gratification by "interpreting" the rule permissively. A determinate rule is less elastic and thus less amenable to this strategy than an opaque one. For example, the United States, when sued by Nicaragua for mining its harbors, considered shielding itself by pleading the "Connally Reservation," which bars the International Court of Justice from exercising jurisdiction in any case that pertains to "domestic" matters *as determined by the United States.*[70] At the time the U.S. Senate voted to accept the I.C.J.'s jurisdiction in this peculiarly indeterminate form, Senator Wayne Morse characterized the Connally reservation as "a political veto on questions of a judicial character."[71] It appears to allow the U.S. to repulse *any* assertion of jurisdiction by the Court. The elasticity of this rule was such that it was universally known as the "self-judging reservation," a submission to the Court in form but not in substance. In the separately stated opinion of four judges of the International Court in the *Interhandel* case,[72] this elasticity nullified the U.S. submission altogether.

Yet, when it came to the lawsuit brought by Nicaragua—a suit potentially involving billions of dollars in claimed damages—the American lawyers did not invoke Connally. Instead, they tried in every other conceivable way to argue that the Court had no authority to hear the case: that the dispute was already before the Organization of American States and before the U.N. Security Council; or that it wasn't a legal dispute at all but a political one; or that Nicaragua, itself not having accepted the Court's compulsory jurisdiction, had no right to implead the U.S. The failure of the lawyers to use the Connally shield is all the more remarkable because, whereas Connally gave the U.S. a self-judging escape from the Court's jurisdiction, all the other defenses left the key jurisdictional decision up to the judges, who eventually rejected them all.[73] Had the U.S. simply faced the Court with a "finding" that the mining of Nicaragua's harbors was a "domestic" matter for the U.S., that ought to have ended the litigation. Instead, the U.S. went on to lose, not only in the matter of jurisdiction but also, eventually, on the merits.[74]

Why wasn't the Connally Reservation's shield used to prevent this outcome? The answer lies in Connally's unexpected determinacy. The reservation, while very open-ended, was certainly not intended to cover a situation in which the CIA had arranged to have mines planted in the harbors of a foreign state with which the U.S. was not at war. Although the term "domestic matter" is not so determinate as to bar differences of interpretation—that, after all, is why its interpretation was deliberately reserved to the U.S. Government and not left to the Court—*no* reasonable interpretation of the concept could be stretched to cover such activity. Even the U.S. Government, anxious to do almost anything to stay out of court, was unwilling to subject itself to the shame and ridicule which would have ensued had the Connally shield been deployed to avoid adjudication. Some, in the State Department Legal Adviser's Office, even feared that if the U.S. tried to use the Connally shield in this mendacious fashion, the judges would take away the shield altogether by holding it irreconcilable with U.S. acceptance of the Court's compulsory jurisdiction. So the Connally shield was left to idle in the armory. Interest gratification, convenience, and advantage were sacrificed in order not to be seen—by the Court, and by the court of public opinion—to be mendacious or absurd.

Such a foreboding of shame and ridicule is an excellent guide to determinacy. If a rule is interpreted by a party seeking to justify its violation in such a way as to evoke derisive laughter in any reasonably objective observer, then the rule must have a degree of determinacy, because the laugh originates in the incongruity between the violator's tortured definition of the rule and its range of plausible meaning. This is not the same as the incongruity between a good faith interpretation of an opaque rule and the definition given that rule by a judge. It should not be mistaken for the feelings which normally follow when a litigant discovers that the law is on the opponent's side; for, it is perfectly possible that a state (or a person) could lose a lawsuit without incurring shame or ridicule, as long as the rule text at issue is sufficiently indeterminate to make various interpretations rationally possible. Even losing on a morally charged issue like school desegregation[75] need not have engendered shame in the first school board to be compelled by the Supreme Court to integrate its pupils, because—in the light of earlier interpretations of the Constitution's "equal protection" clause—separate but equal facilities, until then, had been thought to meet the vague constitutional standard.[76] Only in subsequent cases, involving wilful obstruction of a standard which the courts had already clarified, could one speak of opprobrium, as when local school boards pretended to make all public schools private institutions in a ludicrous effort to escape a rule which had already become quite clear.

Thus, while it may be true in theory, as Wittgenstein has charged, that no "course of action could be determined by a rule because every course of action can be made out to accord with the rule,"[77] yet some rules are less maleable, less open to manipulation, than others. Although Wittgenstein's point has merit—and has recently been wittily adumbrated by Professor Duncan Kennedy[78]—in practice determinacy is not an illusion. The degree of elasticity of words and texts varies, and can be controlled as a deliberate strategy. Like legitimacy itself, textual determinacy is always a matter of degree, and the degree to which a rule exhibits determinacy varies from rule to rule. While no word formulas are entirely without elasticity, yet some are more elastic than others.

The degree of determinacy directly affects the degree of a rule text's perceived legitimacy. That is why the World Court, had its jurisdiction in the *Nicaragua* case been challenged by U.S. recourse to the *Connally* reservation, might well have overruled it for being too indeterminate, either in general, or at least in the circumstance of that case. Such a decision might have used the well-established "void-for-vagueness" rule applied by U.S. courts to refuse to give effect to federal statutes drafted with too elastic a text. A rule which prohibits the doing of "bad things" lacks legitimacy because it fails to communicate what is expected, except within a very small constituency in which "bad" has a high degree of culturally induced specificity. To be legitimate, a rule must communicate what conduct is permitted and what conduct is out of bounds. These bookends should be close enough together to inhibit incipient violators from offering ludicrously self-serving exculpatory definitions of the rule. When everyone scoffs at an exculpatory definition, the outer boundary of the rule's elasticity has been established. A rule's determinacy may thus be tested by measuring how far exculpatory definitions can be stretched before those doing the stretching are—in Ezekiel's phrase—"laughed to scorn."

There is another sense in which determinacy increases the legitimacy of a rule text. A rule of conduct that is highly transparent—its normative content exhibiting great clarity—actually *encourages* deferral of gratification and thereby gives added impetus to rule-conforming behavior. States, in their relations with one another, frequently find themselves tempted to instant gratification, as when they are in a position to take advantage of a power balance in their favor. If they choose, instead, to obey a rule which denies them that gratification, it is likely to be because of their longer-term communitarian interest in seeing the rule reinforced. The U.S. decision not to stop a delivery of Silkworm missiles to Iran, discussed in Chapter 1, is an example. The short-term costs of deferring a realizable advantage may seem to be outweighed by the potential long-term benefits likely to accrue from reliance on the same rule. States frustrated by a rule can visualize future situations when the rule will operate in their favor. This cost-benefit analysis which leads to voluntary deferral of short-term interest gratification depends, however, on the rule being clear enough to support reasonable expectations of long-term benefits from the future operation of the same norm.

Let us consider the case of a foreign ambassador's son who has murdered someone in Washington, D.C. He is arrested by the District police when a message arrives from the State Department demanding his release. The Secretary of State announces that the culprit is to be sent home. Hearing of this, the public is outraged. Patiently, the Secretary of State explains that "almost all" states "almost always" act in accordance with the universal rules of diplomatic immunity, which fully protect ambassadors and their immediate family from arrest and trial. Although in this instance, the Secretary continues, the rule does seem to work an injustice, in general it operates to make diplomacy possible. If the U.S. were to violate the rule this time, it would weaken the rule's future utility, lessening the power of its compliance pull. Alternatively, if the U.S. acts according to the rule, even at some short-term cost to its self-interest, it will thereby reinforce the applicable treaty-based rule text.[79] As the State Department has recently pointed out to Congress, obeying the rule to one's short-term disadvantage can help ensure its future availability to protect U.S. diplomats and their families abroad.[80] A 1984 study by a committee of the British House of Commons—conducted after a shot from the Libyan embassy ("People's Bureau") had killed an on-duty London policewoman, thereby provoking public outrage—also came to this conclusion.[81]

Note, however, that the argument for deferring interest gratification only makes sense if there is a fairly clear understanding of what the rule covers. The immunity of the ambassador's son, in our example, must be part of a clearly understood normative package. It must be evident that other countries, too, will refrain from arresting members of the families of U.S. ambassadors. Such expectations of reciprocity are important, fragile threads in the fabric of the international system; but before the expectation can arise there must be some mutual understanding of its content. The belief that if I act in accordance with a rule you will do so, too, will only pull me toward compliance if our interactions have achieved the level of continuity of an ongoing game, or system, *and we share an understanding of what the rule covers.* If its contents are vaguely defined and fuzzy—if some countries in some instances have extended ambassadorial immunity to the ambassador's children while others have not, or have done so only if no capital crime is involved, or only if the child was actually working for the embassy, or if immunity has been denied to second sons, or daughters, or step-children—then the impetus for gratification deferral in the instant case would disappear. The demand for the arrest and trial of the ambassador's son might then be both reasonable and irresistible. It could quite easily be defended as not violating a "real" rule. It could then also be argued that bringing the son to trial would create no new hazards for American diplomats abroad that did not already exist because of the rule's vagueness. If a norm is full of loopholes, there is little incentive voluntarily to impose on oneself compliant standards of conduct which one knows others can evade because of the rule's opaqueness and elasticity.

An excellent example of this cost of indeterminacy is offered by the U.N.'s rules prohibiting and defining aggression. These were approved by the General Assembly after some seven years of debate.[82] Among the transgressions named in article 3 is the "sending by or on behalf of a State of armed bands, groups, irregulars or mercenaries, which carry out acts of armed force against another state." Article 7, however, says that nothing in article 3 "could in any way prejudice the right to self-determination, freedom and independence . . . of peoples forcibly deprived of that right . . . nor the right of these peoples . . . to seek and receive support. . . ." To confuse matters further, article 5 declares that no "consideration of whatever nature, whether political, economic, military or otherwise, may serve as a justification for aggression," while article 8 adds that in "their interpretation and application the above provisions are interrelated and each provision should be construed in the context of the other provisions." Interrelated they may be, but like a tangled skein. Do these provisions prohibit or encourage aid by one country to an insurgent movement in another? It is not that the individual articles of the convention are opaque, but that the provisions, seeking to reconcile irreconcilable positions, contradict one another. Such a muddled obligation, one would expect, could have little effect on the real-world conduct of states; and one would be right.

It happens—by way of contrast—that, in international practice, the rules protecting diplomats, as codified by the Vienna Convention, have a very high degree of specificity,[83] and they are almost invariably obeyed. So, too, are the highly specific rules, in another Vienna Convention, on the making, interpreting, and obligation of treaties.[84] This says with consummate clarity that *treaties are binding*. Yet, even within the four corners of that Convention are two concepts which are less clear. Article 62 appears to sanction the notion that at least some treaties may be terminated in the event of "a fundamental change of circumstances." However, what that means is defined only in rather vague generalities. Article 53, moreover, provides that a treaty is void "if, at the time of its conclusion, it conflicts with a peremptory norm of general international law," but the term "peremptory norm" is only tautologically defined as "a norm from which no derogation is permitted, and which can be modified only by a subsequent norm of general international law having the same character." These provisions introduce an element of uncertainty. However, while such terms as "fundamental change" and "peremptory norm" may be vague, the elasticity of those terms actually might *increase* the determinacy of the rule in certain circumstances. This paradox cannot be explored here, but we will revert to it in Chapters 5 and 6, when we examine the possibility that uncertainty sometimes may actually make a rule *more* determinate. For present purposes it is enough merely to note once more that clarity and certainty are usually, but not invariably, synonymous with determinacy.

Among other subjects covered by determinate rules which elicit a very high degree of rule-conforming state behavior are those pertaining to jurisdiction over vessels on the high seas, territorial waters and ports,[85] and over aircraft,[86] rules pertaining to copyright and trademarks,[87] as well as those pertaining to posts, telegraphs, telephones, and radio waves. There is also a high degree of determinacy in the rules governing embassy property, rights of passage of naval vessels through international straits and territorial waters, treatment of war prisoners, and even as to the duty of governments to pay compensation—even if not as to the *measure* of that compensation—for the expropriation of property belonging to aliens.[88] There are very many more examples. What is interesting about these rules is that a high level of textual determinacy goes together with a high degree of rule-conforming state behavior.

A rule with low textual determinacy may overcome that deficit if it is open to a process of clarification by an authority recognized as legitimate by those to whom the rule is addressed.

Courts, as one would expect, are among the most credible of these processes of clarification. Yet they are by no means the only component of the international system able to give case-by-case determinacy to otherwise seemingly opaque or conflicting rules. All the members of the international community, individually and collectively, by their conduct and by the expression of their views, contribute to the clarification process. The performance of states in the international community is constantly subject to qualitative evaluation by other states, institutions, and processes which, themselves, have varying degrees of legitimacy. For centuries, to take one example, it was the papacy which determined whether wars among Europan nations were "just" or "unjust," applying progressively specific criteria.[89]

Whether the clarifying process is successful in transforming rule indeterminacy into determinacy depends on the legitimacy that the members of the international system ascribe to the specific process. This implicates such factors of legitimacy as *who* is doing the interpreting, their *pedigree* or authority to interpret, and the *coherence* of the principles the interpreters apply. One would expect that a textually opaque rule could be transformed into a more determinate rule if the vague text were interpreted in actual disputes by respected authorities enunciating clear criteria in one instance and, thereafter, applying these consistently, case-by-case. A good example is the process by which the International Court of Justice took a relatively indeterminate rule pertaining to the division of a continental shelf shared by several states and, case-by-case, has given the rule an increasing degree of determinacy. The indeterminate rule is article 83(1) of the convention negotiated by the Third United National Conference on the Law of the Sea,[90] which says that an undersea coastal shelf shall be shared by neighboring states with opposite or adjacent coasts "on the basis of international law . . . in order to achieve an equitable solution."

If an "equitable solution" standard were clear and simple, it would have been spelled out explicitly in article 83, instead of being left in almost mystical indeterminacy. Nevertheless, the International Court has begun to give the concept practical meaning. In 1969, accepting that the formula lacks "any indication of a specific criterion which could give guidance to the interested states in their effort to achieve an equitable solution" the judges began to define a concept of proportionality which requires a relation "between the extent of the continental shelf areas appertaining to the coastal State and the length of its coast measured in the general direction of the coastline."[91] The equitable principle was further developed by the Court in a 1981 case between Tunisia and Lybia[92] and again in a 1985 decision involving Libya and Malta.[93] The once-indeterminate rule text has thus gradually gained greater transparency as the cases have defined the parameters of an equitable solution which is applied regularly and consistently. Naturally, it was helpful that this development has occurred under the aegis of a tribunal whose institutional and procedural legitimacy is widely acknowledged by states. It should also be noted that article 83's vagueness occurs in the context of an overall treaty which it, unlike the Connally reservation, does not *contradict*. The vagueness of the "equitable solution" text could thus be cured by the Court looking at principles underlying the treaty as a whole, and at other, including customary, international law applicable both to the subject matter (sea law) and the relevant interpretative mode (equity).

Many standards to which state conduct is held accountable do not present these problems, or present them in less acute form. Most rules strive for the highest attainable level of specificity in spelling out what is, and what is not, within the future contingent behavioral expectation of the parties. The movement, generally speaking, is toward determinacy. Even the notion of "just" and "unjust" wars has been replaced, in article 2(4) of the U.N. Charter, with another far more determinate notion: that the first use of force is *never* acceptable if it is used to derogate from the independence or territory of a state. Such move towards *textual* determinacy is a powerful force in the life of the international community, even though the goal, absolute certitude of literary content, is simply unattainable. Instead, the reach should exceed the grasp; that is what words are for. While some subjectivity will always be brought to words by the conceptual gestalt of the listener, much clarity can be gained if the speaker or writer, at least, is unambiguous about that which he wishes to communicate and uses words to express clarity rather than ambiguity or, perhaps worse and more common, merely to hold the podium until the arrival of an apprehended future enlightenment. Such a reasonable pursuit of greater determinacy is, seemingly, a primordial drive of rule systems and the international community is no exception. For example, a coastal state's territorial sea used to be measured—at least figuratively—at the distance from shore that a cannon could be fired,[94] which meant the breadth of sea over which effective coercive force could be exercised. This is a ballistic standard of obvious elasticity. Later, as we have noted, a coastal state's jurisdiction over the adjoining continental shelf was extended to encompass all of the shelf to whatever depth technology permitted exploration and exploitation, another standard of low specificity.[95] Under the most recent Convention on the Law of the Sea, however, the coastal state's territorial dominion is set at 12 miles, its exclusive economic zone at 200 miles, and its exclusive underwater coastal shelf-rights are determined at least in part by a fixed standard that measures the isobath and marine geological formations.[96] These are much more exact yardsticks. It is easier to measure a 2500-meter isobath than to measure equity in fixing the boundaries of states sharing a continental shelf.

Yet the rules applicable to that shelf do use both determinate and indeterminate standards, which coexist in a series of elaborately negotiated and carefully drafted treaties at least one of which binds most states.[97] Disputes about the meaning of these standards, as we have seen, have been submitted by states to the International Court of Justice and the resulting judgments have been carried out by the parties. As a result of the convergence of these various propitious factors, this area of international behavior is now governed by rules, widely accepted, which either employ specific standards (350 miles width, 2500-meter isobath, etc.) or have standards (equitable allocation) which, while initially vague, are becoming more determinate as their textual ambiguity is cured by judicially supplied "process determinacy." The international community thus seems to be moving toward rules in this area which have a powerful pull to compliance.

As we have observed, a rule is more likely to be perceived as legitimate when its contents are relatively transparent, when the content can be determined with comparative ease and certainty. However, further consideration has demonstrated that a rule's determinacy may be ascertained either from its text or from the application of the text in specific disputes by a legitimate clarifying process. The authority supplying this "process determinacy" need not necessarily be a court. It could be other states acting to apply a rule. For example, the emerging but still somewhat vague rule that territory may not be acquired by military force[98] has been clarified by the General Assembly when it rejected overwhelmingly several instances of violent acquisition,[99] or when states acting individually,[100] or through regional organizations,[101] refuse to give practical effect to a military occupation. Obviously such clarification of the rules by states is only persuasive if they are seen to be acting in a disinterested, principled fashion—expressing *opinio juris*—and not simply gratifying their short-term self-interest.

To say all this is also to admit to what appears to be an infinite logical regression, the oft-encountered unclosed circle. If the legitimacy of a rule depends on the legitimacy of a rule-giving institution, what determines the legitimacy of the institution? If indeterminate rules gain legitimacy when they are clarified by legitimate interpretation, what clarifies the rules by which the clarifying institutions and their clarifications are validated? We have sought to elude this conundrum by relying on observed *perception*, but that merely replicates the *logical* dilemma. If process-determinacy is supplied by institutions which, themselves, are *seen* to be of a high order of legitimacy, what controls that perception? Legitimate institutions, like legitimate rules, are those *which are established and function in accordance with ascertainable principles of right process*. We have argued that the legitimacy of these institutions, like the legitimacy of the rules they promulgate, interpret, and apply case-by-case, is a matter of degree. As with the rules, so with the institutions. Nevertheless, this degree of institutions' legitimacy, as with the rules, cannot be ascertained in abstract logic by recourse to the principles of right process being described in this study. Rather, the degree of their legitimacy can only be derived behaviorally, by studying the rule or the institution *in action*, to ascertain the force of its compliance pull on those addressed. This does not prove anything in logical theory. Yet observed phenomena have their own *contingent* logic. Any observed correlation between *properties* of a rule or of an institution and its *compliance pull* is not mere happenstance: it does not occur in a purely random fashion. The observer is not just passively observing behavior. Rather, from the observed patterns of correlation between the properties of a rule or institution, on the one hand, and its compliance pull on the other, the indicators of legitimacy *as they apply within a rule community* can be *deduced*. But they must be *deduced*, not assumed *a priori*. Moreover, the deduction is always contingent and limited in validity to that specific community within which it has been observed to operate. This imposes limits. If a rule exhibiting a high degree of legitimacy is habitually disobeyed, the definition of legitimacy, not only the disobeyed rule, requires further attention. The definition must be wrong. Were the rule validated by absolute logic, however, it would be the rule's desuetude that would demand "fixing." That is the meaning of the contingency which affects the writ of legitimacy theory. But such contingency does not invalidate. If the institutions which exhibit a high degree of determinacy, symbolic validation, coherence, and adherence are those which, in practice, are seen to endow the rules they make or interpret with a high degree of compliance pull, then one may claim to have deduced correctly something of descriptive, but also of *prescriptive*, importance. That importance, however, is rooted in behavioral (dare one say *scientific?*) observation of phenomena, rather than in fixed abstract logic. To place the matter in another context: in the behavior observations made by astrophysics certain things are explained about terrestrial origins, but such clarification, too, may merely postpone absolute finality. It is helpful to know—or to hypothesize—how the earth emerged from our universe, or how it relates to our galaxy, but such explanations do not yet unlock the ultimate mysteries of the relation of all firmament or the origins of matter. Nothing which is *observed* can provide *closure*, but must remain contingent. Before that useful reminder of incompletion, one can only demur, all the while pleading the mitigating caveat that sufficient unto the day are the contingent clarifications thereof.

To revert and summarize: the legitimacy of a rule is affected, in part, by the rule's determinacy. A rule's determinacy may be manifest either by its textual clarity or by the remedial work of a legitimate clarifying process. In passing, however, we have noted that clarity and determinacy are not always synonymous. It is to this point that we next turn to examine the complex relationship between the two concepts.

5

Determinacy and the

Sophist Rule-Idiot Rule Paradox

. . . precision is not to be sought for alike in all discussions, any more than in all products of the crafts.

Aristotle[*]

. . . : moderate indeterminacy does not undermine the law's legitimacy.

Ken Kress[**]

The preceding chapter has attempted to introduce the relationship of the legitimacy of a rule and its degree of determinacy. The aspects of determinacy examined in that chapter are: 1) the transparency of the standard established in the rule text; and 2) the extent to which the rule is accessible to legitimate clarifying procedures. These two aspects have been designated, respectively, the *substantive* (or textual) and the *procedural* (or institutional) sides of determinacy. The present chapter examines a number of other, related aspects of determinacy. As in the preceding chapter, central to the discussion of determinacy will be the hypothesis that the formal literary structure of a rule text is one of the several elements affecting the degree to which a rule is perceived to be legitimate.

At the conclusion of the preceding chapter we warned that a

[*] *Nichomachean Ethics*, Bk. 1, ch. 3.
[**] "Legal Indeterminacy," 77 *Cal. L. Rev.* 238 (1989).

rule's clarity, by itself, is no guarantee that it will exert a powerful compliance pull. This is because clarity, while often an indicator of determinacy, may occasionally produce results which are so at variance with common sense that the clear meaning of the rule is rejected by those whose conduct the rule is intended to govern. A rule which appears to be perfectly clear *unintentionally* may command what turns out to be an absurdity. Indeed, the simpler, clearer, and more straightforward a rule is, the greater is its propensity to produce an unintended absurdity, usually in unforeseen circumstances. Such a familiar sign as "No Running in the Halls" ceases to transmit a clear rule-signal and, instead, becomes ludicrous if the structure happens to be on fire. Of course, the possibility that this sort of absurdity may sometimes occur does not support the view that clarity conduces to absurdity, merely that it is not an infallible indicator of compliance pull.

Let us examine why this should be so, why precision in rule drafting may sometimes even undermine, rather than fortify a rule's determinacy. Let us also ask what can be done about mitigating such odd side-effects.

An illustration of the problem may be helpful. The United States and Great Britain recently signed an agreement which purports to change the rules applicable to a fugitive who has committed a crime in one signatory and has escaped to the other.[102] Ordinarily, when a country in which a crime was committed has sought extradition, U.S. courts[103] permitted the fugitive to resist by establishing that the crime was a "political offense." The purpose of the new treaty is to eliminate that defense, making extraditable anyone believed to have committed murder, bombing, hijacking, hostage-taking, or similar "terrorist" acts. The State Department, pressing the Senate for consent to ratify the new agreement, argued that only in this way can terrorism be contained and punished.[104] Critics responded that "it denies that Americans might sometimes refuse to condemn such actions—for example when used in attempts to escape from police states. . . ."[105]

The U.S.-U.K. agreement is now in effect. It proceeds from the notion that murder, bombing, or kidnapping is always inexcusable and should never be condoned, no matter whether the actor is a wanton criminal or a righteous revolutionary. Nor should it matter whether he or she felt provoked by political repression, economic deprivation, or simply by the desire to seize power. Opponents criticize the new rule for abandoning America's time-honored role as a haven from political persecution. They want to distinguish between persons charged with ordinary crimes and those provoked to violence by repression, preferring that the law take into account not only *what* was done, but also *why* and *to whom.*

The preference for a simple, straightforward rule based on *what* has been stated by Judge Abraham D. Sofaer, the Reagan administration's State Department Legal Adviser, in an important essay entitled *Terrorism and the Law.*[106] Answering opponents of the treaty, he criticized what he described as a recent trend to soften rules against terrorists by making them less clear-cut. As further examples he cited the Hostage Convention,[107] the High Seas Convention,[108] and the 1977 First Protocol to the Geneva Conventions of 1949,[109] each of which prohibits various kinds of violence but exempts persons who take hostages, engage in piracy, or engage in irregular military combat *if* they are fighting against "colonialist, racist and alien regimes."[110] The Legal Adviser condemned these efforts to exempt from the rules persons fighting what some perceive as "good" causes. The result of such exculpation, according to Sofaer, is that "international law has been systematically and intentionally fashioned to give special treatment to, or leave unregulated, those activities which are the source of most acts of international terror."[111]

Sofaer's version of the meaning of these caveats is not beyond criticism.[112] Even if his analysis is correct, however, he does not make explicit *why* persons who commit criminal acts only against tyrants, oppressors, perpetrators of gross economic and racial injustices, and against foreign occupiers of their lands *should* be treated the same as those who commit comparable acts for pleasure, private gain, or as an undemocratic shortcut to power.

It is not difficult to think of reasons why the two might be distinguished. Nowadays, there is wide agreement that colonialism, racism, and alien domination are prohibited conduct.[113] No state any longer publicly asserts a *right* to colonize or oppress. In passing, let us note, perhaps even cheer, this recently acquired abstemiousness in state conduct. Some, while still colonizing and oppressing as if nostalgic for the good old days of gunboat diplomacy, at least make-believe otherwise, in recognition of the strong pull to compliance exerted by the new rules. Outright defiance, however, is rare. When the norms are blatantly disregarded—as by South Africa in its treatment of blacks—then an international community lacking collective enforcement power might, instead, rationally opt to license remedial violence by the victims. For example, the rules could encourage states to give victims refuge, supplies, training, even military bases from which to strike back at their oppressors. Yet, were such conduct licensed, such license presumably would not, as a logical concomitant, also have to be extended to ordinary criminals.

Judge Sofaer thinks all such licensing of violence wrong in principle, however, and he rejects the notion that the international community's rules of conduct should make distinctions between when it is, and is not, permissible. He argues that acts such as murder, hijacking, and hostage-taking should *always* be prohibited and not condoned or encouraged under any circumstances. In this view, anarchy ensues from "the premise that terrorist acts can be lawful in the pursuit of proper goals. . . ."[114] As President Reagan put it, in a world where "there are innumerable groups with grievances . . . the first step in solving some of these fundamental challenges, in gettting to the root cause of conflict, is to declare that terrorism is not an acceptable alternative and will not be tolerated."[115]

Sofaer and Reagan, in other words, believed that the international standard of conduct should turn on *what* acts are committed, unmodified by considerations of *why* and *to whom* they were done. For example, all rebel forces which kill, injure, or blow up property should be dealt with as terrorists, and not ever as prisoners of war. The Reagan administration was especially critical of article 1(4) of Geneva Protocol I of 1977 precisely because it adds *why* and *to whom* factors to exculpate conduct which should always be impermissible. That article extends the protection of humanitarian rules for treatment of military prisoners to insurgent irregular forces when these are engaged in fighting against colonial domination and alien occupation, or against racist regimes, in the exercises of the right of self-determination.[116] "Never before," Sofaer complained, "has the applicability of the law of war been made to turn on the purported aims of a conflict."[117] In a message to the Senate explaining his refusal to seek consent to ratify the Protocol, Reagan said he was acting "at the ideological levels so important to terrorist organizations, to deny these groups legitimacy as international actors";[118] while Sofaer attacked the Protocol as a "significant success" for "radical groups [seeking] to acquire legal legitimacy."[119]

Obviously, U.S. opposition to Protocol I and similar rules is not based on sympathy for racists, colonialists, or alien occupiers of others' lands. Rather, it reflects the fear that exceptions based on *why* and *to whom* would let too many terrorists slip through the net.[120] To make killing, hostage-taking, or hijacking acceptable when done for a "good" cause would send the international rule system down a slippery slope. *The rules would lose their determinacy.* Every criminal could justify resort to violence by claiming political, economic, or social grievances. Rules meant to restrain violence would be swallowed up by vague, elastic exceptions and exculpations. As the rules became unclear, they would cease to exert a pull to compliance.

The trouble with this analysis is that it is not borne out by reality. The Reagan administration, itself, felt little pull to comply with its own clear rules against aid to irregular combatants in such places as Nicaragua, Afghanistan, and Angola. One problem with the Sofaer-Reagan defense of an anti-terrorism rule employing simple *what*-based normativity is that virtually no state in practice ever seems inclined to make a wholehearted commitment to such a rule.

That *what*-based rules, despite their superior, simple clarity, nevertheless may lack compliance pull can best be illustrated by a hypothetical example. Suppose that, in 1938, the Prague government of President Edvard Benes, foreseeing the inevitable dismemberment of Czechoslovakia after the Munich pact, had infiltrated a trained death squad of German Jewish exiles back across the German border, in civilian clothing, to assassinate Adolph Hitler. Suppose they had succeeded, but in the process had also killed a number of innocent bystanders. What ought the international rules to say about this? Should Czechoslovakia, and the assassins, be congratulated or condemned? If the perpetrators were to reach the United States, should they be extradited or given a ticker tape parade?

This hypothetical case challenges the argument favoring a rule that brooks no exculpation, simply making such violence wrong, regardless of circumstances. A clear, simple, *what*-based rule would exert very little compliance pull because, in the circumstances, almost everyone would agree that the terrorists were "justified." If the terrorists thought about it, they would just know instinctively that the rule, no matter how clear, would not be applied and, thus, need not inhibit them.

What is the theoretical explanation for this paradox of a rule's clarity actually undermining its legitimacy? Literature is a good place to look for an answer. In Fyodor Dostoevsky's *Crime and Punishment*, the latent conflict between simplistic clarity and legitimacy arises when Rodion Raskolnikov, a poor student, kills a malevolent pawnbroker with an axe. In a recently staged version by the Soviet director Yuri Lyubimov, the police investigator, Porfiry Petrovich, demands that the world reject exculpatory excuses for crime. Whether Raskolnikov's act should be regarded as criminal, he argues, must be determined solely by reference to *what* he has done, not *why* or *to whom* he did it. "Pity the criminal all you like," he exclaims, "but don't call evil good."[121] Porfiry is not immune to pity but he believes that to allow it to shape the law would destroy society. There is a social compact among citizens, a promise to act lawfully, provided the society punishes those who act unlawfully. For this contract to be effective, the line between lawful and unlawful conduct must be clear, simple and direct, which is only possible if prohibitions are defined as *acts*, not as *motives* or *objectives*. The exculpatory "why?" and the mitigating "to whom?" should in certain circumstances perhaps serve to soften the way society acts against the perpetrator and may even arouse pity, but no more than that. Otherwise, the fundamental social compact would be threatened because the line between what is, and what is not, permissible would become smudged. "Why" and "to whom" are dust thrown into the eyes of the rules, making them indeterminate and eroding their legitimacy.

Porfiry emphasizes the importance of clarity in legitimating a rule of conduct and making it applicable to the real world. The more the rule departs from quantitative measures to embrace qualitative ones, and the more it accommodates exculpatory exceptions based on "good" motives—the more it differentiates between "just" and "unjust" causes—the more difficult it becomes to determine the rule's content. And the more opaque and elastic that content, he would argue, the less likely it is to control actual conduct.

Yet, even Porfiry would probably choose to make *some* exceptions, just as President Reagan made exceptions in favor of the Contras and the Mujahedeen, while almost everyone probably would have made an exception for someone who had killed Hitler. It is Porfiry's dilemma that a blanket policy of excluding all exculpatory *why* and *to whom* factors would create more unpredictability than certainty. A rule without exculpation, while seeming to court legitimacy by its apparent simplistic clarity, may actually appear illegitimate by producing results that appear so extraordinarily unjust, cavalier, unfair, even absurd, as to undermine the rule's ability to exert a strong pull to compliance.

This paradox—clarity *undermining* legitimacy rather than reinforcing it—occurs in various circumstances, but most often when the clear rule is perceived to be unjust. As we noted, in passing, in Chapter 2, the shared sense of justice or fairness of a moral community has a power to pull toward voluntary rule compliance which is different from, yet comparable to the compliance pull which legitimacy exerts on behalf of rules of the secular community. When justice and legitimacy pull in opposite directions, however, the result is to undermine the will to comply with such a rule. To mitigate this effect, in practice, judges and others charged with interpreting or applying rules in a secular community usually try to interpret the secular rules to avoid at least the most cacophonous clashes between principles of justice and a prima facie valid secular rule. Moreover, the rule-makers, in fashioning a norm, are often willing to trade off a degree of clarity for a greater consonance with the common perception of fairness, making exculpatory exception to an otherwise simple and straightforward rule.

These are rather special, exceptional circumstances. Most national legislation is *what*-oriented, just as are most of the rules in the international system. This is meant to promote determinacy, and it succeeds. But there are exceptions, where trade-offs need to be made. For example, justifiable homicide. What homicide is justifiable? The English common law, aligned with Porfiry's proposition, holds that nothing excuses cannibalism, not even when starving passengers in a lifeboat save the many by eating one. English law extends pity, and perhaps even clemency, to persons haplessly caught in such a situation, but it leaves the norm clear and simple: cannibalism is always, simply, illegal.[122] The U.S. Model Penal Code, on the other hand, allows for exculpatory circumstances which can transform an act of cannibalism into sanctioned behavior.[123] The *why* factor has thus been introduced into the rule alongside the *what* factor.

The English common law rule, and Porfiry's proposition, point to what we may call an "idiot norm" while the U.S. Model Penal Code prescribes a "sophist norm." Both the concept of "idiot norm" and "sophist norm"—terms which are useful shorthand for purposes of our analysis—are meant to be neutral denotations. The term "idiot norm" is intended to conjure up the qualities of another of Dostoyevsky's characters: Prince Myshkin, the Christ-like figure in *The Idiot* whose characteristics include his single-minded passion for arrow-like truths, "simple" principles, and comprehensive mastery of self and others in accordance with invariable verities, regardless of dangerous, even absurd, consequences. The term "sophist norm" is here deployed not in the pejorative sense in which it was used by Plato, but rather in its original meaning of intense scrutiny of simple ideas to plumb

their multi-layered complexity. It is this process of skeptical analysis of simple "truths," evolved by fifth-century B.C. Greek philosophers, which led to a more textured understanding of ideas and
of reality.[124] "Sophist norm" should convey to the reader that
same approach to normative conceptualization, a running of the
intellectual gauntlet, yielding a calibrated rule, one shaped with
a careful eye to detail and common sense.

It is evident that an "idiot norm" based on *what*—the definition of conduct by the actor purely in terms of externalized acts—
is much simpler: to *write*, to *understand*, and to *apply* than a
law which takes the quality of the motive and of the victim into
account. The simplistic common law against cannibalism can be
stated in the sentence set to music by Donald Swan: "Eating
people is wrong."[125] The "sophist rule" set out in the U.S. Model
Code, permitting the eating of people in certain circumstances,
could well run to several paragraphs in an effort to be neither
over—nor under—inclusive and requires tough judgement-calls, case-
by-case. Thus the English passengers in a lifeboat would know
exactly what the common law requires of them. The passengers
governed by the Code might be in some doubt. The English passengers, however, would probably think their law distinctly unreasonable, and thus ineffective in guiding situational conduct, a
feeling the Americans in the lifeboat probably would not have
about their Code.

Similarly ambiguous reactions occur when states find their
conduct purportedly regulated by an international version of the
idiot rule which makes no *why* or *to whom* allowances under
circumstances in which, if the rule were to be followed "to the
letter," it would conflict with the popular notion of fairness and
common sense. For example, the U.N. Charter, in articles 2(4)
and 51, sets out an idiot rule pertaining to the use of force. It
says, in substance, that states may not initiate the use of armed
force against another state. They must exercise restraint, responding only after an actual armed attack on them. This rule, on its
face, seems to enjoy a high level of determinacy. And in most
instances of conflict, the rule also makes sense. It is fair to a
global population concerned about survival of the species. It rests

on a simple question of fact: Who struck first? It is usually possible, in these days of outer space sensing devices, to provide persuasive proof as to which of two or more combatants initiated hostilities. Even without such "spy satellite" evidence, the answer can usually be determined by looking to see which party to the conflict is ahead after the first day of fighting. Nevertheless, despite its superficial clarity, the rule—under certain circumstances—does not satisfy the test of common sense or fairness; and thus, deprived of the compliance pull its clear standard was meant to assure, the rule also will not accurately predict the actual conduct of states. This is because a literal reading of the rule can lead to absurd results at the margins of its application. For example it would compel a state threatened by a nuclear attack to wait until it had actually been hit ("armed attack") before permitting the use of force in self-defense.[126] In less dramatic circumstances, the rule would require even a state like Israel or Singapore to wait until after an armed attack before striking back, by which time its minute territory might well have been overrun. Such a rule lacks essential legitimacy, because it is evidently absurd. It is easy to predict that no state would abide by its strictures in at least some situations, as Israel demonstrated by destroying the Iraqi nuclear reactor in an air raid. In other words, the clear meaning of the rule is *not* determinate because the members of the community to which it applies have already decided that, in at least some circumstances, the rule cannot mean what it says. It exerts a feeble compliance pull. Where an arrow-like rule, however clear, encounters a universal sense of its absurdity, oft-times powered by an outraged sense of its injustice, the determinacy—and, thus the legitimacy—of the rule suffers.

This does not mean, unfortunately, that some other, more textured rule—a sophist rule setting out the exact circumstances in which a state might strike in *anticipatory* self-defense before actually being attacked—necessarily would be perceived as more legitimate or would exercise greater compliance pull on governments. Quite conceivably, such a rule (as Judge Sofaer might point out) would merely encourage every malevolent government to take advantage of the holes in the net. A wise cautionary note has been struck by the World Court jurist Professor Manfred Lachs, who reminds us that the plea of anticipatory self-defense has been used by aggressors in "countless instances . . . alleging the need to forestall attack. Pleas of this kind may amount to severe distortions of reality."[127] Thus, it may be necessary to conclude that no rule—neither an idiot law nor a sophist law—on this subject is likely, in present circumstances, to exercise a powerful compliance pull on the conscience or the conduct of nations. It may just be up to politics, in the form of deterence strategy, and not the international rule system, to guide and illuminate state behavior in this area, since neither an idiot rule nor a sophist rule seems able, so far, to express a clear and credible normative consensus.

Idiot rules, it seems, sometimes tend to be unsophisticated in their lack of fine-tuning and are then likely to be perceived—at their margins—as unreasonable and illegitimate in their demands. If a patently absurd or unfair result accrues from the only possible application of the evident meaning of a simple rule in circumstances requiring a more calibrated response, then that rule has suffered *reductio ad absurdum*, a condition which even may undermine its legitimacy in circumstances not at its margin. Mr. Bumble's conclusion that "If the law supposes that, the law is a ass—a idiot" is a most human reaction demonstrating the "legitimacy costs" often inherent in idiot rules. While an assinine national law is still a law and may be enforced, an international rule widely perceived as absurd soon loses its capacity to obligate. In the international—unlike the national—system, once a norm is deprived of its legitimacy, it becomes a dead letter.

Reductio ad absurdum is but one way even a simple, perfectly clear and straightforward rule nevertheless can be indeterminate and illegitimate. If, looking at its perfectly clear text, the observer is led to exclaim "but surely it can't mean *that*," the reader is caught in a cognitive dissonance between the rule's text and its meaning as reinterpreted by recourse to common sense or some imagined "reasonable intent." Surely, the reader thinks, the rulemakers must have had a different result in mind, or would have, had they thought about it. The rule, as it operates, has become incoherent: that is, it operates to frustrate the very thing it was intended to promote. Its words belie its purpose. As Paul said of the law in his second epistle to the Corinthians, "the letter killeth, but the spirit giveth life."

Another way a seemingly transparent rule can be made indeterminate is by a change in the circumstance which made the rule reasonable at some earlier time. For example, the energy crisis produced the fuel-saving 55-mile per hour speed limit on U.S. roads, which was widely obeyed while the crisis persisted. But when, a few years later, gasoline again became cheap and plentiful, the rule began to be generally disobeyed and was only rarely enforced. Thus the clear rule that limited speed to 55-miles per hour became opaque as the public perceived and acted upon the authorities' increasing tolerance for a *de facto* limit of 65- or 70-miles per hour. Being a state law, the rule may still be capable of enforcement by the police. But it is no longer effectuated by a public perception of its legitimacy. There may not be any question, in Professor D'Amato's sense, as to whether article 2(4) of the U.N. Charter or the 55-mile per hour speed limit, is the "law." Also, there is no misconstruing these rules' simple, quantitative standards. They appear to excel in concise, precise inelasticity. Yet, for all their textual clarity, these rules do not describe or predict with accuracy the actual behavior of the real world. Their determinacy is undermined by a popular perception that they can't mean what they so plainly say. The irrationality of the rules—their incoherence: a failure to be instrumental in relation to the purposes for which they were devised—causes us to believe, and act on the belief, that they have become indeterminate. The rules, therefore, have lost some of their compliance pull.

Rationality, some irreducible bedrock of reasonableness and coherence, lies just beneath the surface of our operational notion of rule-determinacy. National courts have noted this by refusing to interpret laws in a literal manner if, to do so, compels a patently absurd result. Paradoxically, some of the simplest, clearest rules, the idiot rules, are the very ones that break down into irrationality at their margins. In this sense, a superficially high level of clarity may hide a rule's indeterminacy, an imagined, or rationalized, lack of certitude which results from dissonance between literal command and reasonableness or coherence.

Sophist rules, we have been told by Porfiry, President Reagan, and Judge Sofaer, are subject to different, more obvious legitimacy costs due to their elasticity. Norms setting out standards of compliance which are measured in complex qualitative terms, or which are hedged by *why* and *to whom* exculpations, may be difficult to apply to real life situations. Even though such rules may accord more closely with popular reason and, thus, with actual behavior, still the rules' sophisticated and exculpatory texture may proclaim that textual agreement as to their content is only an illusion. The very prediction that a sophist rule will prove impossible to apply can, itself, constitute a powerful motive for ignoring it in practice.

The illusory quality of much sophist normativity stems mostly from the difficulty of achieving general perceptive consensus, in actual cases, as to the meaning of a rule standard incorporating such complex phenomena as motive, or provocation. The previously noted rule in Geneva Protocol I of 1977, which requires prisoner of war treatment for guerillas fighting "colonialism, racism or alien domination" was not only hard to formulate, but would be even more difficult to apply to actual civil conflict. Which rebellions qualify? Has Jonas Savimba's army been fighting for self-determination in Angola, this past decade, against the "domination" of "alien" Cubans? What is the implication of the exculpatory *to whom*—"colonialism, racism or alien domination"— for those fighting the governments of Israel and Britain, or, for that matter, for persons thinking of shooting officers of the U.S. Department of the Interior on Indian reservations or in Puerto Rico? Or Soviet officials in the Armenian Republic?

Structurally, the gains in a rule's legitimacy made by recourse to sophist standards thus tend to be dissipated, in practice, when the application of the standard ends up with unilateral, self-serving exculpatory interpretations of those rules by interested parties, interpretations which cannot readily be refuted by recourse to the all-too elastic rule text. For example, applying the proposed international norms known as the Reagan Doctrine, Ambassador Jeane Kirkpatrick has argued that U.S. support for the Nicaraguan Con-

tras is permissible, while Soviet and Cuban support for the Sandinistas is not, because the Contras are democrats fighting a totalitarian regime while the Sandinistas are totalitarians being used by
Russians and Cubans to colonize Nicaragua.[128] A sophist rule
which lends itself to that interpretation, however sensible its intent, is unlikely to inhibit any state from pursuing any opportunity
for short-term interest gratification and will be dismissed from serious consideration by states when they weigh their options.

Thus, while it is not necessarily true that a sophist rule is less
determinate than an idiot rule, it is generally the case that, as rules
become more complex, the determinacy and, so also, the legitimacy of the rule's application and, ultimately, of the rule itself,
becomes increasingly dependent, first, on the degree of common
community understanding of the rule's complex content and, second, on the perceived legitimacy of the process by which the rule
is applied. As we saw in the preceding chapter, this lack of *textual*
determinacy may be redressed by *process* determinacy. If it is not,
then the text will be seen to lack the ability to describe, predict,
and prescribe actual state conduct. It will have minimal compliance pull.

Were it not for the lack of global agreement on the content of
sophisticated rules incorporating *why* and *to whom* factors, and,
even more, the absence of credible institutional processes for applying such inevitably complex, textually indeterminate standards,
most of us would probably reject Porfiry's preference for idiot rules
and opt for the sophist rules whenever possible. The Reagan Doctrine, with its sophisticated distinctions between external support
for "good" insurgents against "bad" regimes as opposed to support
for "bad" insurgents against "good" regimes, undoubtedly has
ethical and political appeal for liberals as well as conservatives. It
also has a considerable pedigree in the normative evolution of the
international system. The "just war" doctrine struggled to make
precisely such distinctions even in the time of Emperor Constan-
tine. Early church theologians, having to reconcile pacifist theology
with imperial military needs, reinterpreted older Greek and Roman
principles to arrive at a Christian norm.[129] In the wake of the Empire's fall, Augustine used the just war doctrine to deny legitimacy

to internal and external challenges to Christian unity.[130] The same motive led Thomas Aquinas further to refine the definition by requiring wars to be (1) waged on valid authority; (2) just with regard to the cause espoused; and (3) animated by a right intention.[131] Grotius, the last classical expositor of the just war doctrine, tried to provide a credible basis for the distinction in natural law rather than in Christian theology.[132]

After the onset of "charter diplomacy" with the founding of the League of Nations and of the United Nations, the sophist "just war" concept was replaced by the aforementioned idiot rule that makes the initiation of force by states invariably unacceptable. The Reagan Doctrine, sensing that the new norm does not accurately describe or predict actual state behavior and, moreover, is, at least in part, unfair or even absurd, proposed a form of system-wide return to a "just war" rule.[133] In practice, however, this meant assistance to the Contras of Nicaragua, the Mujahedeen of Afghanistan, the Cambodian resistance, and to Jonas Savimbi in Angola, while deploring aid to the Irish Republican Army, the Palestine Liberation Organization, and the rebels in El Salvador.[134]

This deductive result suggests the problem with sophist rules. While an idiot rule more-or-less applies itself, sophist rules usually require an effective, credible, institutionalized, and legitimate interpreter of the rule's meaning in various instances. During the Middle Ages, the papacy assumed this role of legitimate and legitimating interpreter of the rule which categorized wars as "just" and "unjust."[135] The process by which the rule was applied provided the process-determinacy which the rule's bare text so evidently lacked. Gregory VII taught that only wars conducted pursuant to papal authority were just.[136] As the papacy declined, however, monarchs became the self-serving judges of whether their cause was just and papal approval became merely "a useful adjunct, if not an absolutely necessary one."[137] With that, the sophist rule withered into illegitimacy and gave way to an idiot rule: first, Vattel's principle that all war was legal (as long as it was fought "by the rules"),[138] and, later, that all war-making (except in self-defense) was illegal.

Since they are less obviously clear, sophist rules need more help from legitimate interpreters than do idiot rules. Thus, in dealing with cannibalism, a judge applying the common law's idiot rule need merely determine whether someone was eaten and by whom. In most cases, that would be an easily ascertained fact. His role is minimal. Under the U.S. Model Code's sophist rule, however, the judge or jury must play a far more important part, deciding not only whether someone had been eaten but also whether the hungry people in the lifeboat would have died very soon had they not resorted to cannibalism, whether they had reason to believe that they would not be rescued in time, whether they followed a fair procedure for choosing who to eat and many other *why* and *to whom* issues. The judge hearing an extradition request under the new U.S.-U.K. rules need merely decide whether there is probable cause to believe that a violent act was committed by the defendant. Under the traditional sophist extradition rule, however, the judge also was required to examine "the capacity of foreign regimes to do justice"[139] as well as the appropriateness of the aims of the terrorists, the methods chosen, the victims selected, and the repressiveness of the regime against which the terrorists were fighting.

In sum, a rule finely calibrated to reflect sophist considerations, embodying a carefully tuned system of regulatory and exculpatory principles, may suffer legitimacy costs due to its very complexity, its elastic texture which invites dispute as to whether the rule is applicable in any particular case. It seems to promote indecisive, self-interested sparring about the relevance of the rule's exculpatory principles to actual, often ambiguous, events. In such circumstances, textual indeterminacy can be seen most clearly as undermining the rule's legitimacy. Even though the sophist text may be the very model of fairness, yet it will fail to obligate the conduct of states in real world conflicts.

In the context of a domestic legal system, this paradoxical vulnerability of rules which are both rational and just but also complex and intricately configured is mitigated by tribunals which are charged with applying the law and clarifying its content in the context of actual disputes; tribunals, moreover, which the society generally trusts to be principled in their reasoning. In the international system, to understate the point, there is a shortage of comparable, legitimate institutions capable of clarifying and validating the sophist norm's standards through case-by-case application. As a result, even what appear to be painstakingly calibrated and perfectly reasonable sophist rules are sometimes deemed of low legitimacy by dint of their illegitimate application, which usually takes the form of self-serving assertions by an interested party—President Reagan and Ambassador Kirkpatrick come to mind—in the course of implementing an action of doubtful normativity. The sophist rule invites exculpatory self-justifications by suspected violators, excuses which cannot be dismissed by that laughter, noted in Chapter 4, which demonstrates a rule's determinacy. A sophist rule, in the absence of a legitimate, impartial interpreter, is likely to be perceived as illegitimate because it can be made to appear to permit anything.

Greater rule clarity, however, is not always the answer. Paradoxically, it can also be a factor in undermining a rule's legitimacy. A simple, utterly clear text may create serious problems of irrationality, unfairness, or perceived incoherence at the fringes of its practical application. This causes the superficially clear text to become constructively indeterminate in the minds of those whose conduct the rule seeks to regulate.

Since both sophist and idiot rules thus seem frequently to incur legitimacy costs, we are left to confront a dilemma, to which an answer must be found if we are to understand how determinacy can raise a rule's compliance pull.

6

Redefining Determinacy

Determinacy is a literary characteristic of rule texts and of rules; it is about transparency. It denotes a rule's clarity of meaning: how effectively it communicates with the parties to a dispute. It also denotes the extent to which the rule's communicative power exerts its own dynamic pull toward compliance, which may not always correlate with its textual clarity.

We have noted, with regret—because it would have simplified matters were it otherwise—that the determinacy of a rule is not simply a textual property; nor is it solely a consequence of the literary form in which it is cast. Although very clear rules constructed around quantitative standards ("2500-meter isobath") and binary categories ("red light to port, green light to starboard") give the appearance of readily accessible determinacy, this can be misleading. If a simple, straightforward norm—we have used the term "idiot rule"—produces what is generally perceived as an incoherent, unfair, or absurd result when it is applied to a real, or even an anticipated, situation, then those to whom the rule is directed—and whose voluntary compliance is evidence of its legitimacy—may not feel much pull to comply. They may instead decide that an absurd result could not have been intended and will ignore or reinterpret the rule. Even the mere expectation that states will ignore or reinterpret a rule can undermine its capacity to command voluntary compliance. Thus a perfectly clear rule may be far from determinate and less than legitimate.

On the other hand, a sophist rule of complex, elastic texture, employing a subjective, qualitative standard to measure compliance and configured by exculpatory *why* and *to whom* considerations, while superficially appearing to have less legitimacy than an idiot rule because it has less textual clarity and certainty, might better predict and influence actual state behavior precisely because it makes more sense or seems more just. It will thus exert a stronger compliance pull.

For example, consider the rule noted in Chapter 4 as a model of clarity: *pacta sunt servanda*—treaties are binding. Its very clarity pressages problems. What if the subject matter of the treaty disappears? What if the circumstances in which the treaty operates are altered so radically as to make nonsense of it? What is the validity of a treaty governing international commercial access to a river port once the river has changed course? In such circumstances, to insist on the immutability of treaty rights would make the rule unfair or absurd. For such exigencies, the international rule-system *implies* into treaty texts a sophist proviso—the *clausula rebus sic stantibus*,[140] which permits a treaty to be deemed to have lost its validity upon a profound change of circumstance. While this reduces the rule's clarity, it actually makes it more sensible. *Rebus sic stantibus* transforms *pacta sunt servanda* from an idiot rule into a sophist rule, protecting it from the perception that it is "a ass." The former port need no longer tolerate uncontrolled access, now that it is landlocked.

At the same time the rule has become far more elastic, thereby creating a new legitimacy problem. Unlike idiot rules, sophist norms usually do not "apply themselves." The determinacy and legitimacy of a sophist rule, as perceived by those to whom the rule is directed, depend in significant part on whether there is a process for the rule's case-by-case application which, itself, is widely accepted as legitimate. Sophist rules lacking this interpretative component tend to be seen as mere hunting licenses for states to do whatever they wish.

A good example of the problem is the aborted effort begun by the United Nations in 1972 to draft a code for the prevention and punishment of terrorism. After first trying, but failing, to agree on a straightforward prohibition of designated terrorist acts, the members tried to seek agreement on a more configured sophist rule.[141] For two years, negotiators sought consensus on a rule with exculpations.[142] The Non-Aligned Group favored a rule that would exempt terrorist acts on behalf of "the inalienable right to self-determination and independence of all peoples under colonial and racist regimes and other forms of alien domination" in recognition of "the legitimacy of their struggle, in particular the struggle of national liberation movements. . . ."[143] The Soviet Union demanded special consideration for "acts committed in resisting an aggressor in territories occupied by the latter, and action by workers to secure their rights against the yoke of exploiters."[144] The advocates of this sort of text, however, made no attempt to stipulate a legitimate process for interpreting the rule, evidently preferring to leave case-by-case application to states. In effect, this would have allowed anyone to justify anything, a consequence the sponsors probably intended.

Those who would make the prohibition and punishment of terrorist acts inapplicable to forces fighting colonialism, racism, and alien domination, or capitalist exploitation, are rightly suspect of wanting no rule at all, and the suspicion cannot be allayed unless the advocates of such exculpatory caveats add provisions for interpreting their rule in a legitimate forum. Similarly, those in the West who propose a new rule to permit states to aid citizens of other states seeking the overthrow of totalitarian foreign-imposed regimes are obliged—for the sake of their own credibility—to suggest a process for making coherent, principled decisions, case-by-case, on the proposed rule's application; else the norm would predict only to chaos and would and *should* not be taken seriously. In other words, if the state system wishes to resuscitate the just war doctrine, it must also revive the legitimizing role of the papacy or its contemporary, secular equivalent.

The tendency of qualitative standards and complex sophist rules to create an appearance of indeterminacy can only be rectified by adding a credible interpreter to supply process-determinacy. Ideally, this would suggest a vision of nations solemnly taking their disagreements before the International Court of Justice. In practice, for many reasons, this is not now a realistic scenario, if only because of the limited number of states party to the general mandatory jurisdiction of that tribunal under article 36(2) of its statute.[145] The I.C.J. can only act as interpreter of a small number of rule texts. Therefore, advocates of sophist rules must explore alternatives. The key is institutionalized multilateralization. Obviously, if all, or virtually all, states in the international system agree on the meaning of a sophist rule in a particular instance, that consensus helps to define and legitimate the rule, even if abstract definitional questions remain unresolved. For example, nations generally agree that South Africa's apartheid violates a fundamental international prohibition on institutionalized racism even though there is continuing disagreement about whether the same rule also is contravened by U.S. policy toward native Indians, Burundi's treatment of the Hutus, or Sri Lankan treatment of Tamils. The rules regarding racism thus are weakened by large areas of indeterminacy; but they are clear enough in respect of the kind of violation practiced in South Africa. Still, the legitimacy of a rule cast in a broad term like "racist" but which only seems to be generally perceived as applicable in one case, or a few instances, remains justifiably suspect.

We have noted that sophist rules do not have the benefit of automaticity—do not apply themselves—the way idiot rules do. Thence the search for the credible interpreter. The *universal* political institutions of the international system in theory could act to apply rules case by case, but, as with the General Assembly, a persuasive consensus is likely to be elusive in all but a few instances such as *apartheid*. Interpreting done by a deeply divided General Assembly does not help. The ineffectuality of such divided verdicts is illustrated by the lawyer's anecdote about flowers sent by colleagues to a judge's hospital room with an attached card reading "Get well soon: 5 to 4."

A universally based system of interpretation such as the International Court, or the General Assembly acting by consensus, however, is only potentially the *best*, not the *only* system for defining the content of elastic sophist rules. Even a forum of limited, but more compatible, multilateral membership—NATO, the Organization of African Unity, or the dispute-resolution mechanisms so commonly employed in international business disputes[146]—would be a more credible interpreter of a sophist rule than the foreign office of a single self-interested state. For example, suppose fifteen democratic states agreed that they would henceforth intervene on behalf of any of their members threatened by foreign-supported subversion or insurrection. Such a rule would gain in determinacy if it were accompanied by a public process of fact-finding which would determine collectively, case by case, whether the stated conditions for intervention actually existed. On the other hand, if there were no such process and each state were free to decide on its own whether there were grounds to intervene, the rule's meaning would be far less determinate and it would be perceived as lacking in legitimacy. Process determinacy—even when supplied by a political grouping with limited membership, but *ipso facto* more so when validated by a global rule community—thus may credibly mitigate the elastic quality of the sophist rule, if the process is generally perceived by almost all its constituents—those to whom the process speaks—as usually operating in accordance with their agreed definition of right process. One may then speak of its high degree of contingent validation.

Alternatively, there also are structural means to ameliorate the idiot rule's propensity to *reductio ad absurdum*. One way is to *de-construct* the category of activity being regulated, prohibiting only narrow categories of acts as to which, by common agreement, no exculpation will be allowed. Thus, "terrorism," as a category of regulated activity, can be replaced by narrower sub-categories like hostage-taking,[147] violence against diplomats[148] and aerial hijacking.[149] As to these, at least, the preponderance of the global community appears genuinely willing to accept a simple inelastic rule without exculpatory exceptions. More can be done along such micro-regulatory lines with collective remedies directed toward violence against children, against persons not owing allegiance to the targeted government, or, perhaps, more generally against civilians not in government service.

The effect of such de-construction is to leave regulated by simple *what*-based rules only those activities as to which there is a general systemic consensus to bar exculpatory *why* and *to whom* considerations under any conceivable circumstances. For example, the U.S. has prosecuted, however ruefully, a hijacker fleeing from Eastern bloc oppression,[150] thereby discharging its obligations (to prosecute or extradite) under the Hague Convention.[151] While such flights to freedom, to paraphrase Porfiry, may generate our sympathy, they do not lead us to overlook the evil of hijacking. The Hague Convention's idiot rule only becomes genuinely determinate when it accurately reflects the nations' overweening revulsion against *any* aerial hijacking, for any reason whatever. A similar example is the accord signed by the U.S. and Cuba in 1973[152] which virtually eliminated[153] hijackings after both states had become exasperated enough to commit themselves without exception to their eradication. Similarly, the 1978 Bonn Declaration, adhered to by Canada, France, Italy, Japan, U.K., U.S., and West Germany,[154] imposed collective measures, without qualifications, against states which refuse to extradite or prosecute hijackers.[155] While every idiot rule has potential for *reductio ad absurdum*, it is possible by narrowing the rule to narrow also the margins at which a sense of the rule's absurdity appears. Similarly, too, even Islamic and Soviet authorities joined in the U.N. Security Council[156] to condemn the Iranian violations of U.S. diplomatic immunity in Teheran in 1979; and judges from Islamic and Socialist countries joined in a unanimous ruling by the International Court[157] rejecting the notion that the taking of diplomatic hostages could ever be excused by alleged wrongdoings—such as espionage—by those seized or by the country they represent.

There are other forms of deconstruction which can help reduce the idiot norm's tendency to deteriorate into *reductio ad absurdum* at its margins. One remedy frequently employed is the narrowing of a rule's application to a smaller sub-system within the international community. The previously discussed U.S.-U.K. Extradition

Treaty is one example. The idiot rule which is the centerpiece of that agreement is less vulnerable to *reductio ad absurdum* precisely because the inelastic rule has not been made applicable to every nation, but only to Britain, where the political system accommodates non-violent change and where even advocates of the violent pursuit of extreme causes are entitled to a seat in Parliament and a fair trial.

This selective, deconstructive approach to the application of an idiot rule was spelled out by the U.S. Legal Adviser in his statement explaining the intent of the agreement to the Senate Foreign Relations Committee. The "political offenses exception," he said, "has no place in extradition treaties between stable democracies in which the political system is available to redress legitimate grievances and the judicial process provides fair treatment. . . ."[158] But he also recognized that the public conscience would not soon be ready to accept a similar extradition relationship with, say, East Germany.[159] Thus, while the U.S.-U.K. Extradition Treaty appears to exemplify an idiot rule, it is really a disguised sophist norm because the rule is applicable only in relations between the U.S. and a nation having an independent judiciary and an open political system. The U.S. and Britain, in other words, have agreed that their process for applying the rule, operable only *inter se*, is contingently legitimate.

The problems arising from both idiot and sophist rules thus can be mitigated, if not altogether eliminated, if that is the desire of states. If it is not, the rules, whatever their degree of clarity, may not achieve much determinacy and will lack legitimacy: that is, they will lack effective pull to compliance and will fail to decribe accurately the realities of state conduct.

7

Symbolic Validation, Ritual, and Pedigree

As determinacy is the linguistic or literary-structural component of legitimacy, so *symbolic validation, ritual,* and *pedigree* provide legitimacy's cultural and anthropological dimension. Once again, the legitimacy of a rule—its ability to exert a pull to voluntary compliance—will be examined in the light of its ability to communicate. In this instance, however, what is to be communicated is not so much content as validity or *authenticity:* the voluntarily acknowledged authenticity of a rule or a rule-maker, or, sometimes, the authenticity (validity) bestowed on a symbolic communication's recipient. Reisman refers to this as "the authority signal."[160] We shall call these validating communications *cues.*

The assent of the Queen to an act of the British Parliament is an example of a cue symbolically validating the new law's authenticity. The mace on the table in the House of Commons is a cue symbolizing the authenticity or valid authority of a law-making institution. An example of a cue intended to authenticate an exercise of authority is the braid on the sleeve of a naval officer, or the exequatur and letter of credence carried by a diplomat. In each case, the cues do not actually bestow the authority, but signal its validity by authenticating it symbolically.

As Magherita Ciacci has remarked, "When legitimacy is claimed by virtue of an established belief in the certainty of immemorial tradition and of the status of those exercising authority, we have an obedience which is due to the person who occupies the traditional position of authority. . . . Such attitudes comprise culturally, and historically rooted habits, charismatic elements as well as rational considerations inherent in the goal, latent or manifest, which the command demands should be obtained."[161]

Symbolic validation, ritual, and pedigree are related but not identical concepts. The *symbolic validation* of a rule, or of a rule-making process or institution, occurs when a signal is used as cue to elicit compliance with a command. The cue serves as a surrogate in place of enunciated reasons for obedience. The singing of the national anthem, for example, is a vocal and visual signal symbolically reinforcing the citizen's relationship to the state, a relationship of rights and duties. This compliance reinforcement need not be spelled out in the actual words of the anthem (as it is not in the American one). The act of corporate singing itself is a sufficient cue to validate the fabric of regularized relationships—loyalty, freedom under law, etc.—which are implicated in good citizenship. We are not really singing about bombs bursting in the night, but about free and secret elections, the marketplace of ideas, the rule of valid laws and impartial judges.

Such symbolic cues may be objects, songs, acts, or spoken words. During the U.S. Senate's debate on joining the United Nations, the Republican leader Senator Arthur Vandenberg reassured his colleagues that "the flag stays on the dome of the Capitol."[162] Everyone understood that cue.

Ritual is a specialized form of symbolic validation marked by ceremonies, often mystical, which provide unenunciated reasons for compliance with the commands of persons or institutions. The entry of the aforementioned mace in the British House of Commons is intended to call to mind the Commons' long and successful struggle to capture from the Crown control of law-making power. Like the U.S. national anthem, it functions as symbolic validation, but of a much more direct, literal kind than the words of the rather diaphanous "Star Spangled Banner." Ritual is often a cue presented as drama, for example, the swearing in of a new U.S. President, in order to validate a community and thus reinforce the rule structure which upholds its unity, its values, its uniqueness in both the inclusive and exclusive sense.

Operating primarily on the symbolic level, ritual serves to communicate and ratify the beliefs and values of a system. It reinforces the rules and authority structure of a community by embracing and involving an in-group and by excluding an out-group which cannot (or will not) share in, or understand, the symbolic communications code. Masonic rites exemplify this, by being comprehensible only to insiders. It is thus a way of confirming common bonds and legitimizing not only a particular action or rule, but the system itself, its entire set of norms and the distribution of roles and authority.[163]

It will be apparent that these functional effects of ritual are interconnected. In ancient imperial China, the concept of *Li*, beginning as a simple rule of ritual sacrifice, gradually evolved into something akin to a code of etiquette, a "politeness of the heart" which constituted a system of "restraint on unbridled absolutism" by leaders and was "considered a tool for the restraint of civilized mankind as a whole. *Li* regulated human emotions that would otherwise be unrestrained, so as to keep people within bounds, and also gave them a refined expression."[164] By formalizing and formulating communication, rites confined what could be said, thereby narrowing the emotive range of expression.

As Confucius observed, foreshadowing the Western concept of the contractarian society, "when rulers were punctilious in their ritual observances, the people were punctilious in fulfilling their duties to superiors." Ritual, he said, thus also "served the function of control because it lent a certain uniformity and therefore predictability to people's [and leaders'] behavior."[165] The third-century B.C. philosopher Hsun-tzu described the purpose of ritual as a form of control on behavior which established principles "to curb contention and wrangling among men, and to train their desires."[166] This curbing of passion, however, was a two-way street because ritual involved—subordinated, in effect—both the rulers and the ruled. The emperor, as well as the various levels of his bureaucracy, and the people in general, were to be "restrained or more readily controlled by the requirements of ritual."[167] Similar observations have been made by scholars of Aztec society. Ritual established "the customary symbols of the rulers' majesty, morality, and responsibility to the gods. . . ." It did so, however, by subjecting the ruler to a superior order that limited his discretionary powers. "At the investiture of the head of state, high priests admonished him of his obligations and duties. Priests could invoke the wrath of the gods upon rulers who were evil or otherwise unfit to rule."[168] Thus both Chinese and Aztec rites were used primarily to validate, but also to formalize and thereby limit, power and its exercise. The oath to uphold the federal Constitution of the United States, in a sense, may be seen as America's ultimate secular ritual, dramatizing and cueing the subservience of a person invested with temporal power to the "majesty" of the law. American life is full of secularized ritual, ranging from parades on the fourth of July to the constitutionally suspect but resilient practice of clergy-led prayers for legislators on Capitol Hill.

Ritual is a form of symbolic validation, and *pedigree* is another. Pedigree, also signaled by cues, pulls toward rule compliance by emphasizing the deep rootedness of the rule or the rule-making authority. This compliance pull, emphasizing the venerable historic and social origins and continuity of rule standards, and rule-making or rule-applying institutions, is redolent with *noblesse oblige*. It links rights and duties reciprocally in a notion of venerable, authenticated status deserving special deference. The cues used in pedigreeing often augment their persuasive power by using symbols—heraldry is an example—of venerable cultural-anthropological significance. Such deep-rootedness of the cues has further instrumental value in securing compliance with rules and commands.

Pedigree is usually earned by longevity of the rule or institution, but can sometimes be conferred on a new beneficiary. For example, when a new state or government is recognized by existing ones the act of extending formal recognition symbolizes authentication: the conferral of rights and obligations as concomitants of induction into a time-honored national or governmental status in accordance with traditional standards of inclusion and exclusion.

A new state's election to membership in the U.N. is an example of corporate pedigreeing by the international community. Validation through such acts of recognition will be examined further in Chapter 8.

Pedigree is a particularly universal form of symbolic validation. In its simplest form, it occurs through genealogical lineage, a phenomenon compelled not by logic and by, at most, questionable utility, but one of near-universal usage. A person is said to deserve to be obeyed—or, in modern social usage, to be "taken seriously" because of his or her lineage. It is a rare event of social discontinuity—the Cromwellian and French revolutions, for example—that succeeds in turning the tables of consanguinity. Anthropologists have "listed descent among the basic jural postulates" in studies of many different societies,[169] while Maurice Cranston explains that the "great merit of this system from the practical point of view, is that it removes from the realm of controversy (except in the case of uncertain succession within a royal family) the choice of the head of state."[170] If old families are good families, old practices and ways are also deemed special. Most societies make some form of linguistic connection between "old" and "venerable." Among the Tswana of Southern Africa, laws fall into two distinct categories: *mekgwa* and *melao*, the former being rooted in antiquity and the latter having received social recognition and approval only within human memory. The former are obeyed just *because they are old*, while the latter take their force from the perception of the legitimacy of the promulgating chief.[171] In the ancient Aztec state the rulers' deep-rooted hereditary relation to the Toltec dynasty "was the sacred source of legitimate power and authority"[172] supplemented by a host of "pedigree nobles."[173] So, too, in the socio-political circumstances of 1000 B.C. China, where the "Mandate of Heaven" doctrine endowed an ancient imperial line of rulers with power. The Mandate of Heaven was part historical, part mystical, and part rational. It consisted of a mixture of portents—venerable omens such as comets, eclipses, droughts, floods, and earthquakes—for which the term *t'ien-t'ung* was employed—and an orderly system or line of succession which was essentially dynastic, called *cheng-t'ung*.[174]

The pursuit of symbolic validation by use of ritual and pedigree is part of the legitimation strategy of all communities, all rule-systems. Study of political legitimacy in ancient China has led to the observation that "ritual and symbol . . . by endowing authority with mystical values and legitimacy, serves not merely to reflect authority but also to re-create and reinforce it. By such means the extent to which people are persuaded to accept a given authority goes far beyond the obedience normally elicited by force."[175] Similar observations have been derived from the study of Aztec legitimation strategy. Rulers routinely made symbolic resources available in order to achieve "political socialization."[176] For example, the government ritually distributed food to the citizenry at state ceremonies, rather as the Christian church promotes its own symbolic validation by the sacrament of feeding the flock at communion, or Judaism confirms itself by the ritual *seder* meal.

Ritual and pedigree are not always merely self-serving but may also cue obedience to others than those performing the rites. In Aztec society, scholars have found, the priesthood existed in large part to provide "supernatural sanction for legitimate state authority."[177] So, too, the Roman pontifices, literally the "bridge builders," whose priestly task it was to reconcile the civil and the divine by appeasing the river god Tiber and reconciling him (by the rite of *Arget*) to the construction of bridges. The *Pontifex Maximus*, the chief priest, thus deployed ritual to validate the power of the emperor, until eventually the two offices merged. Cues may thus be invoked by one authority ostensibly to validate the authority of another. The U.N., in voting to admit a new member, symbolically validates the status of a new state. At the same time, however, the U.N. manifests, and so reinforces, its own authority to bestow status by institutional acts of authentication.

The pull to rule compliance exerted by ritual and pedigree may be quite independent of other, more utilitarian justifications for deferring to authority, such as the coercive police power, the ability of the rule-maker to govern well or the capacity of the rule to effect justice. Those exercising powers in nations and tribes may use ritual and pedigree to say: "because I, the ruler, am pedigreed, or have participated in the prescribed rites, you, the subject, must obey me and my rules." As Graham Greene has so eloquently illustrated,[178] a Catholic priest, ordained by a consecrated bishop's laying on of hands, is apostolically authorized to perform the central mystical miracle of Christianity, regardless of whether he is a good or bad human being, an effective or incompetent shepherd, or even a true believer. This authority, the authenticated ability to "perform" the miracle of transubstantiation, is conferred symbolically by strict adherence to prescribed historically rooted and mystically endorsed ritual. Adherence to the prescribed forms, in this context, means that a bishop's ordination of the priest and his consecration of the bread and wine must both have been carried out by pedigreed officials rigidly following the proper format.

Symbolic validation may use either ritual, pedigree, or the two together, as cues to secure compliance. "Political legitimacy," a study of the highly formalistic regime in ancient China has noted, "can be said to adhere to a regime and its authorities when the governed are convinced that it is right and proper to obey them and to abide by their decisions."[179] If such conviction that authority is "right and proper" is cued by ritual, the rite may be religious or secular, deploying metaphysical or rational cues. In a secular society, ritual is not discarded; rather, it is history and notions of community which ritual evokes symbolically in place of magic and myth.

For example, in Britain the rule that a parliamentary bill becomes law only after receiving the assent of the Crown[180] certainly no longer relates to any mystically based idea of the divine right of monarchs. King James I wrote a book called *The Trew Law of Free Monarchies* which advocated that notion, but it is no longer in print, much less in fashion. Although the present Queen's title still claims that she rules "by the grace of God," it is not now widely believed that the Queen rules, or, for that matter, that if there is a God, he or she is noticeably involved in British government. The monarch's considerable current role does not include ruling, and it is no longer cued by symbols of divine grace but, instead, by reference to venerable traditions. Except in the most formal sense, the modern Crown's pedigree is not claimed to be bestowed by the grace of God; but it is still rendered venerable by virtue of its awe-inspiring millennium of continuity and its authenticity as symbol of the British nation.

A utilitarian explanation for the survival of these historic rituals surrounding British monarchs is that it reflects the importance of historically based constraints on the exercise of governmental power—in lieu of such explicit normative texts as are found in the U.S. Constitution—to the principles and institutions of British democracy. This rationale remains plausible despite the fact that the Crown long ago lost the right to refuse assent to legislation passed by Parliament. Oddly, the very obsolescence of the practice of royal assent helps keep it alive. The act of seeking the Queen's approbation, even when it is clear that she has no choice but to grant it, is not meaningless. It signifies the Government's acceptance of all the accumulated encrustations of customs that define and restrict British governmental powers and practices. The Speaker of the Commons, for example, assures the Queen that the bill has had its customary three readings in Parliament and has passed both the upper and lower houses.[181] This, too, means little in itself. The rank and file in Parliament, as Gilbert and Sullivan put it, always vote at their party's call and never think of thinking for themselves at all. Thus, the governing party usually can command the parliamentary majority necessary to do whatever it wants. Nevertheless—or *particularly*—in these circumstances the ancient ritual of three readings[182] has an importance, for it symbolizes the governing party's subordination to orderly, unhurried parliamentary procedure, comparable to the church's practice of publishing the banns of a proposed marriage on three successive Sundays.[183] In an era of relentless governmental power, these quaint rituals provide a period of delay for reflection by the society as a whole and its mobilizing and opinion-shaping non-governmental institutions.

A bill passed by Parliament which had not received the necessary three readings, or was not presented for the assent of the Crown, would undoubtedly be perceived by Britons to lack legitimacy, not because those ritual forms are believed to be powerful in themselves, but because the failure of the government to perform the ritual would be seen as acting in unseemly haste. More important, it would be understood by the public as repudiating the British parliamentary system's ancient democratic essence, of which these and other rites are still potent cues.

This secular basis for ritual and pedigree was understood even in ancient China.[184] The first century scholar Wang Ch'ung maintained publicly that there was absolutely no instrumental value in ancestor worship and sacrificial rites for the dead because there were no beings to receive such offerings. Yet, he maintained, these rites had value "for the purpose of avoiding the appearance of ingratitude for the virtues and contributions of past men" deserving of particular esteem.[185] In other words, the rites were a ceremonial celebration of desirable modes of conduct personified, a reification and ratification of, and rededication to, laudable attitudes and practices which, thereby, gradually became normative and served as prescriptors of future behavior.

A similar point is made by the story of the Emperor Kao-tsu, who reigned from 206 to 195 B.C. When Kao-tsu founded the Han dynasty he and his followers were "rough and ready fellows" and, to put them at ease, the emperor abolished the "elaborate and bothersome" Ch'in ritual code. Unfortunately, this made a "shamble of court audiences," with the members of his court "getting drunk, hurling insults at one another, and hacking up the wooden pillars of the palace with their swords. To introduce some decorum to his court, Kao-tsu was moved to appoint an erudite named Shu-sun T'ung to provide him with a court ritual consonant with his modest personal capacity for performing ceremonial. The experiment proved a great success. The ritual "served as a powerful tool for dignifying and strengthening the ruler's position and for controlling the behavior of subordinates. It emphasized the large gap between the position of emperor and that of mere bureaucrat, prevented former associates from presuming upon past friendships, and helped keep subordinates agreeably subservient."[186]

Whatever the reasons such cues of ritual and pedigree retain a potent compliance pull, their capacity to validate rules and rulers has been appreciated in all organized societies and at all times. Much of what Max Weber has explained about the role of legitimacy in securing compliance with commands was known, thousands of years ago, in other cultures. Cheng notes in his *Sui History* that the state could be governed by four methods: (1) benevolence and righteousness, (2) regulation by ritual, (3) codified law, and (4) punishment. He concluded that all four were necessary to good order, but benevolence/righteousness and ritual were the "trunk" of governance, while codification and punishment were merely the "branches."[187] In other words, even in imperial China authority sought voluntary compliance by promoting the subjects' perception of the legitimacy of the rulers and the rules, rather than relying principally on coercion. In promoting this perception, rituals and pedigree played a significant part.

The value of symbolic validation appears also to be known intuitively by the community of states. Despite the paucity of available cues, there are significant examples of the still comparatively immature international system—institutions and rules—seeking to legitimize itself, to call itself into validation through ritual and pedigree. One of the oldest and most universal examples was the use of marriage between children of heads of state to symbolize political and social compacts between nations, as between England and Holland, or England and Hanover. The practice was common not only among medieval European royal houses but also in Asia, Africa, and the pre-colonial Americas. For example, in Aztec Mexico, the "head of state established alliances with neighboring states through marriage. . . . Acampitchtli is reputed to have married twenty daughters of the chiefs of the clans that comprised Aztec society."[188]

Some of the newest examples of symbolic international system-legitimation are proferred by the proliferating supranational agencies such as the United Nations Development Programme,[189] the International Bank for Reconstruction and Development ("World Bank"),[190] the World Health Organization,[191] the Food and Agriculture Organization,[192] and the United Nations International Children's Emergency Fund.[193] Of course these organizations are not primarily symbolic. Their very practical function is to distribute benefits to the deserving and the needy, either in tandem, or in competition, with the unilateral donations which are still given by one country to another. Nevertheless, they also exemplify symbolic validation. Their very status as international agencies is partially symbolic, transforming them from a diplomatic conference of sovereign states into entities different from, and to some extent independent of, member nations. By symbolically mingling the donations of various countries, the assistance given is intended to be purged of the aura of direct dependence between recipient and donor, a relationship which has often led to bitterness superseding gratitude. Instead, by symbolic multilateralization, gratitude is directed to an agency in which donors and recipients participate as symbolic equals.

Equality of participation in these agencies is itself potent symbolism. The international system's organizing principle of sovereign equality is a cue communicating the equal entitlement to *rights* of states with unequal power, despite the exceptions which are made as in the case of Bretton Woods institutions such as the World Bank, where voting is by shares, rather than "one-state one-vote" and in the U.N. Security Council, where five "permanent members" exercise the power of veto.

The distribution of benefits by a global agency, with its own officials and symbols, also helps to create a sense of social solidarity—a primitive version of loyalty—between recipients (both persons and governments) and the international system (the "United Nations Family") of which the donor agency is a part, rather in the same way as did the Aztec rulers' ritual distribution of foodstuffs to subjects. This symbolic, as well as utilitarian, function of multilateral, institutionalized benevolence is familiar to anthropologists and sociologists who study the formation of national societies. In Aztec society the "[c]onstruction and maintenance of temples and other public buildings appeased the gods, organized people's labor according to state directives and supported priests and other state functionaries."[194] The Pharaohs similarly sought to serve both personal and socializing objectives in the construction of the pyramids. This concept of legitimation through the symbolism of public works was not unknown, either, to American politicians from "Boss" Curley of Boston[195] to Nelson D. Rockefeller of New York. In formulating the project for the Albany

Mall, Governor Nelson Rockefeller suggested modeling the core of New York's capital on the Palace of the Dalai Lama at Lhasa, Tibet. The Mall's plan incorporated architectural and symbolic elements from Lhasa, Washington, D.C., Brasilia, Versailles, Rockefeller Center, and St. Petersburg and was meant to be "the most spectacularly beautiful seat of government anywhere in the world."[196] Rockefeller understood the symbolic legitimating value of architecture in much the same way as did the Aztec and Pharaonic rulers or the fledgling international bureaucracy responsible for U.N. Headquarters in New York and the Asian, African, and European regional offices.

There are many more examples of the use of ritual and other authenticating symbols to reinforce legitimacy in the international system. The United Nations organization, for example, is authorized to fly its own flag, not only at headquarters but over regional and local offices around the world.[197] The flag has been used at the instigation of the Secretary-General to immunize such risky or controversial tasks as the clearing of sunken ships from the Suez Canal and to provide protection for members of the Palestine Liberation Organization being evacuated from Lebanon during the Israeli invasion.[198] The U.N. also issues stamps[199] which not only are accepted for mail delivery by member states but also generate a tidy independent source of income—some 8.6 million dollars in 1986–87—for the organization.[200] Peacekeeping forces and truce observers under U.N. command and wearing U.N. symbols are stationed between hostile forces in places such as Kashmir,[201] the Golan Heights,[202] Cyprus,[203] Southern Lebanon,[204] and the Iran-Iraq border.[205] They are lightly armed and palpably unable to defend themselves in the event of renewed hostilities; but, with their distinctive emblems, they have come to symbolize the world's interest in preserving a truce or armistice. The blue and white helmets and armbands also symbolize a growing body of rules applicable to peacekeeping operations, thus manifesting and reinforcing the authority of forces that usually are neither as numerous, nor as well armed, as those they must keep pacified. Their role is purely, but effectively, symbolic of the desire of bitter enemies—and the international community—to have respite from combat.

Yet, their token presence has a far more inhibitory effect on the behavior of states than could be explained by their minimal coercive power.[206] It is their perceived legitimacy, symbolically validated, which serves as their shield and, using familiar cues, usually induces more powerful forces to defer to their intangible authority.

The United Nations and its agencies also have headquarters and regional facilities with limited extraterritoriality and immunities.[207] These have symbolic as well as practical significance. The extension of such immunity to the U.N.'s top officials, privileges historically reserved for representatives of states, symbolizes the emergence of that organization as an autonomous international actor, gradually becoming pedigreed in its own right by the passage of time and the tacit consecration of states. Additionally, the agencies are represented in various countries by resident representatives whose functions and privileges, in practice, do not differ greatly from those of ambassadors. Although it is not widely known, the organization also levies an income tax (staff assessment)[208] on its employees who, with the exception of Americans, are immune from national taxation in symbolic recognition of the fact—noted by the U.S. Supreme Court in the domestic federal context[209]—that the right to tax necessarily encompasses the right to destroy.

A few more examples. Symbols and rituals are also firmly embedded in state diplomatic practice. The titles ("ambassador extraordinary and plenipotentiary"), prerogatives and immunities of ambassadors, consuls and others functioning in a representative capacity, are among the oldest of symbols and rites associated with the conduct of international relations.[210] The sending state, by the rituals of accreditation, endows its diplomats with pedigree. They become, in time-honored tradition, a symbolic reification of the nation (possessed of its "full powers" or *plenipotentiary*), a role which is ritually endorsed by the receiving state's ceremony accepting the envoy's credentials, ceremonies which, incidentally, are as old as they are elaborate and which are performed with as remarkably faithful uniformity in communist citadels as in royal palaces.[211] Once accredited and received, an ambassador *is* the embodiment of the nation. The status of ambassador carries with it rights and duties which inhere in the status and do not depend on the qualities of the person or on the condition of relations between the sending and receiving state. To insult or harm this envoy, no matter how grievous the provocation, is an attack on the sending state. Moreover, when an envoy, acting officially, agrees to something, the envoy's state is bound thereby, even if the envoy acted without proper authorization.[212] The host state is entitled to rely on the word of an ambassador as if his or her state were speaking.

Ambassadors of great as of tiny nations are entitled to equal and full diplomatic courtesy, symbolic of the equal rights of states regardless of their unequal power. In the sixteenth century Alberico Gentili, regius professor of civil law at Oxford, cited this ancient precedent:

> certain ambassadors of the Germans, noticing some persons in foreign dress sitting in the section assigned to the Senators at Rome, asked who they were, and on hearing that this honor was granted to the ambassadors of those nations who excelled in valor and in friendship for the Romans, exclaimed that no one in the world surpassed the Germans either in arms or in fidelity. Thereupon they walked over and sat down among the Senators.[213]

In this way, too, the system validates the symbolic, principled compromise between the reality of obvious power-inequality and equality of states' entitlement to fundamental rights of membership in a community of states.

The venerable ritual practices of diplomacy are almost universally observed and the rules that surround diplomacy are widely recognized as imbued with a high degree of legitimacy, being both descriptive and predictive of nearly invariable state conduct and reflecting a strong sense of obligation. When the rules are violated—as they have been by Iran and Libya in recent years[214]—the response of the international community tends to be to rally around the rule, as the Security Council[215] and the International Court of Justice[216] demonstrated when the Iranian regime encouraged the occupation of the U.S. embassy in Teheran. Violations of the elaborate rules pertaining to embassies and immunities usually lead the victim to terminate its diplomatic relations with the offending state;[217] but it also leads to general community-wide reaffirmation of the basic rules. An offended state, on the other hand, usually takes care not to retaliate by means that the rules do not permit. Thus, when a British policewoman was shot and killed by a sniper firing from within the Libyan embassy (People's Bureau) at London's St. James's Square, the authorities reconsidered, but wisely did not seek to abridge or amend the rules of immunity, this despite the outrage of a British public which saw the murderers depart safely. Instead of yielding to such passion, Britain proceeded by the rules, expelling the offenders and barring their government from further diplomatic representation in the United Kingdom.[218]

Related to the pedigree process of diplomatic accreditation, with its symbolic status of privileges and immunities, is the prevalent idea of sovereign immunity. That set of rules and practices has its roots in the medieval notion that the "king can do no wrong" and the monarch's claim that "I am the state." Nowadays, most rulers can be sued in their own courts. Among themselves, however, nations generally continue to treat their sovereigns and presidents as sacrosanct. All property of foreign recognized states and also those activities and enterprises carried on in the foreign government's name remained similarly immune until the 1950s.[219] Only in the last three decades have most nations begun to limit the immunity of foreign governments' expanding *commercial* activities.[220] Even so, sovereign immunity from suit, or at least from execution of judgment, continues to be granted everywhere to officials and property engaged in *public*, or non-commercial, undertakings.[221]

Symbolic validation rarely is the only force pulling towards voluntary compliance with a rule. International sovereign immunity rules do not generate strong compliance pull solely by virtue of their symbolic validation but also because they facilitate the conduct of intergovernmental relations free from harassment by lawsuits and property attachments. The rules are also designed to reserve to governments and intergovernmental processes the resolution of disputes between nations. They bar judges and litigants from becoming the unauthorized agents for precipitating crises in international relations. While this utility no doubt reinforces the rule of immunity, so, too, does the ancient and anachronistic ritual by which governments rededicate themselves to honored traditions and authenticate rules promoting orderly, restrained interaction.

If the utility of the rules of immunity alone were sufficient to assure their legitimacy—their capacity to ensure voluntary compliance—the symbolic cues associated with immunity would not have been preserved so carefully, despite their evident anachronism. The rituals attending the validation of an ambassador's, or a sovereign's, pedigree status—while once rational symbolic representations of such political realities as the divine right of kings—are now non-rational and rather burdensome symbols, retained only because of their historic venerability. They continue to be re-enacted ritualistically today because they symbolize an etiquette, an international code of *Li*, which is thought to bridle the passion of nations and facilitate orderly communication and transaction of business.

Anachronism, however, is fragile. Often a characteristic of pedigree and ritual, it cannot survive literal-minded scrutiny. Its claim to validate is based on allegorical qualities. This very fragility of non-rational, non-instrumental symbolic practices contributes to a feeling that it would be risky to scrap them precipitously. They are old beams in an old building. One cannot really know how much the entire structure leans on any particular one.

Perhaps that is another part of the continuing power of ritual and other practices of symbolic validation. The rules validated by venerable ritual, especially by those rituals which appear anachronistic in form, are understood to have taken a long time becoming universally accepted, and new replacements cannot simply be legislated into the public psyche. Each time the penumbra of ritual validating a rule is not adhered to, that rule dies a little, and often there is no other of comparable clout ready at hand to take its place. Despite the above-quoted story of Emperor Kao-tsu, who first abolished and then re-invented court rites, it is safe to assume that his resurrection of ritual was possible only because it had only briefly and imperfectly been suspended. Real pedigrees cannot be purchased except with the currency of time and practice. A new rule simply, and quite aside from its merits, cannot instantly claim quite the same degree of legitimacy as an old one. The symbolic function of an anachronistic cue is to underscore the venerable age of the rule which it serves.

A study of ancient Chinese ritual has shown that the "manipulatory dimension of ritual and symbol" cannot be "purposively fabricated by individuals or groups with particular goals in mind. . . . No one makes up ritual or symbol any more than anyone makes up language. Ritual and symbol arise without intention or adaptation to conscious purpose; they seem to be collective products worked out . . . over long periods of time. . . . Ironically, it appears that rituals and symbols must in some way already be regarded as 'legitimate' in order for them to confer legitimacy on those who employ them."[222]

How else can one explain the punctilious adherence of the Union of Soviet Socialist Republics to the following ritual:

> At the entrance to the building of the Praesidium the Ambassador is greeted by the Military Commandant. Officers in ceremonial uniform greet and salute the Ambassador in the vestibule. The Military Commandant accompanies the Ambassador to the outer hall. In the outer hall the Head of Protocol Department introduces Soviet officials attending the ceremony to the Ambassador.
>
> After the announcement of the arrival of the Ambassador to the Chairman of the Praesidium, the Head of Protocol Department invites the Ambassador, the officials accompanying him and the Soviet officials into the hall for the presentation of Letters of Credence.
>
> The Ambassador, together with the diplomatic personnel from the Embassy and the Soviet officials, enters the hall: the Head of the appropriate geographical Department of the Ministry of Foreign Affairs stands on the right of the Ambassador, on the left is the Head of Protocol Department.
>
> Simultaneously, the Chairman of the Praesidium of the Supreme Soviet enters through the opposite door in the hall: on

his right is the Secretary of the Praesidium, on his left the Deputy Minister of Foreign Affairs. The Ambassador stops one or two paces short of the Centre of the hall, opposite the Chairman of the Praesidium, and greets him with a slight bow. The Head of Protocol Department presents the Ambassador to the Chairman of the Praesidium.

The Ambassador then delivers a speech. If the speech is delivered in a foreign language, an interpreter translates into Russian.

After the translation of the speech into Russian, the Ambassador hands his Letters of Credence to the Chairman of the Praesidium, together with his predecessor's Letters of Recall, and returns to his place.

The Chairman of the Praesidium delivers a speech, in reply, which is translated into the language in which the Ambassador delivered his speech.

At the end of the speeches and translations, the Chairman of the Praesidium and the Ambassador approach one another and shake hands. The Chairman of the Praesidium introduces the Secretary of the Praesidium and the Deputy Minister of Foreign Affairs to the Ambassador. In his turn the Ambassador introduces the members of the Embassy diplomatic personnel accompanying him.

The Chairman of the Praesidium accords the Ambassador a private audience in an adjoining room, at which the Secretary of the Praesidium and the Deputy Minister of Foreign Affairs are also present. All the remaining officials return to the outer hall, where coffee or tea awaits them.

After the audience the Chairman of the Praesidium invites the Ambassador and the Head of Protocol Department and all those present at the ceremony to be photographed in the main hall. After the photograph the Ambassador bids goodbye to the Chairman of the Praesidium and with the other officials and the Head of Protocol Department departs for the Embassy or his Residence in the order of arrival.[223]

Evidently, although this is a revolutionary socialist government, it nevertheless understands the uses of symbolic validation, even when the instrumental ritual is redolent of medieval royal mystique. Even—perhaps *especially*—the new and the revolutionary acutely craves authentication by ancient anachronisms. In this case, the ceremonial can be traced at least to that used by Byzantine emperors receiving foreign envoys in their magnificent "cosmic robe" studded with celestial symbols to indicate the imperial person's descent "from heaven itself" and including representations of all the known continents to signify his "immense terrestrial jurisdiction."[224] The rituals established by this Eastern court soon spread to the West and North, with the Duke of Apulia presenting a copy of the "cosmic garment" to Henry II of Saxony in the eleventh century, from whence the model spread to other European kingdoms.[225] While some of the excesses of the ancient rites and symbols have been stripped away in modern usage, a surprising residue remains and is still cherished.

On the other hand, when a rule supported by venerable rituals and pedigrees is swept aside in the name of modernity or convenience, much else besides may also be discarded. An illustration is provided by the 1985 decision of the U.S. government, for reasons of national security, to order a large-scale reduction in the number of diplomatic and support personnel at the three Soviet missions to the U.N. (the U.S.S.R., Byelorussian S.S.R., and Ukrainian S.S.R.). The U.S. action was not supported by evidence of espionage or other illegal activity on the part of any incumbent Soviet representatives. Although this order could be defended as "legal" in the sense that it was not specifically prohibited by treaty texts,[226] its effect was to end a venerable, long-standing international conference practice, a rule or custom encrusted with the ritual of diplomatic politeness, going back at least to the 1814–15 Congress of Vienna. This rule has long allowed each participating nation at diplomatic conferences to determine for itself the number and composition of its delegation,[227] a practice maintained by the authorities in Vienna even when the extravagant demands on hospitality threatened to break their treasury.

Will the violation of this venerable tradition of diplomatic politeness make it more difficult to hold conferences? Only time will tell how important the largely symbolic, Li-like anachronism has been to the system of rules which facilitate the conduct of modern diplomacy.

Before the U.S. violated that rule, it always had been the U.N., itself, which regulated and authenticated the credentials of the representatives sent by member states. Now, the host country (to which the diplomats usually are not accredited) has insinuated itself into the process, thereby affecting also the symbolic independence of the U.N. Once belief in a symbol, ritual, or pedigreed status has been challenged successfully, its efficacy undoubtedly diminishes. It was less shocking, although still widely resented by other members, when three years later, the U.S. expelled the Nicaraguan ambassador to the Organization of American States in the absence of any showing that he had engaged in espionage or other illegal activities.[228] The lower shock-index registered by this second transgression reflects the diminishing power of diplomatic courtesy to shape expectations and influence conduct. The legitimacy of the system of rules and institutions is undermined when its validating symbols and rituals are dishonored. To what extent a rule, system, or institution is undermined cannot be known until after the beam has been removed. At that point it may be too late to restore the structure's fragile support, its capacity to function in a world of voluntarist compliance.

Then, again, as with forest fires so perhaps with old rules: some wanton destruction may prove a useful prelude to renewal. Perhaps the tremendous improvements in long distance communications brought about by telephones, computers, and "fax" machines will make personal diplomacy largely redundant, replacing it with direct bilateral or multilateral communications among national capitals and between international organizations and the member governments. That would require new rules and practices. To say the least, however, it would be foolhardy to write off an existing old rule system and its colorful validating symbols and rituals before the emergence of some equally serviceable palimpsest.

8

True Cues and
Symbolic Validation

In international law and diplomacy, a sovereign, a government or regime is recognized by other nations if it is legitimate and it is legitimate if it is recognized by other nations. Recognition not only "sees" legitimacy: it also confers it.

Maurice Cranston*

Just as determinacy appeared perfectly straightforward, at first impression, but became more complex as one probed deeper, so too with symbolic validation. Sometimes cues succeed in communicating legitimacy; at other times, symbols fail to validate. Fortunately, these deviations occur in accordance with norms which are readily understood. To take what is perhaps the prime instance: the cues used to confer legitimacy succeed only when those addressed perceive them as symbolic of *truth*. That truth may be historic or contemporary, political or metaphysical, allegorical or real, but if the validating "magic" is to work, the cue must not be perceived as *false*.

Symbolic validation exerts a compliance pull on those to whom the cues of ritual or pedigree are communicated. But cues can do this only if, at some level, they evoke reality. A false cue can be illustrated by the uniform of an admiral of the Serbian navy.

* From *Legitimism to Legitimacy: Legitimacy/Légitimité* (A. Moulakis, ed., 1986)

Serbia ceased to be a sovereign state more than half a century ago, and when it did exist, was landlocked. While official insignias and the braid used to denote rank usually serve as effective legitimators of authority, they will fail if the factual basis for the authority, as cued by those symbols, is known to be false. It is therefore useless to try to use symbolic validation to enhance the authority-claim of an officer of the Serbian navy except in respect of those who are ignorant of the geo-political facts. Yet symbolic validation sometimes is used fraudulently, creating confusion about the legitimacy of the bestowing authority, the symbols used, and, also, of that which is sought to be validated.

As we have observed, the legitimacy of rules and institutions exerts a compliance pull on those addressed. For example, the validation of basic institutions of the international community—the state and its government—is symbolically cued by the rite of *recognition*. The rules governing the practice of recognition are endowed with an impressive pedigree. Individual governments extend recognition to new nations and new rulers. International organizations do somewhat the same when they admit a new state to membership or accept the credentials of diplomats representing a new regime. Both kinds of recognition purport to validate a sovereign; they help a new state or government attain status in the community of nations, which, in turn, authorizes it to be treated as a presumptive equal—at least as to entitlements—by its peers.

This can be illustrated by negative inference. A good example is the effect of *withholding* recognition on the so-called "African homelands" established by the Republic of South Africa. The nations of the world, acting through the U.N. General Assembly, have condemned these puppet Bantustans and called upon all states to refrain from recognizing their independence. That call has been heeded by almost all nations. Effectively, by non-recognition, the statehood and concomitant entitlements to which the Bantustans aspire has thus been symbolically denied them. They have been blackballed from the international community: the reality of their statehood has been withheld by refusing them its symbols.

The importance of recognition is that symbolically it conveys to the recipient crucial entitlements in relation to other states and governments. Article 2 of the U.N. Charter, echoing the 300-year-old text of Hugo Grotius's introduction to the *Law of War and Peace*,[229] declares that the organization is based on the principle of the *sovereignty* and *equality* of all its Members. Both terms, as we shall see in Chapter 12, are symbolic and partake of some poetic license. Nevertheless, in one of its most important resolutions the General Assembly, by consensus, has reiterated that sovereign equality is the essential right of all states.[230] Membership, in less highly embossed words, is a certificate that entitles the holder, presumptively, to the rights and benefits, as well as the obligations, of a peer among peers.

Such entitlement, even stripped of its bravado, is neither unimportant nor taken for granted. Only quite recently has the community of states become a society of peers. In the preceding chapter we noted Gentili's report on the German ambassadors' effort to establish their formal equality in ancient Rome. This, however, was an uphill struggle against the then-prevalent position. In ancient Chinese, Greek, Roman, Anglo-imperial, and, even in Grotian times, equality was either formally denied all other nations by the omnipotent "middle kingdom," or was restricted to a select company of symbiotic societies. The kingdoms, principalities, and other entities under the umbrella of the Holy Roman Empire were quite unequal, even in the formal sense. The notion of the sovereign equality of states may be said to have made its debut, in modern Western civilization, with the Peace of Westphalia.[231] Even thereafter, both in colonial and other non-Western societies, quite different principles—manifested by hegemony, tributary and vassal status, imperial dominion, and spheres of influence—long continued to hold sway.[232] Until quite recently, the empires of Western Europe operated on a system of capitulatory regimes[233] and tutelage over "protectorates."[234] The rights and duties of states accorded by the European rule-system were restricted to "civilized" states, which arbitrarily excluded most of Africa and Asia. Within the British Empire, "dominions" like Canada, Newfoundland, Australia, New Zealand, South Africa, and India passed through non-severign stages of sub-equality during which their national governments enjoyed many of the attributes of sovereignty over domestic affairs and some powers pertaining to foreign relations, but were not, or were only partially, accepted as equal or sovereign participants in the international system.[235]

Against this historic background of subordination, it is understandable that modern states and governments crave symbolic validation as a badge of their right to exist and function as sovereign and equal among peers.

When this symbolic validation is bestowed nowadays, however, it does not invariably coincide with empirical reality. In one sense, the entire concept of sovereign equality seems flushed with embarrassing hypocrisy. The Gambia and the Soviet Union are far from equal, and even the U.S.S.R. is not truly sovereign in a world of economic, ecological, and epidemological interdependence. Indeed, sovereignty and equality of states are antithetical concepts in the sense that formal equality exists only as a set of entitlements of states within a community of rules, and such a rule community *ipso facto* limits the sovereignty even of powerful states to do as they will with their weaker peers. Most informed observers of the international system understand, therefore, that the notion of sovereign equality must be taken *cum grano salis:* its meaning being restricted to such a degree of sovereignty and equality as is commensurate with the international system's objectives of peace, human survival, and socio-economic development. Even understood in this restricted fashion, however, symbolic recognition is heartily desired by those entitled to it; and it is sometimes blatantly denied to those that appear to qualify. Conversely, the symbolic validation of recognition is sometimes bestowed as a matter of political strategy on the unqualified, even in the noticeable absence of the reality it is supposed to symbolize. Both recognition and non-recognition thus can be powerful cues or blatant mis-cues. For example, India became one of the original members of the League of Nations in 1920, its status, rights, and duties as a member of the international community being thereby symbolically validated. Yet India was not objectively entitled to this cue. It did not win its independence from Britain until 1947.[236] A more radical distortion is the case of Byelorussia and the Ukraine, which are members of the U.N. but have almost none of the empirical attributes of sovereign and equal status. The government of the Soviet Union, which had insisted on the U.N.'s admitting these two of its constituent federated states, would surely be the first to object if the world began to take those cues literally.[237] That the nations have not done so is evidence of their ability to distinguish between real and bogus cues.

Sometimes the perception that a cue is communicating a lie may result from a misunderstanding of what the cue actually is intended to represent. As we have observed, membership of a state in the United Nations, properly understood, is not meant to symbolize the actual equality of all states—that would be a lie—but only the equal capacity of each state to acquire such peer rights as the community attributes to statehood. Even understood this way, the Charter lies a little. It proclaims sovereign equality,[238] yet only the "Big Five" enjoy the privilege of the veto in the Security Council.[239]

Only a Polyanna would expect all inequality to have been banished. Thucydides observed, at the time of the Peloponesian wars that "the strong do what they can and the weak do what they must."[240] This has not changed much in two thousand years. Nevertheless, the Soviet Union seemed to understand that Afghanistan was—somehow—its peer, at least in the sense that Moscow had to pretend not to have invaded it, and eventually had to withdraw its occupying forces under U.N. auspices. The practices of symbolic equality, formally enunciated by Kant and discussed in Chapter 13, nowadays stipulate, for example, that the ruler of tiny Bhutan must receive exactly the same number of volleys fired in salute by a U.S. honor guard as the leader of its leviathan neighbor, China. This is more than a fancy, for, while perfect equality has not been achieved, and may even be undesirable, its symbols nevertheless communicate a real aspiration of the international system. The effect of ritually validating the equal capacity for rights and duties of rich and poor, strong and weak, is to legitimate not only the recognized state, but also that substantial body of international rules which purports to treat states (or governments) equally, and to create a presumption against rules, or interpretations of rules, which would arbitrarily distinguish between the rights and duties of states solely on the basis of power or wealth,[241] or which would perversely exacerbate existing inequalities.

Thus, much importance attaches to the symbolic validation which pedigreed authorities—states and international organizations—extend to new peers in the ritual act of recognition. Whenever recognition is denied a new state or government, or when a state or government is excluded from the councils of the United Nations, that is considered a serious penalization, a deliberate withholding of a coveted status. For evidence of this, one has but to recall the importance attached by all sides to the twenty-year battle over the question of which government—communist or nationalist?—should represent China in the U.N.[242] It would be quite wrong to try to understand that conflict in narrowly utilitarian terms, since both contending governments—Beijing's communists and Taipei's nationalists—did not need the U.N. forum as a microphone to make their wishes known to the international community. Rather, the intensity of that struggle illustrates their appreciation of symbolic validation's importance in cueing a government's entitlement to the full range of rights and privileges that come with peer status.

Understandably, as Grotius observed, it is the weaker states which most value the symbols of equality. They need them: to tame the conduct of more powerful nations, much the way we have observed the rituals of Li being used by subjects as a symbolic shield to contain the power of ancient China's emperors. Less privileged nations believe that ritual incantation of their symbolically validated status as sovereign equals at least narrows the options of the powerful when they are tempted to take advantage of their military and economic pre-eminence.

For somewhat similar reasons, the International Court of Justice concluded that the U.N., itself is entitled to some of the most important symbolic attributes of a state.[243] The judges' opinion pointed out that nations have assigned tasks to the organization which it can only be expected to perform if it is accorded at least some of the status of an independent actor in the international system. For example, like a state, it must have the capacity to pursue claims on behalf of its personnel when they are injured in the performance of official duties. Symbolic form, the Court thought, must follow function.

We have observed that the ritual of recognition is intended as symbolic validation of a state's or government's existence and its entitlement to equal status in the international community. But recognition illustrates the important caveat that cues can validate only when they are perceived as true or appropriate: that is, when they symbolize a reality which is not seen to be false by those to whom the symbol is addressed. However, to complicate matters further, this veracity or falsity of a cue is not always self-evident. Even in international relations, perceptions of reality—the birth of a new nation, or a change of government by military coup, for instance—give rise to Descartian and Berkeleyian[244] epistemological and cognitive questions. How do we know what is real or true? The answer to this question is provided by the international community in distinctly pragmatic fashion. For the most part, states and international organizations seek to determine by empirical tests whether a state or a government is functioning. Is effective control exercised? Is there stability? Is there an ability and willingness to behave like a state or government and to discharge the concomitant obligations of statehood and governance? Sometimes an entity behaves like a state for some purposes but not for others. Then, it may be accorded—like the U.N. or such entities as Liechtenstein, Monaco, San Marino and the three Micronesian nations—a quasi-state status. In most instances, most governments and most international organizations strive to make form follow function, to shape the cues to validate perceived reality, so as to employ true cues rather than fictional ones. This is not only because untrue cues undermine the potency of the symbols, but because they harm the credibility and authority of those who misuse them.[245]

For example, in a bloody 1971 civil war, Pakistan was split in half. A new state, Bangladesh, arose in what had been Pakistan's eastern region, and claimed validation as a new institutional participant in the international rule system, one entitled to the equal capacity for rights that inhere in recognized statehood. The claim of Bangladesh to be legitimated by symbolic acts of recognition—by nations and by international organizations—had various practical implications. Understandably, recognition was strongly resisted by Pakistan. This created practical, but also symbolic, problems for states and international organizations. Should U.S. postal authorities forward mail addressed to "Dacca, Bangladesh"? What role, if any, should the Universal Postal Union play in such a situation? To which national treasury should the World Bank address the bill for a quarterly payment due on a loan to Pakistan for construction of a dam in the region which became Bangladesh? Should the United Nations admit Bangladesh to membership, and how soon? Does it matter that the General Assembly has passed a resolution[246] that is a thinly disguised criticism of India's role in facilitating Bangladesh's independence? Should the U.S. recognize Bangladesh, thereby being able to establish diplomatic relations and having an influence on the new state during its inception, but courting the animosity of Pakistan? How quickly should symbolic recognition follow "the facts" of Bangladesh's self-proclaimed independence?

In practice, entities (governments, international organizations) which, by international custom or treaty, have the power to decide whether to extend such symbolic validation, will generally strive to do so when it is warranted by generally perceived reality. Keeping the cues true has the multiple benefits of preventing cognitive dissonance between the worlds of reality and of symbols while protecting the potency of symbols and the credibility of those charged with symbolic validation.

This is illustrated by the examples given. The letter would probably be forwarded to the new state.[247] Asked about mail service to an unrecognized secessionist territory, the Director-General of the Universal Postal Union (UPU) replied:[248]

> The UPU regulates the international postal service between the postal administrations of Member countries, i.e. between territories which *de jure* and *de facto* are part of the sovereign states members of our organization. For obvious political reasons, the UPU Acts do not govern the exchange of mail with seceding territories. In that case, the exchange of mail with the

seceding territory is regulated *de facto* according to circumstances and possibilities until the said territory achieves independence and is admitted to UPU membership. A bilateral agreement is sometimes concluded between the government or the provisional government of the said territory and a friendly neighbouring state in order to regulate, at least temporarily, the conveyance of mail; for example, mail to the northern part of Cyprus usually transits through Turkey.

However, in order to help maintaining postal relations in case of disputes, conflict or war, UPU has adopted resolution C37 . . . which grants certain powers to the International Bureau.[249]

From this it is evident that the UPU seeks to extend its own brand of partial, informal, functional "recognition" to any regime which in fact exercises control over territory and population, even though it must proceed cautiously so as not to antagonize "the sovereign states members of our organization." While individual states and the U.N., for political reasons, have refused to validate the secessionist Turkish state in Northern Cyprus,[250] the UPU accepts the reality of that entity's existence for purposes of mail delivery and it informally approves the pragmatic solution. Form seeks to follow function.

As for the World Bank, it would use its considerable leverage to encourage Bangladesh and Pakistan to agree to the transfer of the obligation to the new state, perhaps as the price of its gaining membership in the Bank.[251] The U.N., also seeking to align form with function, did vote to admit Bangladesh in 1974,[252] and among those joining in that result were many states that earlier had voted for the resolution implicity critical of the way the new state had come into being through Indian intervention.[253]

Each of these questions is addressed by different governmental and intergovernmental authorities. When they act, they often advance reasons, which serve as rhetorical and conceptual bridges between the worlds of reality and of symbolism. The reasoning evidences states' and international organizations' understanding that validation, if it is to be a powerful cue, must be congruent with the general perception of reality, or, at least, not be contradicted by readily apparent empirical evidence. It must employ what states in general perceive to be a true cue. To be effective, cues should act as shorthand confirmation of what is widely known or believed, not the opposite. But true cues do more than confirm reality: they endow it with the *ergo* predicate: "I am a state, therefore I have rights and duties."

Realistic cueing has been defended against efforts at self-interested manipulation by impartial authorities charged with refereeing the international rule-system. In 1948, the International Court of Justice was asked by the U.N. General Assembly to define the standards determining membership in the organization.[254] It replied by pointing out that article 4 of the U.N. Charter lays down five conditions: an applicant must be (1) a state; (2) peace-loving; (3) willing to accept the obligations of the Charter; (4) able to carry them out; and (5) willing to do so. This is a test of a state's effectiveness as a member of the community. Again, form was urged to follow function. If an entity can perform as a member state, the legitimacy of its claim to statehood status should be symbolically validated by the collective act of bestowing membership. A further question was put to the Court: could members of the U.N., in deciding whether to admit a candidate, impose *additional* conditions before voting to grant a pedigree? The issue arose because the Soviet Union had said publicly that it would veto certain Western-supported candidates for membership unless the West, which at that time commanded a majority of votes, would agree in advance to support several Soviet-sponsored socialist candidates. The Court held that this additional condition was impermissible, that the five-part standard in the article 4 text established "not merely . . . the necessary conditions, but also . . . the conditions which suffice." Members must apply the written standard; they were not "free to import into the application of this provision conditions extraneous to the conditions laid down therein. . . ."[255]

There has also been a clarification of the related but different matter of contested governmental credentials, a problem which sometimes arises when several governments claim to be a member state's legitimate authority and send rival delegations to a U.N.

organ, such as the Generaly Assembly. Which delegates receive the Assembly's symbolic imprimatur obviously has a practical significance. The legal adviser to the Secretary-General prepared a memorandum which declared unequivocally that the test here, too, should be based on article 4. "Where a revolutionary government presents itself as representing a State, in rivalry to an existing government," he wrote, "the question at issue should be which of these two governments in fact is in a position to employ the resources and direct the people of the State in fulfillment of the obligations of membership. In essence, this means an inquiry as to whether the new government exercises effective authority within the territory of the State and is habitually obeyed by the bulk of the population."[256] Again, the effort is directed to bringing symbolism into line with perceptions of reality.

The same memorandum, addressing the related question of admission to U.N. membership, asserts that there have been numerous instances when members have voted to admit states by applying the article 4 test even though they, themselves, had not yet recognized those applicants. The legal counsel recalled that, in an instance comparable to that of Pakistan and Bangladesh, Colombia had declared to the League of Nations that its vote to admit Panama, a seceded former province, was not to be taken as its recognition of that secession.[257] Counsel also reminded the members that Burma and Yemen had been voted into the organization at a time when a majority of states had recognized neither. Counsel's point was that questions of the validity of a delegation's claim to represent a member state, like questions of membership, should be determined strictly in accordance with information relevant to a government's functional ability to carry out its systemic duties and obligations, a test which might be different from the one applied by member governments when deciding whether their nations, individually, should recognize the same regime. That latter decision might turn on other functional considerations irrelevant to the U.N., such as whether the new regime had indicated a willingness to assume pre-existing bilateral obligations between the two nations.

That subjective attitudes for or against a new state or a new regime should not be determinative in these matters was further urged in another opinion of the U.N. Legal Counsel, this one responding to a request by the General Assembly for guidance on a different credentials issue. He advised that it would be wrong for members to vote to reject the credentials of a delegation—it was South Africa's credentials which prompted the question—solely on the ground that the state it sought to represent had been violating its obligations under the Charter. Such exclusion, he wrote, "would have the effect of suspending a Member State from the exercise of rights and privileges of membership in a manner not foreseen by the Charter." Counsel added that "Article 5 lays down the . . . requirements for . . . suspension. . . ."[258] That article requires an affirmative vote in both the Assembly and the Council, thereby making suspension subject to veto by a permanent member.

What is being said by the World Court and the U.N. legal counsel is that states and governments which are "facts" (as measured by the article 4 standard in the text of the Charter) are *entitled* to join the organization and participate in its organs. It is impermissible, in this view, to deny symbolic validation and its commensurate entitlements to nations and governments which can be seen to exist and which meet the functional criteria for bestowal of validation. The cues must seek to refer to perceived reality; form should accord with function. A self-proclaimed regime may be denied validation only if it does not exercise effective control. A new state should be denied membership only if its existence is still precarious or if it does not want to, or cannot, assume the duties of membership. A state which is already a member should not be denied the rights and privileges of membership except as part of the onerous procedure for imposing collective punishment, which requires the consent of the Security Council including all five permanent members. This functional or empirical standard for validation, like any general principle, does leave room for doubts and differences of fact-interpretation in borderline cases, but it narrows the ambit of acceptable reasons a state may advance for voting to reject an applicant for membership or questioning a representative's credentials. For example, it is not permissible to vote to deny membership on the ground that the president of a new state is black, or that the government has come to power in a coup. The standard for symbolic validation has a fairly high degree of formal determinacy, making it possible to identify bogus, self-serving deviations.

It is important to appreciate that a realistic use of validating cues is not a concession to their impotence. On the contrary, cues used in a way that accords with reality help significantly, by deploying the symbolic power of the *ergo* predicate, to reinforce the reality symbolized by them. What the UPU, the World Bank, the General Assembly or the French government does when it "recognizes" the existence of a new state or government is to accord institutional legitimacy, which is of great practical significance to the beneficiary—in getting the mail delivered, a loan advanced or repayed, etc.—and may well be guided by such utilitarian considerations. However, these acts of validation have an additional symbolic dimension. By using symbolism tactically, they help the new entity consolidate its authority. Conversely, the withholding of symbolic validation undermines its authority. Symbolic validation, properly employed, does not merely mirror objective-functinal reality. In T. S. Eliot's phrase, it pins that reality to the page.

Given symbolism's potency, it is hardly surprising that states and international organizations are sometimes tempted to use symbolic cues to manipulate and change an unwanted reality. This need not be a malevolent motive. For example, consider the statements made by U.S. government officials in explaining a decision to recognize the state of Israel on the very day it declared itself independent, long before its ability to survive and exercise effective control of its territory had been established factually. The U.S. spokesman said that the U.S. purpose in extending recognition was to help create those very facts. "I should regard it as highly improper for me," he said, "to admit that any country on earth can question the sovereignty of the United States of America in the exercise of that high political act of recognition. . . . Moreover, I would not admit . . . that there exists a tribunal of justice or any other kind, anywhere, that can pass judgment upon the legality or the validity of that act of my country."[259]

A note of caution should be sounded before continuing. International law distinguishes between recognition (by the U.S., for example) of 1) a *state*, 2) a *government*, 3) admission of a state to *membership* in the U.N. or other multilateral organizations, and 4) acceptance by an organ of that organization (the General Assembly) of the *credentials* of delegates representing a member government. All four of these, however, require a deliberate act by governments which are validated members of the international community (in the case of recognition) or of the international organization (in the cases of membership and acceptance of credentials).[260] All four instances, moreover, are acts of symbolic validation and, for our purposes, may therefore be treated together. The differences are marginal for our purposes. It should also be noted that U.S. practice, and that of most other nations, has not been consistent, and the U.S.—in common with several other nations including Australia and Britain—from time to time has sought to abandon altogether the practice of recognizing new governments, substituting the act of establishing, or maintaining diplomatic relations with a new regime.[261] For the most part, however, the U.S., like most others, continues to extend symbolic validation to new states and new regimes in the traditional manner.

What is *not* traditional, however, is the extent to which U.S. practice in extending its symbolic cues is politically influenced. Thomas Jefferson, reflecting the republican philosophy of his new nation, added a new criterion to those which a new regime had to meet before it could expect recognition: that it should rest on the will of the people "substantially declared."[262] This view was restated by President Woodrow Wilson when he conditioned "mutual intercourse" with other governments on "order based upon law and upon the public conscience and approval."[263]

That is how it remains. The United States continues to be one of the few practitioners among nations of this subjective or political-tactical test for symbolic validation. It does not accept that a state or government is entitled to be recognized when it has met some mere "objective" standard of functional existence, or that recognition must be withdrawn when it no longer meets the standard. Washington withheld recognition from the Russian revolution between 1919 and 1933, even though the Soviet regime was known to be in full control. A similar period elapsed before it recognized the functionally effective communist government of China. Explaining its reluctance in the latter instance, the State Department said that "the United States policy of not extending diplomatic recognition to the Communist regime in China proceeds from the conviction that such recognition would produce no tangible benefit to the United States or to the free world as a whole and would be of material assistance to Chinese Communist attempts to extend Communist dominion throughout Asia." The statement denies that a regime, merely because it exists as a fact, is entitled to validation. "In the view of the United States diplomatic recognition is a privilege and not a right." It is "an instrument of national policy. . . ."[264]

This is a minority view among the nations of the international system. Or, perhaps, it is merely that few other states so openly and boldly reject the idea that their symbolic recognition behavior ought to be based solely on objective evaluation of functional considerations. In sharp contrast are the words of Sir Roger Makins, then the British ambassador to the U.S., explaining in 1954 his country's functional attitude to Chinese recognition: "The practice of Great Britain has always conformed fairly closely to the *de facto* principle. If a government is in effective control of the country in question; if it seems to have a reasonable expectancy of permanence; if it can act for a majority of a country's inhabitants; if it is able (though possibly not willing) to carry out its international obligations; if, in short, it can give a convincing answer to the question 'Who's in charge here?,' then we recognize that government. We are not conferring a favor, we are recognizing a situation of fact."[265] In practice, it should be added, even U.S. recognition behavior more often than not accords with the Makin formula. It is only in cases where a new regime is viewed with extreme disfavor (or favor) that Washington may choose to use the validating cue in defiance of the facts.

Nevertheless, for our purposes it is the extreme cases which are interesting, and what makes them so is less what the U.S. does than what its leaders say. At the level of theoretical explication of state conduct, there are two polar positions with respect to recognition. The United States leads a small group of states which openly proclaim that functional "facts"—the effectiveness of new nations and new governments—confer no entitlement to symbolic validation. They assert that recognition of a new state or government is entirely optional and governed by no rules except our political sensibilities or self-interest. In proclaiming this view, the U.S. is not alone. In the United Nations, it was not the United States but the Soviet Union which first applied a subjective, qualitative approach to membership and accreditation. The Soviets, over U.S. protest, from time to time have asserted that the decision to admit a state to U.N. membership, or to accept the credentials of a delegation is a political decision which cannot be circumscribed by so-called objective standards for determining whom to validate. Later, the U.S. itself took this view, battling to keep the delegates of communist China from taking the Chinese seat. More recently still, African and Arab members respectively, have led efforts to reject the credentials of delegations from South Africa and Israel,[266] despite the legal counsel's aforementioned caution against such distortion of reality and of the Charter text. At times the U.N.'s majority has succumbed to the urge to use its control over cues to change, rather than to symbolize, reality. For example, the General Assembly, with the support of the United States and a majority of Western and third world nations, has continued to seat the delegation of a Cambodian regime which would fail any objective, functional test because it does not control any significant part of the country it claims to represent. This is sometimes justified on the ground that the regime which is in effective control should not be rewarded for having invited the foreign aggression which installed it.[267] That argument, however, proceeds from the hypothesis that cues should be used to create a reality which ought to exist, even though manifestly it does not. Used this way very sparingly and briefly, symbolic cues may have some constitutive effect, erecting a bridge from present reality to a preferred tomorrow. The early U.S. recognition of Israel undoubtedly helped that nation consolidate its independence. In 1988, the U.N. General Assembly was asked to upgrade the Palestine Liberation Organization's representation from that of observer for an organization to that of observer for a state, even though no such state, objectively, can be said to have been in existence. Conversely, the U.N.'s rejection of the Bantustans' claim to symbolic validation—arguable on the facts[268]—no doubt helps to keep them from enjoying the rights and privileges of peer status, as did states' non-recognition of Biafra's secession.[269] However, this creationist strategy has its limits. When cues are used regularly and for prolonged periods in disregard of the generally perceived reality—when form disregards function—the symbols lose their efficacy. To put the matter bluntly, symbolic cues should confer entitlements on those objectively entitled. Where the objective entitlement is in doubt, symbolic validation may help to secure it. But if the gap between objective reality and that which is cued symbolically does not close, the cues will be seen to be bogus, the validation will fail, and the symbols will be tarnished.

It should be noted that we have, here, two separate, if related aspects of the issue under consideration. The first is whether there is an *entitlement*. Do states and governments have a right to be recognized by other states, admitted to the U.N., and have their credentials accepted by U.N. organs, once they have met certain objective functional standards? This is a question addressed by jurisprudence when it asks whether recognition is a "declaratory" or "constitutive" act. It need not concern us further in this context, because our province is the second aspect of the issue: what happens when validation is wrongly given or withheld, when untrue cues are used by states or international organizations? What happens to the legitimacy of the bestower, the bestowee, and to the compliance pull of the validating symbols when they are invoked against the evidence? That is the question here under consideration. There is another, related question which we will address in Chapter 9: What happens when the process of legitimation is applied *incoherently*, that is, when not only the facts, but the underlying standards for extending symbolic validation are ignored or applied selectively? Although the systemic implications of mis-cueing extend to far more than merely the ritual of recognition, that microcosm provides a handy context within which to address these questions. What happens when the objective functional standard for recognition is not applied, or when lip-service is paid to a prescribed standard but, in practice, it is manipulated or applied selectively to arrive at politically preferred results?

The Chinese recognition issue raised all these questions. For years, the United States government argued that its refusal to recognize the communist Chinese regime, and its opposition to accrediting that regime's delegation to the General Assembly, were justified by the continued control of part of China by the U.S.-supported Nationalist regime. The civil war, it urged, was far from over and the results were still undecided. Yet, during all that time, it was readily apparent that the Nationalist-controlled territory of China (Taiwan) was minute compared with the area and population under Communist rule. It was also clear that the Nationalists could never reconquer the mainland. The U.N.'s twenty-year-long delay, under U.S. pressure, in seating the functionally effective Chinese regime thus created a divergence between the U.N.'s symbolic world of validated members and the actual world of functioning states and governments. The case demonstrated that when this dissonance between function and form occurs and is sustained, the cues usually fail to evoke compliant behavior; the rites fail to bestow legitimacy. Indeed, the legitimacy of the rites suffers, as does the legitimacy of the pedigreeing institution.

Once there is dissonance between the cues and reality, reality is likely to make itself heard and the cues are debased. The U.N. Secretaries-General, Dag Hammarskjold and U Thant, both negotiated with excluded regimes: the former with the Beijing Chinese Government, the latter with the authorities in Hanoi.[270] In 1972, almost seven years before the U.S. was ready to extend formal recognition, President Nixon and Secretary of State Kissinger visited Beijing and signed diplomatic agreements. Non-recognition stood humiliated, exposed as a lying cue.

Nevertheless, some "real" consequences may flow from non-recognition or non-admittance to the U.N. Pedigreeing ritual can affect reality even when it does not reflect it, although usually only in a very limited sense. The Beijing Government, for as long as its representatives' credentials were rejected by the U.S.-led majority in the U.N., could not speak through the microphones of the Security Council or the General Assembly. As a non-member, it was not eligible for loans from the World Bank. Yet these results were almost universally seen not as reflections on the communist regime's lack of legitimacy but as a consequence of the political clout then still exercised in the U.N. by the United States.

The primary effect of that dissonance between the symbolic and the real, however, was to undermine the power of the symbols to pull toward compliance. As there was no question in anyone's mind, after 1950, that the Beijing regime was entitled to the Chinese seat under the applicable U.N. standard for accreditation, the Nationalists, while continuing to hold the seat, increasingly found themselves denied the fruits of legitimacy. Undersecretary-General Sir Brian Urquhart has judged their continued presence at the U.N. as "largely meaningless."[271] Their delegates became diplomatic "Flying Dutchmen," a sort of ghostly presence largely devoid of substance. Few of the other members' representatives took them seriously when plans for U.N. initiatives were being shaped by consultations. On one occasion when the Nationalist delegate tried to veto a Security Council decision, the British ambassador, who was presiding, peremptorily ignored the Chinese vote.[272] On the other hand, the unaccredited representative of Beijing was invited to the U.N. to seek a settlement to the Korean War. Dag Hammarskjold visited Beijing and maintained a close and fruitful relationship with the communists' Foreign Minister (later Premier) Chou En-lai.[273] All this demonstrates that the validating, legitimating effect of symbolic recognition virtually ceases when the symbols cue not cognitive congruence but dissonance. As mythology often asserts, the "magic" does not work if it is invoked for impure ends.

Even if this is so in the context of an international organization's symbolic recognition practices, one would expect any nation's decision to recognize or to withhold recognition—however congruent or dissonant with objective functional reality—to have more resonance. For example, it might be supposed that the national courts would consider themselves obliged to follow the cues emanating from the nation's foreign office. The judiciary after all, is part of "the government." Also, judges tend to be uncharacteristically reticent in matters of foreign affairs, in part in deference to the need for national coherence in the dangerous world of international relations, but also because they cannot easily inform themselves about political conditions in a foreign place. U.S. courts for these reasons do tend to defer to the executive branch, pleading the constitutional doctrine of the separation of powers. "It is for the executive and legislative departments to say in what relations any other country stands toward it" said the U.S. Court of Appeals for the second circuit, in holding that a suit begun in 1917 against an agent of the Imperial Government of Russia could still be pursued in 1927, a decade after the Czar's overthrow, because the U.S. had not yet recognized the victorious Soviet authorities.[274] In another case, the Supreme Court thought that the issue of which "government is to be regarded here as representative of a foreign sovereign state is a political rather than a judicial question, and is to be determined by the political department of the government. . . . Its action in recognizing a foreign government . . . is conclusive on all domestic courts. . . ."[275]

There are real consequences of such judicial deference to recognition. Much in domestic litigation can hinge on this symbolic act of validation. In the last-mentioned case, the issue was whether the statute of limitations had run during the period when the real (Soviet) government, not yet recognized by Washington, had been barred from pressing a claim in U.S. courts. The Supreme Court held that the statute had indeed run, because, theoretically, the claim could have been pressed by the recognized—but defunct—Kerensky regime. The judges were not deterred from this result by the objective-functional fact that the Kerensky regime had been in control of Russia for only a few months before the October 1917 revolution. They considered themselves "bound to accept"[276] the executive's symbolic fiction as controlling the outcome of the litigation.

There are other examples. The will of a U.S. testator leaving a bequest to someone in Latvia could not be executed because Washington still refuses to recognize that there has not been an independent Latvian state since it was occupied and absorbed by the Soviet Union in 1940. In consequence, the New York surrogate's court concluded that it must reject the validity of notarial acts in connection with the state made by the Soviet authorities in Latvia. "Questions of recognition of governments," the judge explained, "lie exclusively within the realm of the executive branch of our government and our courts can give no effect to the act of an unrecognized government which either by implication or otherwise would indicate recognition of that government."[277]

The judge could not but be embarrassed by having to decide the case on the basis of facts that everyone knew to be wishful thinking. In any other person, the same symptoms of reality-rejection would be labeled a psychosis. After all, some 160 other countries recognize, however reluctantly, that Latvia is now part of the Soviet Union, while the exiled government still recognized by the U.S. bravely exists at a Washington, D.C., address.

Not surprisingly, some U.S. judges have refused to heed symbolic cues which they perceive to be so patently false. In *Salimoff & Co. v. Standard Oil Co. of New York*,[278] the highest court of the state of New York was faced with a suit between Standard Oil, an American company, which had purchased petroleum from the Soviet government, and Salimoff, the owner of lands from which the oil had been extracted, whose assets had been expropriated without compensation after the 1917 revolution. The case reached the U.S. Circuit Court of Appeals in 1933. Salimoff, pointing to U.S. non-recognition policy, took the position that he was entitled to the proceeds of the sale because the oil lands had been seized by what he claimed were authorities no better than bandits, incapable of passing good title. As evidence, he produced the fact of the regime's non-recognition by the U.S. The Court, rejecting that argument, said it "will not sit in judgment on the validity of the acts of another state done within its own territory."[279] Was the unrecognized Soviet regime a "government" to whose decrees a U.S. court would give credence or were the rulers mere bandits? The judges decided that while the "government may be objectionable in a political sense," it "is not unrecognizable as a real governmental power which can give title to property within its limits."[280] Form was brought into line with functions. Unanimously, the court found that the Soviet regime, factually, *was* the effective "government in Russia,"[281] To reach that finding of "fact" the court had to look beyond the cues emitted by the State Department, to the real world.

The second instance is a 1961 case, also in New York, in the Appellate Division of the Supreme Court. In that case, *Upright v. Mercury Business Machines Co.,*[282] the Mercury company had purchased typewriters from an East German government-owned manufacturer. The nation and government of East Germany, although functioning for more than a decade, had not been recognized by the U.S. Nevertheless, Mercury openly imported the machines. However, when the manufacturer sought payment, Mercury refused. The debt was assigned by the manufacturer to Upright, an American, who tried to collect it. Mercury argued that the courts should not help Upright because his claim was identical with that of the unrecognized East German government.

This contention was emphatically rejected. "A foreign government," the court said, "although not recognized by the political arm of the United States Government, may nevertheless have a *de facto* existence which is juridically cognizable," and which "may affect private rights and obligations arising either as a result of activity in, or with persons or corporations within, the territory controlled by such a *de facto* government."[283] As far as suits of this sort are concerned "only limited effect is given to the fact that the political arm has not recognized a foreign government."[284]

The court added: "It is a false notion, if it prevail anywhere, that an unrecognized government is always an evil thing and all that occurs within its governmental purview are always evil works."[285] Non-recognition "does not mean that the denizens of such territories or the corporate creatures of such powers do not have the juridical capacity to trade, transfer title, or collect the price for the merchandise they sell to outsiders. . . ."[286] In a more recent case, a federal judge in the Southern District of New York held that the as-yet unrecognized Republic of Palau was entitled to be treated as a "foreign state for purposes of jurisdiction." The court declined "to close its eyes to the *de facto* degree of sovereignty which the Palauans have exercised" in a period of political transition.[287] The judge found as an independently established fact that the "foundation laying period has ended and the transition to sovereign equality has begun."[288]

Thus it would appear that even in U.S. courts, which are ordinarily subservient in such matters, there is a reluctance of judges to close their eyes or to comply with evidently false foreign relations cues.

Such defection attests to the resilient preference accorded true cues, a preference which is natural. Symbolic cues exert a strong compliance pull, and are effective in conferring legitimacy, as long as they are true. When the cues are palpably false, their capacity to exert such compliance pull is diminished. When cues habitually are used to symbolize a false reality, the cues and, perhaps the validating entity, begin to lose their potency as instruments for conferring legitimacy. Conversely, the withholding of symbolic validation can have a negative effect on the legitimacy of an entity, but not if that withholding is patently in conflict with the perceived reality. It is today widely acknowledged even among African delegates that the General Assembly's rejection of the South African delegation's credentials was both a tactical and conceptual mistake. South Africa still maintains a highly effective mission at the U.N. (it has not been expelled), and speaks regularly before the Security Council (where its credentials have not been rejected). Its delegates' ostracism has not inhibited the Secretary-General's negotiations with the South African authorities over such matters as the future of Namibia because he, certainly, is in no doubt as to "who's in charge."

The Assembly's action in rejecting the credentials of South Africa's delegates has proven unproductive. Pretoria has escaped having to pay its annual U.N. assessment, and its representatives have not had to be present to hear the world's unanimous condemnation of their racial policies. More important, the misuse of the credentials process has undermined the integrity of the rule by which the U.N. purports to validate delegates and their governments. This seems to have been understood, because subsequent efforts by Arab states to have the Assembly also reject the Israeli delegation's credentials have foundered on states' resistance to setting another bad precedent. There is genuine concern not to be pushed further down a slippery slope into cognitive dissonance between objective reality and the cues used in symbolic validation.[289]

In summary: Cues used to validate symbolically are potent to the extent they are perceived as true by those to whom they are addressed. When cues cease to refer symbolically to what is perceived as historic, social, political or metaphysical reality they fail to validate and, instead, squander their "magic." In the gray area, when the cues refer to an ambiguous reality, they may sometimes be effective not only in validating, but also in reinforcing, that reality. But where the reality is clear, institutions charged with conferring symbolic validation quite properly resist pressure to abuse—and thereby diminish—their power to bestow legitimacy by resort to false cues.

The role of cues is to validate nations, institutions, and rules. The cues, for example, reinforce the perception that a government or a rule is entitled to respect because its pedigree has been certified by those whose own pedigree is itself established, and in accordance with the requisite procedures and standards. When validating cues are generally perceived to be misapplied—if the clerk of the British House of Commons were to take the mace to a "strip joint," for example, or the Secretary-General chose to license the U.N. flag and symbol for use by the manufacturers of commercial products[290]—then the symbolic validation would not occur; instead, the symbol and its bestower would both suffer the erosion of their authority to confer legitimacy. A core of self-preserving integrity thus motivates most institutions and persons to defend the integrity of the symbols at their disposal.

9

Validation and Coherence

We have examined in some depth the symbolic validation of new states and governments by their peers, the cueing familiarly known as recognition. When this is done as a collective act of the members of an international organization, it is called admission to membership or acceptance of credentials. All these confer symbolic validation and, thus, a degree of legitimacy.

These validating rituals matter because the status of the new state or government is thereby enhanced: that is, it acquires status-legitimacy which carries entitlements and obligations akin to those of its peers. But this legitimation only occurs, symbolically, if the symbol represents, and the cue communicates, what is perceived reality or, at least, not unreality. The General Assembly's decision[291] to permit the exiled regime headed by Prince Sihanouk to speak for Cambodia, in preference to the government firmly installed by the Vietnamese invaders, may be politically justifiable but it puts the accreditation process of the U.N. at the disposal of a fiction. The result may be as costly to the legitimacy of the U.N. as to the symbolically rejected government of Cambodia.

We have noted that symbol and reality also diverged dramatically when, at various times, the General Assembly denied validation to the effective regimes of China and South Africa. These decisions failed to accord with generally perceived reality and bent the organization's own "who's in charge?" standards for representation of states and accreditation of delegates. While this did some injury to the unvalidated governments, it also demonstrated the weakness of counterfeit ritual.

The failure of validating "magic" to work in such circumstances warrants further attention. What accounts for it? We have already observed that this failure in part is due to cognitive dissonance. The power of symbols derives from their almost-Pavlovian ability to reinforce by the merest signal something already known or believed by those addressed. When, instead of reinforcing the known, the cue compels the beholder to choose between it and what is known, it is the sensed reality, rather than the symbol, which is usually chosen.

However, there is a further reason why states and international organizations tend to ignore false validation cues; why they deal with states and governments which are perceived to be in functional control, even when these have not been formally validated and ignore states and regimes which have been validated formally but fail to function in practice. The reason is that in such cases of cognitive dissonance the cues do not merely lie, *they are being applied incoherently: that is, in a way not consistent with the rules* purporting to govern that act of symbolic validation. Put affirmatively: the integrity of the process by which a new state's status is recognized by a community organization like the U.N. will determine whether that symbolic act is successful in actually conferring the incidents of equal entitlement. The legitimacy of a state's, or government's, pedigreed status depends in part on the *coherence* with which the standard extending or withholding symbolic validation has been applied. The Ukraine's membership in the United Nations, for example, cannot validate its status as an equal nation among nations because it is clear that it fails to fulfill the organization's own criteria for eligibility, just as naming a horse to the Roman Senate does not legitimate its status as a senator even after it has undergone the rituals of induction. Conversely, the Assembly's rejection of South African credentials failed to undermine that government's status as the legitimate—not the *just,* or *best,* or *representative*—voice of the Republic. The rejection failed because the Assembly's action was not coherent with its applicable rules. It was both out of synchronization with reality and also utterly incoherent with the standards for accreditation professed by Charter text and practice: a point, as we saw in Chapter 8, which was confirmed by the organization's legal counsel. The effect of such incoherence was noted long ago by Aristotle, who wrote in the *Nichomachean Ethics* that a rule commands obedience rightly if it "has been rightly enacted, not so well if it has been made at random."[292]

The Charter, the World Court, and the U.N.'s legal counsel all agree that the applicable standard for validation of credentials is one not dissimilar to the British "who's in charge?" test for recognition. In South Africa's and Cambodia's cases the usual test was ignored. Moreover, the Assembly's failure to apply it in those two instances contrasts not only with its normal rules of procedure for validation but is also incoherent with its practice in respect of other *reprehensible* regimes. It has been willing to accept the credentials of representatives of Uganda's Idi Amin and Chile's General Pinochet as well as of foreign-imposed governments of Grenada, Czechoslovakia, and Afghanistan. These delegates, although sent by authorities established or operating in flagrant violation of rules of the international system, nevertheless were accredited without serious difficulty. The U.N. refused to embark on evidenciary excursions into the likeableness, representativeness, or legality of the regime so long as it was undeniably in charge of the state it purported to govern and able to assume the duties of a member. Yet likeableness, representativeness, and legality were determinative when it came to South Africa's and Cambodia's delegates, thereby making the Assembly's process of symbolic validation both dissonant with perceived reality and also incoherent with the applicable rules and practice.

In these two cases, the Assembly's decision lacks reality and coherence because the usual standard—"who's in charge?"—was replaced by another: "who *ought* to be in charge?" The symbolic validation thus conferred only the illusion of legitimate status on the regime nominally headed by the exiled Prince Norodom Sihanouk, and withholding of pedigree failed to erase the effective reality of the South African regime.

The occasional deviation by the Assembly from reality and from its own professed standard for pedigreeing, has given rise to what Professor Ronald Dworkin, in a different context, has called, a "checkerboard" effect.[293] Blatant checkerboarding in the application of a rule or standard undermines legitimacy in three related, but different, senses. *First*, it clouds the legitimacy of a particular instance in which the status-endowing process of symbolic validation has been misapplied. It causes the attempt at extending, or refusing, validation to be perceived to be illegitimate and, thus, incapable of conferring or withholding legitimacy from the state or government in question. The cues fail. *Second*, checkerboarding undermines the U.N.'s accreditation rules or standards by showing that they only apply to some, but not all, candidates. The inconsistent application of a rule or general principle undermines its capacity to elicit compliance. *Third*, feckless application of a standard to various parties derogates from the legitimacy of the process or institution by which the rules are applied or pedigree is conferred. The unequal or illusory application of objective standards for delegates' accreditation thus damages the credibility of the U.N. as a legitimate bestower of valid "sovereign and equal" status on states and governments. Checkerboarding vitiates the cue's compliance pull, releasing states to act in nonconformity with what the U.N. has done to legitimate, or withhold validation, in a particular instance. This, in turn, erodes the power of the organization more generally to cue the behavior of its members. Indeed, officials of the U.N. themselves begin to act in non-conformity with the organization's decisions.

A bogus application of, or a failure to apply, the usually implemented standard undermines the legitimacy of the standard and of the authority applying it, without having much effect on the legitimacy of the entity whose status is thereby blatantly misconstrued. The point here is not merely that the denial of validation to delegates of the regimes actually in power at Pnom Penh or Pretoria sends a cue which is demonstrably false, but also that the standard for validation, itself, has been undermined by its incoherent application. Such evident incoherence saps the validation process of its symbolic power to affect status. To recover, the process needs to pull itself together around one standard—preferably one which will produce results congruent with perceived reality—and apply it with consistent integrity: that is, no checkerboarding.

In other words, if the Assembly wished to retain its present policy toward South African and Cambodian credentials, it would need to revise its standards for accreditation and start to apply them consistently. The untruth apparent in the validation process as it has operated in the Cambodian and South African credentials cases is evidenced by a kind of cognitive dissonance, which needs correction before the Assembly's power to validate can be said to be restored to a high degree of persuasiveness. This problem of cognitive dissonance is observable, *first*, between the factual reality which U.N. accreditation ostensibly symbolizes and the generally perceived reality "on the ground"; and, *second*, between the principle, rule, or standard that is supposed to govern the cueing process—that those actually in charge are to be validated while others are not—and the Assembly's actual performance in these aberrational cases.

In other words, the Assembly's validating cue has developed two credibility gaps. The first arises by *external* reference. That is, when the Assembly seats a delegation of a government which does not govern, or refuses to seat the representatives of one which does, each member of the community of states can see for itself that the cue is being misused in an effort to legitimate one not entitled, or to withhold legitimation from one entitled. What does "entitled" mean in this external context? The answer must be sought, and is usually quite readily ascertained, from the nature of the entitlement which validation confers. The placing of the crown on Charlemagne's head validates his imperial power. If the same crown had been placed on the head of a horse, the cue would have failed to impart legitimacy. The status of emperor carries an implicit job description which excludes, as a first cut, non-humans. If a horse obviously cannot rule the empire, it is equally useless to pretend that the government in Taipei can negotiate on behalf of China with other members of the U.N. on the grave matters on that organization's agenda. It is the nature of that agenda—from economic development to human rights—which dictates that basic "job description" which can be met only by those exercising actual power over real nations.

A different organization—for example, a global society of governments-in-exile, or of constitutional regimes illegally deposed, or of "captive nations"—would have an entirely different purpose. By admitting aspirants, it could even afford them another kind of legitimacy: not as the effective government of an actual state with the rights and duties enabling it to transact the business of the global community, but as an aspirant organization seeking to invoke the available appeals to justice or sympathy.

A different credibility gap can become evident by *internal* reference: that is, when the General Assembly's action in accrediting, or failing to accredit, a delegation is compared not with the sensed external reality but with the standards for accreditation developed by the organization. It would be perfectly possible, for example, for the U.N. to change its own rules to admit only states, or accredit only delegates of regimes, which are democratic, or which always obey international law. The result might be a much smaller organization, but it would be one which, with integrity, could exclude not only South Africa and Cambodia but many others who could not clear the higher hurdle. To maintain its validating power, however, the new standard would have to be applied to Morocco as to Israel (both have what the U.N. has deemed "occupied territories"), to Burundi as to South Africa (both have regimes cursed with racism), and so forth. Whatever the standard for applying a symbolic mandate, it will fail to legitimate if it is not applied coherently.

There was a time, not long ago, when most states in the international system regularly acknowledged and tried to address the cognitive dissonance problem by practicing a dual-level recognition policy. States and governments were recognized *de facto* if, by reference to the perceived external reality, they were seen to exist and exercise effective power. However, if they had also come into being in accordance with—or, at least, not in violation of—the rules of constitutional and international law and appeared willing to carry out their international obligation, they were recognized *de jure.* Thus it was that Britain extended *de facto* recognition to Mussolini's Italian invasion of Ethiopia as soon as it became clear that the aggressors were in control of the country, even while Ethiopia's exiled Emperor Haile Selassie and his government in London continued to be recognized *de jure* until 1938.[294] The *de facto* validation, in this scheme, carries with it most, but not quite all, of the rights and duties accruing to states and governments in international systemic practice. The *de jure* regime which has lost *de facto* recognition retains a few rights, usually those functionally appropriate to a government-in-exile. Similarly, for a few years after the Soviet invasion of Hungary, the General Assembly preferred neither to accept not to reject the credentials of delegates sent by the imposed Kadar regime, thereby allowing those delegates to linger in a legitimacy limbo, speaking and voting only on sufferance without being formally validated.

While this two-tier approach has its advantages, in actual practice the *de facto/de jure* split-level approach to validation has largely been abandoned in recent years.[295] "With the decay of the doctrine of dynastic legitimacy," the U.S. *Digest of International Law* points out, "constitutional legitimacy is no longer made the test of the international title to govern."[296] Indeed, "it has been suggested that the distinction should be disregarded. . . ."[297]

Evidently the Assembly is not likely to revise its accreditation standards to reflect its reasons for rejecting the representatives of those in power in Pnom Penh and Pretoria. This understandable reluctance, however, means that the process of accreditation has lost not only some of its congruence with reality but also a degree of coherence. Both losses deduct from the ability of the U.N. to confer or withhold status legitimacy. That, in turn, also subverts the U.N.'s own legitimacy. In practical terms: these rules and procedures have squandered some of their compliance pull by idiosyncratic implementation. In effect this means that nations—and, indeed, the U.N. itself—might feel less obliged to be governed by those symbolic cues. It could cause members to surrender to the temptation to turn the accreditation and admissions process into a political game without rules. If the membership process itself is seen to lack legitimacy, then it might no longer be able to impart legitimacy to members, nor could it pull toward compliance with the rights and duties of membership. Eventually, the very notion of a community of states becomes one of doubtful validity.

None of this is likely to follow solely from the Assembly's occasional failure to play by its own rules. The bleak vision, however, is not fantastic and it introduces our discussion of coherence by emphasizing the costs of incoherence. Inexorably, more nations in more instances will be tempted to ignore those rules and standards which are seen not to be applied with integrity in each case.

Coherence is essential to legitimacy. This legitimacy-destructiveness of incoherence and the constructiveness of coherence can be formulated in a revised version of that apparent tautology first mentioned in Chapter 3: *The legitimacy of a rule is determined in part by the degree to which that rule is practiced coherently; conversely, the degree to which a rule is applied coherently in practice will depend in part on the degree to which it is perceived as legitimate by those applying it.* On closer examination, it will become apparent that this formulation is not tautological. Rather, it asserts the *reciprocal* dependence of its two variables: rule-conforming practice and perceptions of a rule's legitimacy.

This reciprocal dependence of coherence and legitimacy appears to be sensed by the community of states. In the General Assembly there is evidence of a feeling of unease about those cases in which the members ignored their own professed standards for validation. Those instances cannot be expunged from the organization's social memory, but the downward spiral can be arrested by return to rule-coherence. That this is understood by the members may explain their marked reluctance to make another special checkerboard case by rejecting the credentials of the Israeli delegation, as some Arab states have urged.[298] Most U.N. members, while they may have been willing to strike what was presented as a symbolic blow at South Africa, do not favor the erosion of the accreditation ritual to the point where every government's right to be represented becomes subject to the vagaries of its popularity. Neither do they want to promote the Assembly's irrelevance, its descent into a fantasy-world of delegations representing the non-governments of non-states while the real actors of the real world conduct their business elsewhere. To prevent this from happening, the accreditation standards need to be shored up, protected from further erosion of their coherence.

While we have focused on one standard, that applicable to the validation of states and governments by their peers acting unilaterally and collectively, the same mutual dependence between coherence and legitimacy is evident in respect of all standard-applying or rule-interpreting institutions, as the ensuing chapter will attempt to demonstrate. We have focused on status-validation or recognition, at this point in the discussion, because it serves as a convenient bridge from symbolic validation to coherence since it illustrates the efficacy of both indicators of legitimacy.

The concept of *coherence* has been developed in a pioneering study by Ronald Dworkin,[299] in which he contends that it is a key factor in explaining why rules are treated as compelling.[300] Using the term "integrity," Dworkin speaks of its two aspects: *moral* and *adjudicative*. By the former he means that a substantive rule has integrity when it relates in a principled fashion to other rules of the same system, and, by the latter that, in applying a rule, conceptually alike cases will be treated alike. In the next chapter we shall return to this useful mode of analysis.

First, however, let us examine further the notion of *coherence*, beginning with its relation to the better-understood idea of *consistency*.

When we speak of treating alike cases alike, we address a problem of the cases' connectedness. This idea of *nexus* is central to the definition of coherence. It is also related to, but not the same as, simple consistency. The Assembly's failure to accept the credentials of the South African government is both *inconsistent* with seating the delegates of other disagreeable, law-breaking regimes and *incoherent* with the Assembly's own professed "who's in charge?" standard. This inconsistency and incoherence could both be cured either by reversing the faulty application of the standard to South Africa, or by revising the standard and applying a new one across the board. But suppose the new standard were applied only prospectively—for new states and governments, while retaining the old standard for "grandfather" states and governments already in the organization. The applicable standard would then be coherent (i.e. one rule would apply to old states and governments and another to new, which might be thought to be a conceptually defensible arrangement) but it would still lack consistency as long as there were two categories of members and delegates governed by different standards. A dual-tier standard—a common phenomenon in national legal systems, for example, in the regulation of the environment, with newcomers subject to more stringent regulation than old-timers—does not necessarily offend against coherence, despite its inconsistency, so long as there is a rational, determinate connecting principle of general application which is accepted by all as justifying the differential—i.e. inconsistent—treatment.

In other words, consistency requires that "likes be treated alike" while coherence requires that distinctions in the treatment of "likes" be *justifiable in principled terms*. Consistency in a rule text is no guarantee of its coherence. Similarly, a rule which is consistently applied may yet be incoherent. Coherence demands a different level of connectedness between instances covered by a rule than does consistency. To illustrate the element of nexus at the heart of the concept of coherence let us use the recurrent international debt crisis. The world's debtor nations are estimated to owe some 1,010 billion dollars to the world's creditor states.[301] A few net debtors, like the United States, are rich. Some lenders, notably the U.S., are also borrowers. Most borrowers, however, are poor, although a few (like Brazil) are in an intermediate category of rising affluence. As the full extent of the debt burden of countries like Brazil, Mexico, Nigeria, and Peru has become apparent against the background of falling earnings from their commodity exports, several debtors have said they would act unilaterally to alter the terms of their indebtedness. A few have simply refused to continue to repay their creditors.[302] Some have agreed to pay interest but have postponed repayment of principal.[303] Others have limited the amount of debt repayment to a fixed percentage of earned foreign exchange.[304] Still others have negotiated a stretching of their repayment schedule.[305] A few debtor states not only continue to repay promptly to ensure their future credit-worthiness but deeply resent the defaulting states which have dried up the capital transfer market.[306] Lender nations, for the most part, have threatened to blacklist defaulting states even while tolerating some variations in special cases.

The debt crisis can be seen as a web of bilateral interactions. Yet it is also a pandemic phenomenon which seems to call for multilateral, even global, systemic solutions. The third world nations, through such multilateral mechanisms as the United Nations Conference on Trade and Development (UNCTAD), have pushed for such a global approach. But what are to be its parameters? The lenders point to a contractual obligation to make full repayment. The borrowers speak of the impossibility of crushing blood from a stone and of "fairness" and "justice," while arguing the immorality of the starving of children to boost the level of bank earnings.

At the 1987 UNCTAD conference,[307] various proposals were mooted. Some states called for a compassionate wiping clean of the debt slate. Others demanded reiteration of the rule requiring full, timely repayment and sought endorsement of the sanctity of commitments. Still others called for a compromise, since neither of the extreme positions could hope to command general support.

Suppose there *were* a will to compromise, rather than see the world's capital markets descend into chaos. What kind of arrangement could be made if both debtors and lenders were to agree that about half of the total current global debt should be repaid and the other half forgiven? Suppose that this were regarded by both sides as "fair"—in the sense of giving each side something—and that both sides were to agree to such a "bottom line." Some such solution is perfectly conceivable. While it is less "just" by the standards of both lenders and borrowers than would be each side's optimal solution (full repayment or no repayment), it is also less "unjust" to each than the outcome most favorable to the other. But how would the compromise solution be implemented?

One way might be to forgive the total debt of states whose names began with the letters A-M, while requiring full, prompt repayment by states with names starting with N-Z. Such an idiot rule—as we categorized it in Chapter 5—would certainly have the merit of determinacy. It would largely apply itself. It would also be "fair" in the sense that it would "split the difference" between debtor and creditor states as a whole. Yet, as Dworkin points out, such a "checkerboard" compromise is likely to be widely rejected, not so much because of its unfair inconsistency in the treatment of debtors as because of its incoherence (its "lack of integrity" to use Dworkin's term). The plan's incoherence indicates its illegitimacy.

To be legitimate, Dworkin has written, an agreed compromise reached by deliberation "must nevertheless aim to settle on some coherent principle whose influence then extends to the natural limits of its authority."[308] That means the compromise must connect what it does with some *rational principle of broader import*. The alphabetic compromise asserts a principle that distinguishes between countries—those which must repay and those to be forgiven—by the location of each country's name in the alphabet, a "principle" which cannot be defended on any rational basis. The alphabetic compromise, like the flipping of a coin, is an admission that *no* rational principle can be found that will produce the desired result. Thus the decision is left to chance: the "draw" of the alphabet. This is a procedure for deciding not to decide, for bringing to bear no generalizable rule, no principle to justify the basis for making a decision. It thus lacks coherence because it lacks nexus. It fails to connect to a rational principle. It also establishes no basis for a continuing pattern of systemic interaction—it connects the particular decision to no sense of on-going community—because, even if there were other debt crises in the future, this "luck of the draw" approach to its resolution would be even less defensible. The alphabetic solution would no longer be random, the second time around, and would thus have lost its sole utility. For example, prescient nations would deliberately seek to skew the outcome by changing their names. The alphabetic solution would also be a poor candidate for validation in other contemporary contexts such as the allocation of deep sea mining licenses by the envisaged new international authority. Indeed, nothing of importance in international life is ever likely to be solved by the alphabetic principle except seating arrangements at multinational conferences.

The alphabetic "principle" is thus neither consistent nor coherent. It neither treats all the same, nor does it make defensible distinctions.

Another approach would be to take a fixed percentage off the amount owed by each debtor state, thereby distributing an amount of forgiveness equal to half of total global indebtedness. This rule at least would have the merit of consistency, treating all debtors alike. But it would lack coherence, because it would treat rich debtors with huge deficits like the U.S. in the same way as those in direct need, without rational explanation. Indeed, the sheer size of the U.S. international debt would consume so much of available debt relief that most nations would be denied meaningful help. The across-the-board forgiveness of a consistent percentage of each nation's debt would be incoherent with the very purpose of the proposed remedy.

In sharp contrast, a coherent half-loaf compromise could be achieved by recourse to any one of various principled approaches. For example, debt forgiveness could be distributed on a sliding scale based on the debtor's comparative degree of poverty, or one which inverted each state's per capita income, or on the basis of demonstrated willingness to achieve liquidity by matching the proportion of debt a poor state chooses to repay annually. Such methods of implementing the half-loaf compromise incorporate principles of distribution which commend themselves rationally by making distinctions in entitlement which may be acceptable to all, despite—indeed, *because* of—the scheme's inconsistent treatment of debtors.

Such connection does not ensure that the solution achieved necessarily works well, or that the principle it employs is wise, or just, or even helpful. A principle that all debtors should *always* be forgiven a part of their debt, for example, seems likely to make borrowing impossible, could be extremely inflationary, and would fundamentally alter the conditions under which loans are made. Coherence also does not ensure that any particular result would be fairer or more just than that achieved by some other principle, or even a purely random result. *Coherence legitimates a rule, principle, or implementing institution because it provides a reasonable connection between a rule, or the application of a rule, to 1) its own principled purpose, 2) principles previously employed to solve similar problems, and 3) a lattice of principles in use to resolve different problems.*

Coherence, in particular, should not be understood as the consistent application of a principled rule only to cases that look factually *the same*. Coherence also denotes that the rule applied to a dispute about how to distribute a certain quantity of debt relief should employ distinctions which are widely acceptable (or, at least, not unacceptable) in solving quite different problems of distributive entitlements. Thus the alphabetical approach to debt relief is unacceptable because that approach is not employed in implementing any other scheme for allocating limited resources where hard choices must be made among claimants. The across-the-board 50 percent solution is only slightly less unacceptable as a general remedy. On the other hand, any of our proposed principles for implementing the debt compromise on a need-driven basis could be—indeed may already be—applied to the settlement of other kinds of issues: for example, the question of how to assess U.N. members' dues.

A half-loaf compromise is not necessarily the most just, or the most economically efficacious solution to the debt crisis. But it may be a legitimate one if what is widely perceived as a coherent principle for distributing the half-loaf is found. Alphabetic allocation of benefits—the checkerboard compromise—will not do, because it treats various states differently in accordance with a method of allocation which simply cannot be justified by any underlying rational principle. It is not difficult, however, to find in existing international practice several principles of rational allocation that would meet the test of coherence. The resulting formula could be expected to exercise a powerful pull to compliance.

This connection between a rule's authority and its coherence is recognized by the civil law of Germany which distinguishes between *Gesetz*—a law made by legislative fiat[309]—and *Recht*. The latter is a legal right by virtue of its coherence with the "ultimate principles" of the legal system, and this imbues *Recht* with a superiority which allows it to "transcend the realm of enacted written law."[310] Dworkin makes a similar distinction. In his view, a rule which is incoherent loses its purchase even if it achieves part of an otherwise desired outcome. "Even if I thought strict liability for accidents wrong in principle, I would prefer that manufacturers of both washing machines and automobiles be held to that standard," he states, rather "than that only one of them be. I would rank the checkerboard solution not intermediate between the other two [no strict liability and universal strict liability] but third, below both, and so would many other people." Such "compromises are wrong, not merely impractical."[311]

Dworkin is not here condemning *compromises*, but "wrong" or invidious principles for arriving at a compromise. If we inquire further into this distinction, it may be possible to illuminate the reciprocal connection between coherence and legitimacy.

10

Coherence and Legitimacy

Legitimacy is the generic label we have placed on factors that affect our willingness to comply voluntarily with commands. These commands may be direct ("go on green; stop on red") or indirect, in the sense of referring back to a more general underlying rule or principle ("each member of the U.N. is to be treated by all others in accordance with the principle of equal entitlement"). Such commands emanate from institutions and from rules. Those institutions and rules perceived to have a high degree of legitimacy generate a correspondingly high sense of obligation on the part of the persons or states to whom a command is addressed. Evidence of that sense of obligation is to be found primarily in compliant behavior. But there may be evidence of it even in cases of noncompliance. Thus, a failure to act in accordance with a command emanating from a rule or institution of high legitimacy may give rise to a feeling of guilt, which may surface as a government's disingenuous denial of default, or in citizens' street demonstrations against their own government's "illegal" behavior.

A government's failure to comply with a legitimate rule usually arouses the concern of other states, even those not directly affected by the breach. A state's failure to discharge its normative obligation frequently is seen by such other states as threatening their interests indirectly: by undermining the legitimacy of a rule of which they approve and on which they rely, and by weakening the fabric of the community's rule system as a whole.*

It is true, however, that in the international—as opposed to a national—community, the failure of members of the community to obey a command is still an accepted way to try to bring about change or reform in the rule or institution from which the command emanates. The prospects of success in that venture will depend on whether the refusing state convinces enough of its peers that a better new rule should be substituted for the one it has refused to obey. This, in turn, will depend, in part, on whether its rationale for defying the existing rule is couched in terms which give the community a persuasive alternative rule. One form of this persuasion consists of demonstrating that the proposed alternative is more coherent than the old one. For example, when the U.S. decided to force the three Soviet Socialist Republics to reduce the size of their missions to the U.N. in New York, Washington might have—but did not—put forward the notion that no delegation to an international conference should exceed in size a certain percentage of all the delegates. As in that instance, however, most breaches of the rules do not generate such proposals for a new rule because even the violator silently acknowledges the legitimacy of the existing one, and has no interest in making a coherent generally applicable new norm of its aberrant behavior. To cite another example, when the U.S. bombed a mental hospital during the invasion of Grenada, or when the cruiser *Vincennes* shot down Iranian civil flight 655 in the Persian Gulf,[312] the U.S. expressed regret and offered compensation to underscore its assertion that what had occurred was entirely accidental and that no principle was being advanced to defend what had happened. Indeed, the U.S. strove by various means—offers of apology, sympathy, and compensation—to repair the damage it had done, inadvertently, to rules which it values as pillars of civilized community behavior. Its efforts seemed to reassure most states, which had a stake in the violated rules, even if none of their citizens were killed in its

---

* The invasion of Panama by U.S. forces in December, 1989, evoked just such a negative reaction from most equally vulnerable Third World and small nations, a militant defensiveness but little mitigated by those nations' lack of sympathy with the ousted Panamanian leader Manuel Ántonio Noriega.

violation. On the other hand, had the U.S. taken the position that, in a military conflict, it should be permissible to bomb mental hospitals and down civilian aircraft that get in the way of combat, then virtually every member of the international community would have had to line up in condemnation of such an abhorrently revisionist norm. Indeed, the Soviet response to its downing of Korean Airlines flight 007 over Kanchatka foolishly invoked an exculpation which, when extrapolated in people's minds into a coherent general norm, aroused widespread ire, expressed by a clear resolution passed overwhelmingly by the Council of the International Civil Aviation Organization.[313]

It thus seems that in the international community, perhaps even more than in national legal systems, great emphasis is placed on rule coherence. Rules, to be perceived as legitimate, must emanate from principles of general application. State behavior is judged in terms of its effect in reinforcing, undermining, or amending the generalized norms of the system. In a community whose rules are so largely derived from the persistent patterns of its members' conduct, each action is judged by all states in terms of its projected effect if *all* were to act similarly. Therefore, it is not only the legitimacy of rules formally established by treaties or U.N. Security Council resolutions which is constantly subject to the test of coherence, but a broad panoply of actions taken individually or collectively by the members of the community.

Idiosyncratic, aberrational rules and actions—those incapable of being validated by the test of coherent generalization—are easily exposed as illegitimate "checkerboarding." Checkerboard solutions make even gainers feel like losers. For example, a rule that only blue-eyed persons may vote, or park on the street, or receive passports ought to lead even a gainer to worry about the effect on an entire system of rules and institutions if it accommodates such bizarre distinctions. Bad distinctions—in the sense of distinctions incapable of being defended by reference to the generalized logic of the rule—illegitimate the rule to which they adhere. They make it incoherent. A rule that property taxes will be levied only on houses with even-numbered addresses would be perceived as illegitimate by almost anyone, not only those adversely affected. It is demonstrable, however, that this illegitimacy can be cured if the checkerboarding can be justified by a logically defensible, generalizable principle. The rule taxing only even-numbered properties, for example, would be more legitimate if all odd-numbered properties, being on the same side of each street, had received a 20-year tax abatement as compensation for yielding several feet of frontal property to facilitate widening of the roadway. In other words, before a rule which is facially inconsistent in its application can be dismissed as incoherent it must be established that it not only applies inconsistently to what, on the surface, appears to be "likes," but also that no rational principle of general application can justify the inequality. If a rule is inconsistently or unequally applied, its legitimacy should be questioned. If the inequality cannot be explained to most persons' satisfaction by reference to a generally applicable principle then the rule's resultant incoherence will deplete its legitimacy and thereby weaken its pull to compliance.

A rule's inconsistencies—its sophist exceptions—must advance a *rational* basis of distinction if the rule is to have coherence (and, thus, legitimacy). In this context, the definition of the term *rational* is intended to convey an intrinsic, usually logical, relationship not only between a rule, its various parts, and its purpose, but also between the particular rule, its underlying principle, and the principles underpinning other rules of the society.

The idea that coherence is a key indicator of legitimacy may be illustrated by reference to three recent developments in the international community: the emergence of a "right" to *self-determination*, the development of a notion of *state equality* as exemplified by the voting system of the United Nations, and the entrenching of free and non-discriminatory terms of trade—the *Most Favored Nation* system—in the General Agreement on Tariffs and Trade. Each of these rule systems has undergone stress as a result of a fundamental change in the circumstances to which the rules apply. Practice with each led states to a crossroads where choices had to be made between simple consistency, a more sophist coherence, or a state of rule-lessness. In the first example, the failure to negotiate a transition from straightforward consistency in the rule's application to a more complex but still principled or rationally coherent rule led to the erosion of rule-legitimacy and to a rise in anarchic state behavior inexplicable except in terms of narrow and oft-times deluded self-interest. In the second, a special privilege inconsistent with the equality principle was sacrificed voluntarily by states which could no longer justify their preferential status. Arguably, the sacrifice was deliberately made in order to shore up the faltering legitimacy of the rule-system. In the third example, rule-coherence, and, thus, legitimacy, has been preserved by a deliberate sacrifice of consistency in favor of a more sophist rational principle.

The first case-study concerns the evolution of what, for a time, may have been the most dynamic political concept of the twentieth century. The notion that national or ethnic groups are entitled to "self-determination" has transformed both the world's cartography and political sensibility. Its functional origins are to be found in the settlements made at the end of World War I and, implicitly, in article 25 of the Covenant of the League of Nations which conceived of it as a "sacred trust"; but the aspiration's philosophical roots penetrate the deepest layers of human history and tribal consciousness.

The U.S. delegation to the Versailles Peace Conference arrived with firm instructions to apply ethnic criteria to resolve all European territorial disputes. In order to argue the principle of self-determination most effectively, Wilson saw to it that his team included historians, geographers, and ethnologists[314] in addition to the usual diplomatic, political, and economic advisers. The delegation was thus able to make extensive use of data concerning the demographics and ethnic sentiments of various population groups.[315] Wilson himself insisted, during the negotiations, that there be "a settlement on a basis of facts,"[316] by which he meant "racial aspects, historic antecedents, and economic and commercial elements."[317]

The Conference used more than fifty technical commissions composed of specialists appointed by the major powers. These were charged with considering every kind of territorial, economic, ethnographic, and strategic problem,[318] and they conducted twenty-six on-site investigations to consult the people concerned.[319] Although national interest and political considerations sometimes carried the day, the Peace Conference "got further away from mere dictatorial methods of control and nearer to the methods of scientific and dispassionate inquiry . . . than any former conference."[320]

A clear application of the principle of self-determination occurred with respect to the Danes of Schleswig. Despite being annexed by Prussia in 1864, northern Schleswig was, and remained, ethnically Danish.[321] The government of Denmark formally requested that a plebiscite be held and the Supreme Council[322] of the Peace Conference ordered a commission to study that option. It was to be guided by the "principle 'that the frontier between Germany and Denmark shall be fixed in conformity with the wishes of the population.' "[323] Even the Italians, who actively fought against other plebiscitary proposals, supported the Schleswig vote.[324] After the people of Northern Schleswig, on February 10, 1920, voted in favor of incorporation into Denmark, their preference was honored.[325]

Italy's support of the Schleswig plebescite was remarkable because Rome's demands for expansion based on strategic and commercial self-interest ran directly counter to the ethnicity of populations on its own periphery. In pursuing those interests, the Italian government set itself against its American counterpart. Wilson was determined to resist Italy's efforts which he saw as violating his own commitment to the primacy of self-determination. Italy and Yugoslavia both claimed Eastern Istria, Fiume, and Dalmatia, territory formerly within the Austro-Hungarian empire.[326] Discounting the Slavic majority in large parts of the disputed territories,[327] Italy justified her claim on the grounds of geographical unity and logistics.[328] The American experts on the Adriatic question "were all convinced that any arrangement that deprived the Jugo-Slavs of either northern Dalmatia or Fiume would be vicious and unwise . . ."[329] At the Peace Conference, President Wilson informed Italy's Orlando that "he could not consent to any people being handed over without their consent."[330] "Was it not possible," he asked rather disingenuously, for Italy "to obtain all she desired by means of a plebiscite?"[331] Despite Wilson's importunings, however, Italy and Yugoslavia eventually settled their border dispute by direct negotiation leading to the Treaty of Rapallo.[332]

That disregard for the new principle was exceptional. The creation of Czechoslovakia, by contrast, was a dramatic victory for self-determination. In June of 1918, Wilson's Secretary of State, Lansing, announced that America desired "that all branches of the Slav race should be completely freed from German and Austrian rule."[333] Three months later, the United States recognized the Czecho-Slovak National Council "as a *de facto* belligerent government."[334] Wilson refused to discuss any settlement concerning the Czecho-Slovaks without their participation.[335] The Supreme Council at Versailles determined that the historic frontier between Bohemia and Germany would be the boundary of the new state.[336]

Still, the principle could not be carried beyond a certain point. Although Polish and German enclaves would thereby become minorities,[337] the Supreme Council apparently believed this to be inevitable, since a more demographically-exact frontier "would have left Czecho-Slovakia so entirely defenceless as to be really incapable of independent life . . ."[338] Even at this incipient stage in the development of the principle of self-determination, idiot-rule consistency was proving its tendency to *reductio ad absurdum*, which we now recognize as one form of perceived incoherence. Wilson's acceptance of historic modification of purely ethnic boundaries was a "pragmatic decision justified on the grounds that Czech self-determination would be negated unless the new state were permitted to be economically viable and strategically defensible."[339]

However, Wilson consistently fought most other attempts to deviate from strict adherence to his principle. He was not altogether successful in opposing the separation of the Saar basin or Rhineland from Germany. Seeking to prevent a German resurgence, France's Clemenceau insisted upon the creation of a buffer Rhenish Republic.[340] That, too, posed a clear conflict with the principle of self-determination since its four million inhabitants were ethnic Germans who had no desire to be severed from their homeland.[341] Wilson instructed his chief adivser, Colonel House, to oppose even a temporary separation,[342] and the latter complained angrily that the French "do not seem to know that to establish a Rhenish Republic against the will of the people would be contrary to the principle of self-determination. . . ."[343] A compromise led to the creation of the Saar territory, which was not to be independent but administered through the League of Nations. While the inhabitants were not allowed to be represented in the German Reichstag, their schools, language, laws and German nationality were left untouched.[344] A far different result might have emerged had Wilson been less obdurate.[345]

The resurrection of independent Poland also resulted directly from the deliberate application of the principle of self-determination. The American group appointed to examine various options came down firmly on the side of Polish independence on incontrovertible historic and ethnic grounds.[346] President Wilson specifically incorporated this conclusion into his Fourteen Points: "An independent Polish State should be erected which should include the territories inhabited by indisputably Polish populations. . . ."[347] The Supreme Council then appointed a territorial Commission to determine the frontier of the new nation.[348]

Despite these remarkable instances of the redrawing of the map of Europe in accordance with the principle of self-determination, that radical rule, so recently proposed by Wilson, did not govern all post World War I settlements. In some instances it was compromised (as in the Saar and Fiume) and in others it was simply overruled by other considerations. Despite his avowed intention to make self-determination the guiding principle of the peace, Wilson gradually discovered that "other principles needed to be considered in the peacemaking, and these sometimes seemed to clash with the requirements of self-determination."[349] Even he came to accept that—at best—a textured sophist, rather than an idiot, rule was in the process of evolving in international practice. The dispute over Fiume, for example, implicated a heady mix of demographic, strategic, and economic concerns which contradicted one another and were each pressed with great passion. The Italians claimed that possession of Fiume was essential to prevent an attack on Italy from across the Adriatic.[350] They also pointed out that the majority of the population of the city of Fiume was undoubtedly Italian.[351] The Yugoslavs countered by emphasizing that the majority in the area (including the suburban hinterland of

Fiume) was preponderantly Yugoslav, and that Fiume was the most suitable and best situated port for their new country.[352] The question was not whether to have self-determination—both Italy and Yugoslavia gave lip-service to the principle—but to which geographic area it would be applied. As we have noted, the Supreme Council proved unable to reconcile these competing claims, and the parties resolved the dispute by direct negotiation, producing a pragmatic result that derogated from the Wilsonian principle.

Alsace-Lorraine also presented a conflict between the self-determination principle asserted by the French inhabitants and rival versions of the same principle invoked by the German settlers. The issue was not whether the principle applied, but to *whom.* After annexing the province in 1871, Germany had encouraged between 300,000 and 500,000 German citizens to relocate there.[353] During this same period, approximately 500,000 French Alsatians departed,[354] and Germany deported more after the outbreak of war in 1914.[355] Given these population transfers, it is not surprising that, at the Peace Conference, France rejected Germany's request for a plebiscite to determine the province's future.[356] Clemenceau argued that to hold a plebiscite now "would be to sanction the wrong done in 1871 by admitting the lawfulness of that act of violence."[357] The Allied Supreme Council chose to support "the historic rights of an earlier community . . . over the desires of the existing inhabitants . . ."[358] and Alsace-Lorraine was thus incorporated into France. This irredentist embroidery of the self-determination principle had earlier been foreseen by President Wilson's eighth point, in which he had called for the correction of "the wrong of 1871."[359] This could be reconciled with self-determination—as it surely was in Wilson's own mind—but only with a more complex, contoured version of the deceptively simple principle.

The dispute over Upper Silesia was a particularly thorny one, juxtaposing the principle with historic and economic, as well as ethnic facts in a virtually inextricable tangle of interests. Coveted by Poland and Germany, Upper Silesia contained valuable mines and industries.[360] Pure ethnic Germans officially made up approximately one-third of the population. Poland claimed that the inhabitants were predominantly Polish,[361] which, according to the German census of 1910, was technically true.[362] However, the "Wasserpolaks" of the region had lived under German rule for seven centuries and spoke their own dialect.[363] When a plebiscite was held, Germany obtained a large majority of the votes.[364] Poland and France, however, refused to accept that result and the matter was referred to the League Council in 1921,[365] which divided the region in such a way as to give Poland most of the mines and industries.[366]

The principle thus was applied only imperfectly. More important, it was not made generally applicable but was confined almost entirely to the territories of the defeated powers. Few postwar claims of self-determination were made against states that had not been on the losing side in the war. Britain applied a version of self-determination to its partition of Ireland.[367] That, however, was exceptional. Another claim concerned the Aaland Islands, an archipelago at the entrance to the Gulf of Bothnia. Sweden had ceded both Finland and the islands to Russia in 1809.[368] Prior to Finland's declaration of independence from Russia, an assembly of representatives from the islands expressed their desire to rejoin Sweden.[369] The American commission recommended in favor of this solution to Wilson, since the population was "almost purely Swedish in race and language,"[370] and had expressed a clear desire to unite with their ethnic cohorts. To manifest this desire, the Aalanders, citing Wilson,[371] asked the Peace Conference to organize a plebiscite.[372] Finland, although lately itself a beneficiary of self-determination, argued that its sovereignty over the islands was incontestable, and that a small minority of the people of a state had no right to demand separation or independence.[373] Its representatives pointed out that there were numerous Swedes living elsewhere in Finland, and that the Aalanders constituted only one-fourteenth of that ethnic group.

The Supreme Council at last appointed a Commission of Inquiry to visit the islands and make recommendations. Its report began by observing that the principle of self-determination had not been mentioned in the Covenant of the newly established League.[374] Thus, it declared "the principle had not yet attained the status of a positive rule of international law . . ."[375] This led it to conclude that, despite the wishes of the inhabitants, Finland should retain sovereignty, particularly in view of the islands' geographic and economic ties to that nation. The report noted that the Finnish government had promised to protect the Aalanders' autonomous status and preserve their language.[376] As for independence, an alternative to the proposed union with Sweden, the Commission thought the islands lacked the resources to make that a viable option.[377]

If self-determination was imperfectly applied in Europe, and almost exclusively to the territories of vanquished powers, it was applied hardly at all to Europe's overseas colonies. The German and Turkish possessions were transferred summarily to Australia, Belgium, Britain, France, Japan, New Zealand, and South Africa, albeit as "mandates" constituting a "sacred trust of civilization" under nominal supervision of the League of Nations. The victors not only did not diminish, but actually increased the size of their overseas empires without making a serious commitment to giving the people of the acquired territories control of their future. After World War II, however, the self-determination principle came to be applied far more generally and vigorously. The United Nations, in a marked contrast to the League's practice, actively supervised and enforced the "sacred trust" by cajoling the administering nations speedily to "develop self-government, to take due account of the political aspirations of the peoples, and to assist them in the progressive development of their free political institutions. . . ."[378] Former German, Japanese, and Italian colonies were closely scrutinized by U.N. organs and committees in order "to promote . . . progressive development towards self-government or independence . . ." in accordance with "the freely expressed wishes of the peoples concerned."[379]

The principle, now ratified in the Charter and practice of the United Nations, was specifically made applicable to the colonies. But it was not limited to them. This is made clear by the first article of the Charter, which specifies the obligation to develop "friendly relations among nations based on the principle of equal rights and self-determination of peoples. . . ." The principle thus is cast in terms of universal applicability. The term "peoples," moreover, recognizes the importance of the ethnic dimension in determining *who* is entitled to invoke it.

Few obligations of the international system were ever taken more seriously than this one during the decades following World War II. Beginning with India, Burma and West Africa's Gold Coast, Britain voluntarily and, for the most part, peacefully, granted self-determination and independence to nearly one billion persons. These newly independent nations, in turn, joined the Latin American states to press the rapid decolonization of French, Dutch, Belgian, Spanish, and Portuguese empires. As a result, United Nations membership almost tripled between 1945 and 1980. In that brief period, self-determination undoubtedly became the most powerful idea operating in international relations. It evinced remarkable compliance pull, convincing colonial powers not to use their potentially preponderant military power to hold on to their possessions by force.

No other explanation alone can account for the U.S. grant of independence to the Philippines, or the British withdrawal from India and Africa. Some of those responsible for drafting the U.N. Charter were amazed at the speed with which decolonization occurred.[380] Within a decade, France, for example, had readjusted its thinking. It had abandoned a policy of assimilation—which had held that Africans, Asians, and Caribbean peoples were to become French citizens, electing members to the National Assembly in Paris from a string of "overseas departments"[381]—and, instead, had adapted to a new policy of granting independence. To understand the resultant wrench to the national psyche, it is helpful to recall that Algeria, before its independence, had been home to more than one million non-Arabs who regarded themselves as more French than the French.[382] Moreover, the distance from Marseilles to Algiers is only 478 miles, one-fifth that between Hawaii and Los Angeles. This painful adjustment was no doubt in part compelled by the determined Algerian liberation movement, but it was also made easier because nations, including France, at that time attributed great legitimacy to the self-determination principle.

Self-determination's period at the center of events, however, was very brief. Its decline can be seen as the mirror image of what had happened in the aftermath of World War I. Even as members of the United Nations pressed the Western Europeans to account for their stewardship in African, Asian, and Caribbean possessions, and repeatedly demanded the acceleration of preparations for self-determination, large Latvian, Lithuanian, Estonian, Polish, German, Romanian, Hungarian and Slovak-inhabited territories in Europe were being annexed arbitrarily by neighboring states. In some instances, entire populations were put to flight as part of the rearrangement of Eastern European boundaries. As Europe had denied self-determination to the colonies in Africa and Asia after World War I, the new nations that emerged from those colonies after World War II were notably indifferent to the fates of Estonians, Latvians, Lithuanians, Poles, Romanians, Finns, and Slovaks.

Soviet control in Eastern Europe was challenged only by Marshall Tito in Yugoslavia, who sought safety in the formation at Bandung in 1955 of a non-aligned movement. Tito, with Col. Gamal Abdel Nasser of Egypt, Prime Minister Jaharwalal Nehru of India, and President Sukarno of Indonesia, made the perfection and protection of self-determination the movement's first order of business. Nevertheless, although that may have helped protect Tito's defection from the Soviet sphere and promote decolonization in Africa, Asia, and the Caribbean, the non-aligned, for the most part, refused to join in censuring the Soviet Union for the Warsaw Pact nations' invasion of Hungary in 1956 or of Czechoslovakia in 1968.[383] To the nations which had come into being in response to the self-determination principle, it did not seem an urgent priority to reiterate the rule's applicability to Europe. Thus began the rule's decline into incoherence almost from the moment of its greatest success. In the 1950s and '60s, the coherence of the principle of self-determination seemed increasingly to depend upon its redefinition as a set of rules applicable only to non-Europeans, a notion of as little rational persuasiveness as had been its opposite: the confinement of the principle exclusively to Europe after World War I.

After 1945, inconsistency began to appear more and more in the application and denial of self-determination. Two examples are particularly salient. The first is India, which became independent as the world's largest example of voluntary compliance (by Britain) with the principle of self-determination but which thereupon used its armed forces, first, to deny self-determination to the state of Kashmir, which had a rather persuasive claim based on ethnic, religious, and legal grounds,[384] and, later, to occupy Goa. The second example is Nigeria, the most populous African state, which, after being granted self-determination by Britain, thereafter denied it to its ethnically and religiously distinct Ibo region (Biafra).[385] In this Nigeria received both global and regional support. Only four African states, and one non-African, recognized Biafra's independence.[386]

As we have observed, a rule's inconsistent application does not necessarily undermine its legitimacy as long as the inconsistencies can be explained to the satisfaction of the community by a justifiable (i.e. principled) distinction. All sophist rules make such distinctions while usually retaining their coherence. However, while some textured sophist rules may succeed in preserving their coherence by employing justifiable principles of distinction, others fail, resort to checkerboarding, and sink into incoherence.

A distinction must now be made between two phenomena: (1) the sophist rule's *indeterminacy*, which can only be ameliorated by a legitimate process for clarifying its meaning case-by-case; and (2) the same rule's potential further problem of *incoherence*, which emerges if the principles underlying it fail to connect rationally with other rules, or with parts of the same rule. It is the second of these to which we now direct our attention.

The gradual descent of self-determination into unprincipled conceptual incoherence became textually evident in the Declaration on the Granting of Independence to Colonial Countries and Peoples which was adopted by the General Assembly on December 14, 1960.[387] That declaration, largely the work of the newly independent former colonies of Africa and Asia, reiterated "that all peoples have an inalienable right to complete freedom, the exercise of their sovereignty and the integrity of their national territory. . . ."[388] The notion of "integrity . . . of territory" means, if anything, a right to deny self-determination to those seeking independence, or union with a neighbor. The resolution, nevertheless, demanded the taking of steps to implement a right of dependent peoples to independence: immediately "without any conditions or reservations in accordance with their freely expressed will and desire"[389] and regardless of the level "of political, economic, social or educational preparedness. . . ."[390] The incoherence of the unreconciled notions espoused by this new normative charter reappears all over its text. For example, the Declaration stated that the right of self-determination was to apply only to "territories which have not yet attained independence"[391]—which made it conveniently inapplicable to Hungary, Kashmir, or Biafra. Most telling, however, was article 6 of the Declaration, which stated: "Any attempt aimed at the partial or total disruption of the national unity and the territorial integrity of a country is incompatible with the purposes and principles of the Charter of the United Nations." In other words, while Nigeria had been entitled to the independence it achieved on October 1, 1960, Biafra—a part of Nigeria—was not to be similarly indulged. The resolution utterly fails to make this inconsistency coherent by reference to a rational basis for distinguishing between those entitled and those not. Before its independence, Nigeria had been part of the "national unity" of the British Empire. Decolonization, like other secessionist movements, inevitably disrupts some national territorial unity. No attempt is made to explain why British, French, or Portuguese "unity" is expendable while Nigeria's or India's is sacrosanct.

The resolution's attempt to justify a new restriction on self-determination could be traced back to the case of the Aaland Islands or, further still, to theories of manifest destiny which had formed part of the rhetoric of the North in the American civil war. But the notion of the sanctity of existing boundaries was the very one *against* which the concept of self-determination had been developed after World War I. To the extent self-determination is applicable to some places at certain times—the defeated European powers after World War I, and the overseas empires of Western Europe after World War II—but inapplicable in other places or at other times, the principle is weakened not merely by inconsistency but, more, by its obvious incoherence.

That incoherence could only be cured by the nations formulating a new rule based on rationally defensible distinctions between the cases to which the principle would apply and those to which it would not. This has not happened and, thus, the power of the principle of self-determination has diminished and so has belief in the legitimacy of the U.N. system which oversees its application and is authorized to issue the commands which could give it effect. The Algerian right to secede was asserted by a large majority of members, including the U.S. Yet, the right of Biafra, only a few years later, received almost no support from governments, and was not once taken up in United Nations forums. Other contradictions abound. The General Assembly first criticized, but then failed to press, the Indonesian government when it invaded Portuguese Timor at the very moment it was being decolonized and its people were attempting to exercise their right of self-determination.[392] The right of self-determination of the people of the former colony of Spanish Sahara (Western Sahara) has been defended somewhat more diligently by the international community through organs of the U.N.[393] against the efforts of Morocco to absorb the territory without its inhabitants' consent. Yet, even here, the United Nations has failed to speak unambiguously.[394] Unless such muddled and inconsistent efforts by the international community can be reconciled on the basis of a rational, principled distinction, it may be impossible to escape the conclusion that the rule creating a right of self-determination will remain incoherent and unable to regain its power to secure voluntary compliance.

Perhaps most damaging to the legitimacy of the rule and to the United Nations as the institution overseeing its application was the U.N.'s direct complicity in deliberately turning over the Dutch colony of West Irian to neighboring Indonesia despite the manifest and profound objections of an indigenous population which much preferred independence or union with its kin in Papua, New Guinea.[395] On the other hand, it is open to conjecture that the U.N.'s most recent role in securing Soviet withdrawal from Afghanistan and South African agreement to self-determination for Namibia have begun to restore the prestige both of the principle and of the Organization. Such restoration, however, requires that nations work out a new, coherent principle: not an easy task, given the sensitivity of states to secessionist movements.

It is obvious that an idiot rule will not serve. Nations cannot be expected to accept the principle that any group wishing independence is entitled to it, no matter how few in number and regardless of the socio-economic or strategic consequences. To win acceptance as legitimate, any new rule must make a persuasive distinction between "peoples" entitled and not entitled to self-determination. The search for such a principle will be hazardous but, perhaps, instructive.

We have observed that a principle may be coherent even though it employs sophist distinctions and inconsistencies, so long as its differentiations are logically persuasive to those addressed. In the search for such a coherent, textured principle, it is thus appropriate to start by examining the actual conduct of states, while keeping in mind that state behavior may be evidence of a widely accepted, if inchoate, general principle or merely of rampant opportunism unchecked by any recognized applicable rule.

Is there a rationally coherent principle which could reconcile, or at least accommodate, all this inconsistent state practice? Could a rational distinction be made between Algeria and Biafra, so that the former but not the latter would be entitled to self-determination because Algeria is separated from France by water while Biafra is a contiguous part of the Nigerian land mass? Surely the rationality of that distinction cannot be defended, nor is it a distinction which has been accepted by the nations. Many states—the U.S., the Philippines, Canada, Indonesia, India, China, and the Soviet Union—have entire "states," provinces or regions separated from the rest by bodies of water. None would be willing to grant those inhabitants a right to "opt out" solely on the basis of an "ultramarine" principle. Surely it is not rationally acceptable to argue that the Canadian province of Prince Edward Island or Britain's Isle of Man has a right to self-determination and secession while Quebec, Scotland, or Kashmir, being part of a mainland, do not. The water-defined principle fails the test: it evidently does not treat likes alike, but neither does it state a rationally justifiable basis for treating some "likes" differently. Why, in this era of super-rapid communication across natural barriers, would states—any state—accept a right to self-determination which is applicable only to situations defined by an unimportant accident of geography? The "water principle" as a basis for distinction does not hold water. It lacks plausibility, deprives self-determination of its teleological energy, and thus renders it incoherent. True, one must not expect too much: in the real world, rules collide, much as interests do. However, in creating the textured exceptions that distinguish a sophist rule, exceptions which define the circumstances in which the rule's main thrust must yield to some countervailing exception, the yielding must be justified, if legitimacy is not to be lost. Such justification must put forward a principle of distinction which is plausibly, rationally connected with the enterprise which the rule of self-determination seeks to advance. How plausible a distinction is, can only be determined in theory by its capacity to manifest nexus and, in practice, by the degree to which it is perceived as plausible by the community to which it is addressed.

Next, it could be urged, in search of a justifiable basis of distinction, that the Arabs of Algeria are entitled to self-determination because they are ethnically different from the French of Western Europe. But that does not work, either, because Biafran Ibos of Nigeria are at least as different ethnically and religiously from their Nigerian compatriots, the Hausa and Yoruba, as Algerian Arabs are from the French. The distinction does not explain why the international community failed to validate Biafra's attempt at self-determination. Finally, economics might be advanced as a rational, principled justification: that the Ibos, and Nigeria as a whole, have fared better economically by remaining as one large nation than they might, had the tribes formed separate nations. But a case—probably a better one—can be made that Algerians, and France, too, might well have prospered more had they remained united. The quality of Algerian wine, certainly, and of life, perhaps, has suffered since independence. In any event, the notion that economic considerations should trump political, cultural, and social ones has always proven a very fragile principle upon which to found a persuasive general rule of human behavior.

None of these three rational justifications for distinguishing between "likes"—the Algerian case and the Biafran one—can be said to make a new, more textured principle of self-determination persuasive, logically credible, and, thus, coherent. None proposes a new rule which states would be likely to adopt as an abstract concept or as a basis for governing their conduct. The compliance pull of a rule based on such distinctions would be very slight.

Let us make one further attempt to formulate a coherent new principle of self-determination capable of distinguishing rationally between the Algerian and Biafran cases, using the notion of an entitlement to *equality*. The proposed principle is this: self-determination is a right applicable to any distinct region in which the inhabitants do not enjoy rights equal to those accorded all people in other parts of the same state. Conversely, the right is not applicable to regions of an existing state if its inhabitants enjoy the same rights as inhabitants of any other part of the country.

As justification for distinguishing between "likes," this works somewhat better. It is an evidently rational basis for distinction which re-establishes the principle's coherence. The natives of British colonies did not have the same right to select members to the Westminster Parliament as had the inhabitants of the Sceptered Isle, nor were they subject to precisely the same legal and judicial systems. Since the colonials did not enjoy the same status as the British in Britain, it would be *rational* to entitle them to claim a wholly separate one. The distinction connects, logically, with the principle of the equality of all persons, which also underlies the rule of self-determination. By the same token, the Welsh would not be entitled to independence, because they do enjoy the same rights and status as all other British nationals. This rational principle of distinction also explains, in practice, the different treatment accorded the self-determination claims of Algeria and Biafra. Even though French Algeria did elect members to the French Assembly and Senate before independence, these were chosen by two "colleges" in which one-tenth of the population (primarily non-Arab) had equal representation with the other (Arab) nine-tenths.[396] The majority of Arab Algerians thus were not remotely equal in status to French Algerians or the French in France. Biafrans, on the other hand, although subject to a pogrom shortly before their revolt, normally did—and do, today—enjoy legal rights and capacities equal to those of other Nigerians.[397] *For that reason* their claim to self-determination was less convincing. In sharp contrast is the brutal treatment accorded the Bengalis of East Pakistan by a government dominated by West Pakistanis. This probably convinced most states that the secession of Bangladesh was entitled to relatively speedy recognition. Even states with secession problems of their own, who were concerned that Bangladesh should not set a precedent for an unlimited, wide-open invitation to secession based on ethnicity, nevertheless seemed swayed by the harshness with which the province's separatists had been repressed.[398] Today, the same principle would argue that Puerto Ricans are entitled to self-determination as long as they remain unequal American citizens of a dependent Commonwealth, but they would lose that right were they to opt for the equality explicit in statehood.

This proposed version of a new, coherent principle of self-determination makes the validity of each claim turn on whether the claimants are denied equality of treatment in the political entity from which they seek to separate. Such a denial would "trigger" the right to opt out. Such a right need not always be exercised. The people of Puerto Rico could choose to remain affiliated with the United States on terms which favored them in some respects and disfavored them in others: but as long as the terms of the association were unequal they would retain the right to opt out. A denial of *good* treatment, however, would not give rise to a right of secession if every group in the political entity is treated equally badly.

This version of the principle of self-determination achieves coherence, but at some cost to justice. To claim that a generalizable principle is rationally coherent is not the same as asserting that it is *just*. A justice-based rule might well support the exercise of a right of self-determination by any group that desired it, or else, by any group within a mistreated population, even if all nationals of the state were equally mistreated. Justice might argue for the emancipation of some, even while leaving behind others who are less self-assertive. The proposed coherence-based principle, on the other hand, denies the right of self-determination in those circumstances. It justifies treating some "like" differently from others, in the sense of advancing a reasoned argument for making a distinction between the claim to self-determination of a group denied equality and the same claim advanced by a group treated badly but equally. In defense of the rationality of that distinction, despite its apparent injustice, it might be argued that when an entire population—as opposed to a targeted minority—is the object of maltreatment, then their appropriate remedy is revolution, not an act of self-determination by one segment of the society.

The right to secede on the basis of *unequal treatment* is rationally justifiable as a coherent principle because secession may be the only remedy available when the oppressed are a distinct, politically disempowered *minority*. If that is the rationale, then a further distinction may be necessary between unequally treated majorities (not entitled) and minorities (entitled). Thus, rationally, blacks would not have a claim to secede from South Africa (as in the Bantustan African "homelands") because they constitute the country's majority which should pursue its liberation within the existing South African boundaries: by revolution, if necessary. On the other hand, if the tables were turned and a black revolutionary regime were to come to power and then were to oppress the white South African minority, the principle might well support that minority's right to a Eurostan "homeland," on the rational ground that other forms of self-emancipation—through politics or revolution—are not readily available to an oppressed minority.

This version of a coherent principle of self-determination has the advantage of being both rationally justifiable and according loosely with contemporary state practice. This suggests that the theoretical justification for the principled distinction being made is also persuasive in practice. As we have seen, all nations currently refuse to validate—by recognition and U.N. membership—the "independence" of the several black tribal Bantustans carved by an oppressive white regime out of the territory of the white-ruled Republic of South Africa. The U.N. and the community of nations have agreed not to legitimate such "self-determination" not only because the governments of these states remain suspect as South

African puppets, but also because South Africa's black majority is entitled to full participation in the control of the entire country, not just to small, disposable enclaves.

While this sophist version of the right of self-determination is rationally coherent—which is to say it makes distinctions on the basis of principles of general applicability which are rationally connected to the purpose the right seeks to advance and that the reasonableness of the distinctions appear persuasive, as evidenced by the prevalent conduct of states—it is not free of theoretical and practical problems. Suppose the area in which an oppressed, secession-minded minority tribe lives is rich in oil and minerals, while the rest of the country has no resources at all. The proposed general principle would permit that tribe to create its own state. Yet it might be very unreasonable to allow such a richly endowed region to secede, if, to do so would leave the rest of the country hopelessly impoverished and even more miserable than previously. Such consideration, in fact, guided the United Nations in its collective use of force in the 1960s to suppress the secession of the minority Baluba tribe of Zaire, which occupies that nation's principal asset: the mineral-rich province of Katanga.[399] We have already observed that comparable concerns for national security guided the Allied Powers after World War I in drawing defensible boundaries for the new state of Czechoslovakia, even though the incidental effect was to deny self-determination to some ethnic Germans. Evidently, such further concerns must somehow be accommodated in a coherent general principle if it is to be perceived as legitimate.

We have now postulated rather a complex sophist rule, one which gives the right of self-determination to a distinct "people" in a specific region, but *only if* they are a minority in the larger political unit from which they seek separation *and if* their exercise of the right does not unduly deprive the other inhabitants of their economic prospects or national security. The apparent complexity of this rule makes plain that if it were adopted by the community of states, there would be need for an institution of acknowledged legitimacy to apply it, case by case. Without such process determinacy, the rule would lack serious pull to compliance. One reason its application could prove difficult is that disputed facts tend to be extraordinarily hard to assess in the middle of a civil conflict. For example, once an ethnic or religious secessionist movement begins to generate violence, all members of that group are popularly thought to be linked with that secessionist movement and the rest of the population may begin to discriminate against them, often in response to what is perceived as a security problem. An instance is the recent spread of anti-Tamil bias in Sri Lanka. Another is the hardening of Unionist Protestant anti-Catholicism in Northern Ireland. Indeed, provoking such a downward spiral in inter-group relations is a stated objective of many secessionists. The avowed aim is to radicalize the moderates in their group by exposing them to discrimination. Once that has happened it may be difficult to determine whether such discrimination *caused* or *was caused by* secessionism. In such controversial circumstances, only a legitimate third party institution could hope to give a decision which is recognized as a legitimate application of the rule.

If this illustrates the difficulty of finding and implementing a new self-determination rule those difficulties should not obscure the costs of failing to try. In the absence of agreement on a new, coherent concept of self-determination, this briefly dynamic principle will founder in incoherence and desuetude. It is already of much diminished utility as a descriptive and predictive guide to state conduct. Using a somewhat different frame of reference, one might say that, as a rule of state conduct, it is losing its power to obligate, or its psychological power to persuade, because the rule has failed to retain its coherence and, thus, its legitimacy. This will leave a rule-void, unless a new, coherent principle is at hand, one which is rationally justifiable, persuasive, and applied not merely to one but to most instances in which the claim to self-determination arises. While it is possible to see the outlines of such a rule, there appears to be no present inclination on the part of the international community to undertake the task of getting it drafted and adopted, despite the evident lack of legitimacy of what is left of the contradictory rules in the U.N. Charter and the Assembly's 1960 Declaration on the Granting of Independence to Colonial Countries and Peoples.

It is not necessarily a disaster that there once was a rule capable of validating a particular set of claims and a designated type of conduct, but that there is no longer such a rule, or that the rule now lacks legitimacy. No rule may be better than a bad rule or one which has outlived its utility. It is for this reason that the international system recognizes the principle of desuetude, which sweeps away the litter of discarded norms.[400] Nevertheless, it is doubtful whether the international system is well served by the decay of self-determination. Yet this is what appears to be happening. In 1948, for example, it was not particularly difficult to figure out whether, by the then-applicable rules, Ceylon (Sri Lanka) was entitled to independence. Today, it is all but impossible to say whether the systemic rules operate to support, oppose, or are indifferent to the status of the Northern Marianas, the demand of the population of Gibraltar and the Falkland Islands to remain British, the Catholic Irish demand to reunite Northern Ireland with the Irish Republic, the Tibetan desire for autonomy, the Palestinian claim to a homeland, or, for that matter, the campaign for an independent Tamil nation in North-Eastern Sri Lanka. This rule-incoherence has been brought about by a rapid change in the kind of issues that give rise to the demand for independence in the post-colonial era. As yet, there is no clear conceptual agreement among states whether to extend the "old" principle of self-determination to that new context, to let the rule lapse, or to devise new principled rational distinctions of sufficient determinacy to convert a simple, *too* simple, idiot rule—*either*: territories and peoples that want independence should be allowed it *or*, alternatively, no post-colonial peoples are entitled to self-determination—into a coherent sophist rule that enumerates the additional or different conditions that must be met before a desire for independence can give rise to a systemically validated claim. Now that the business of decolonization is finished, a new rule would have to steer a course between encouraging the breakup of viable nations on the one hand and, on the other, rejecting all further claims by oppressed minorities. Such a rational mid-course would recognize some right to self-determination by some "peoples" in some circumstances. In the preceding sentence, the word "some" merely represents a conceptual void. How that blank is filled—that is, how persuasively distinctions are made between those entitled and those not entitled to self-determination—will determine the coherence of the rule and, thereby, affect its perceived legitimacy.

At this point a brief recapitulation may be useful. The legitimacy of which we are speaking is quite unlike Austinian coercive power, being power of another kind: the kind which creates an obligation in the minds of policymakers and of attentive publics. In our example of self-determination, if the applicable rule is perceived as valid by states, then even bystander nations feel an obligation to support those rules and those ethnic groups which seek to exercise their rights. States' perceptions of the extent to which a rule is legitimate determines, in part, their sense of an obligation to adhere, and secure the adherence of others, to the rule. It is precisely in shaping such perceptions that coherence plays a vital role. When states act consistently, it is easy enough to perceive the operation of a rational, consistent principle in influencing patterns of state conduct. But when states do not act consistently, no principle of general application appears on the surface of what looks like an erratic pattern of conduct. States may thus conclude that there is, and can be, no legitimate rule to command their adherence. That conclusion will be appropriate unless the lack of consistency can be validated by reference to a textured principle that makes coherent, rationally justifiable distinctions which follow the contours of state conduct. If such distinctions are logically possible, however, then seemingly random state conduct may actually be suggesting a new rule, one with a ready-made and evidently powerful pull to compliance. In short, like the person who discovered that he had been speaking prose all his life, states may discover that they have not only abandoned an old, no longer coherent rule but have fashioned, in practice and without conscious intent to do so, the basic structure of a newly emergent successor.

Even a textured sophist rule based on a coherent principle may be disregarded in practice; but it is harder for the leaders of nations to ignore a rule which, despite surface inconsistencies, nevertheless is legitimated by an underlying coherent principle. The decision not to adhere to such a rule has higher costs than refusal to comply with an absurd rule, or one which has fallen into desuetude. As Dworkin says, speaking of the national political context, "a state that accepts integrity [coherence] as a political ideal has a better case for legitimacy than one that does not. If that is so, it provides a strong reason . . . why we would do well to see our political practices grounded in that virtue. It provides, in particular, a strong argument for a conception of law that takes integrity to be fundamental, because any conception must explain why law is legitimate authority. . . ."[401]

Translating this into the international context we might say that an international community that accepts rule-coherence as an ideal has a better case for legitimacy than one that does not. A rule purporting to govern state behavior is more likely to be perceived as legitimate if it is grounded in a coherent principle than if it is not, and therefore will exert a stronger pull to compliance. It thus makes sense to regard coherence as fundamental to any theory seeking to explain the legitimacy of an institutionalized system and of its rules.

Dworkin, although addressing persons, not nations, is particularly helpful in analyzing *why* legitimacy is "grounded in" coherence.[402] The answer lies in the nature of *community* or system. Coherence assumes the existence not merely of random interactions between states which happen to occupy the same space but a conscious acceptance of specific "responsibilities . . . flowing from a more general responsibility each has of *concern* for the well-being of others. . . ." Thus, if the world of states is to be recognized as a community, each state, to borrow once again from Dworkin, must "treat discrete obligations that arise only under special circumstances, like the obligation to help a friend [ally] who is in great financial need, as derivative from and expressing a more general responsibility active throughout the assoication in different ways."[403] Those "different ways," themselves, must be justifiable by general principles of rational distinction. Further, this concern—based not on special relationships such as exist, for example, between NATO nations, but on general obligations of *all* states to *any* state—must, in a system or community, "show not only concern but an *equal* concern for all members."[404] This mutual concern is both compatible with a concept of modified sovereignty and with distinctions, so long as the distinction "fits a plausible conception of equal concern."[405]

For instance, as we have noted, the United Nations Charter, makes the claim in article 2 that the system "is based on the principle of the sovereign equality of all its Members." This is implemented, in article 18 by the rule that "Each member of the General Assembly shall have one vote" and by article 27's rule that "Each member of the Security Council shall have one vote." However, article 27 complicates this simple idiot rule by adding that most substantive decisions of the Security Council require not only the support of a majority of nine members, but "the concurring votes of the permanent members. . . ." Britain, China, France, the U.S., and the U.S.S.R.

This "veto" seems to undermine the coherence of the general principle of "sovereign equality" established in article 2. The non-veto-endowed states appear to be deprived of their formal equality. Does the preference given by the Charter to the five permanent members adversely affect members' perceptions of the system's legitimacy? If so, members' sense of obligation to the system as a whole and to its many rules and projects could be expected to be undermined.

Not surprisingly, nations not endowed with the veto do consider it an affront to the integrity of the system, and that perception may be growing. Even in 1945, at the drafting of the Charter, the smaller nations—a majority even then—opposed the special preference.[406] But a case could be made for it which left the equality rule rationally coherent, if inconsistent. Back then, the Big Five paid most of the organization's costs and were expected to assume most of the military, as well as fiscal, responsibilities for carrying out the Charter's mandate. It made sense that they should have a greater say in key decisions. It could also be argued that, since the fledgling organization could not expect to compel any of the "Big Five" to act against its will, the veto merely acknowledged an obvious reality. The record of the drafting negotiations also shows that the Big Powers promised to use their veto only in situations having the most serious impact on their basic interests.[407] They also agreed that when the Security Council was considering measures for the peaceful settlement of disputes, any party to a dispute—including permanent members—would abstain (art. 27). At the time this seemed a significant compromise and may even have reassured the reluctant majority that the veto, while inconsistent with state equality, did not undermine the rule's coherence and legitimacy. The rule of state equality could be understood as coherently modified by a rational principle of distinction: that states bearing the greatest institutional responsibility should also have the greatest say in critical disputes. The distinction accords with the general principle of equality by relating exceptional privilege to exceptional responsibility and limiting the privilege to a narrower category or institutional activity.[408]

Unfortunately, if those indeed were the coherent conceptual justifications for the privileges granted the Big Five in 1945, they are no longer so rationally justifiable today. This, in part, is due to changes in the realities of the global system and, also, to the way the veto has been used in practice. In 1945, the Big Five really were the world's major powers, having vanquished the Axis and inherited the postwar leadership. Their special status had a certain plausibility. Today, Britain, France, and China are middle powers, economically inferior to resurgent Germany and Japan. Even India, Brazil, and Nigeria might now have as good claim to preferred status as have Britain and France: if not on strictly economic and military grounds, then on geographic and demographic grounds. The once-rational justification for Big Five privilege has lost its persuasiveness. Collective security, the area in which big military powers were expected to bear the principal responsibility, has virtually disappeared from the U.N.'s agenda, to be replaced by peacekeeping, an activity for which the neutral states of northern Europe and the third world have accepted primary responsibility. To make matters worse, the veto has not been employed sparingly. As of April 1987, it has been used 56 times by the U.S., 114 times by the Soviet Union, 29 times by Britain, 16 times by France, and 3 times by China.[409] The problem is exacerbated because an important self-restraining commitment—to abstain when a member is a "party to a dispute"—has not been kept. The U.S., for example, did not abstain from vetoing a 1986 resolution calling on it to execute the World Court judgment in a case brought by Nicaragua.[410]

It appears that this problem of creeping U.N. Charter incoherence has been recognized. While the Charter has not been amended—a very difficult procedure—nevertheless, Britain, China, and France, while casting occasional negative votes in the Council, have quietly made it a practice rarely to do so except in the company either of a majority of the Council, or of the U.S., or the U.S.S.R.[411] In this way, these three permanent members of the Council have voluntarily contributed to the *de facto* remission of their veto power.

That these three nations lately should have adopted a self-restraining practice which, in effect, reduces privileges which have come to be unjustified illustrates their consciousness of the role of coherence in legitimating the system of rules which is the U.N. Charter: a legitimacy in which all members have a stake. The General Agreement on Tariffs and Trade of 1947[412] provides another illustration of nations' understanding of the important legitimating function performed by coherence. The GATT's most basic provision is the "Most Favored Nation" (MFN) clause, article 24, which prohibits members from giving "any advantage, favour, privilege, or immunity granted by any contracting party to any product originating in or destined for any other country" which is not immediately accorded "unconditionally to the like product originating in or destined for the territories of all contracting parties."[413] The purpose of this provision is to encourage free trade by discouraging cartelization and exclusionary measures leading to trade wars. Nevertheless, the treaty is sophist in its textured approach, recognizing several categories of exception based on countervailing historic, social, or economic considerations. For example, the continuation of trade preferences already in force (within the British Empire and Commonwealth, in particular) was permitted by article 1(2). With Western European integration in mind, article 24(4) also allows the MFN's obligation of equal treatment to be suspended in the case of "customs unions" and "free trade areas." There is also provision in article 18 which allows states with "low standards of living" to take certain discriminatory measures to protect their fledgling industries.

Only after large numbers of underdeveloped nations had become independent and had joined the GATT—they now number over 50 of its nearly 100 members—did it become apparent that article 18 did not suffice. What these new members demanded was the very opposite of the MFN principle. They wanted preferential access to the large, affluent markets of developed countries for the products of their new industries and, at least initially, they needed it at tariff rates which would give an advantage to their products. It is significant that the GATT and its members with developed economies have sought to accommodate, however imperfectly, these seemingly contradictory tendencies in a coherent new principle which both retains MFN among the developed traders, yet accommodates a Generalized System of Preferences (GSP)[414] for the poor. It achieves this by advancing justifiable distinctions in the context of a treaty the very essence of which is the duty consistently to treat "likes" alike.

Under GSP's terms, preference may be given to specified goods of developing countries "without according such treatment to other contracting parties."[415] The MFN principle, nevertheless, is kept relatively intact by seeking to ensure that such concessions are not used by developed countries as a way of giving themselves reciprocal preferential entry into developing countries' markets and also by casting GSP in transitional terms based on short-term needs. Indeed, within the category of needy states, a special category of "least developed" is created for which further provision is made.[416] Underlying all these textured adaptions of MFN is the general recognition by developed and less developed states that, while a world of uniformly low tariffs is in the general interest of world trade over the long-run, yet in the short-run it may not be in the best interest of a large number of poor nations.

Despite many problems and alleged violations occurring within this system it illustrates a comparatively successful adaption of a rule which had become incoherent—that is, incongruent—with its own underlying general principle. That general principle had never been an idiot rule approach to tariffs. Rather, MFN had never been shaped as the core of a bundle of considerations, some of which required quite sophisticated texturing of the rules. From the very beginning, the objective of ensuring free trade had to be balanced against the objective of encouraging the development of economic and political integration among states, especially in Europe and Latin America, many of which traditionally had been one another's implacable enemies. This could not be done by insisting on simple consistency, but only by textured sophist rules. Such rules retained coherence, however, by making exculpatory exceptions that were general, rational, and principled, and by making the rules' implementation subject to highly credible and mandatory dispute-settlement procedures.[417] While the 1947 treaty did not envisage the precise circumstances of large-scale decolonization and third world development, the later emergence of GSP, while superficially at cross-purposes with MFN, can be seen as coherent with the treaty's original balance between general objectives and the specific short-term detours necessary to get there.

While GSP is inconsistent with MFN, it is coherent with the underlying purpose of GATT, which is to increase trade among all its parties, because without GSP the new third world nations' share of trade would shrink under the weight of MFN. The GSP exception to MFN also applies a principle of distinction (i.e. between those entitled to GSP and those not) which connects coherently with distinctions commonly made in other rules and regulations of the international system. Redistributive principles employed by GSP are commonplace throughout the international rule system to justify distinctions which suspend a rule's consistency, yet preserve its coherence.

To summarize: The degree of a rule's legitimacy depends in part on its coherence, which is to say its connectedness, both internally (among the several parts and purposes of the rule) and externally (between one rule and other rules, through shared principles). This connectedness between rules united by underlying principles—both manifest in a rule's mandate and, often, also in its textured exceptions and exculpations—manifests the existence of an underlying rule-skein which connects disparate *ad hoc* arrangements into a network of rules "governing" a community of states, the members of which perceive the coherent rule system's powerful pull towards voluntary compliance.

In considering these examples of coherence and its effect on the perception of a system's legitimacy as well as on the sense of obligation to comply with its rules, we have been making an unstated *assumption* about the existence of a "community" of nations. That unexamined assumption, all along, has underpinned much of our analysis. We have assumed, but not demonstrated, that there really is a political community with a *system* of principles, rules, and decision-making processes. If this assumption is false, the quest for coherence becomes irrelevant. The coherence factor would be a chimera, as would be the search for legitimacy itself. The right of states to assume that obligations really are owed, that rules and principles do connect, that the system indeed is endowed with legitimacy and, in turn, can validate texts by reference to defined standards for rule-making: all this turns on the fundamental assumption of *community*. The quest of states for coherence in the rules governing their conduct, however, not only assumes community but is also evidence that states share the sense of membership in such a rule community.

Another way to put this is that the actors in a "community" perceive themselves as participating in a continuing game, that the game has rules which enable the participants to score against one another. But, above all, in a community the highest priority is accorded to keeping the game from ending. Almost everyone in the U.N., including the British ambassador, probably believes that the British veto has become an anachronism. That is why Britain strives not to be placed in the position of having to cast a sole negative vote. Yet, if a British veto were actually cast, and it were simply disallowed by a President of the Council wielding the power of the gavel, the U.N. might well unravel. Every member, not Britain alone, would understand that their associational rules had been torn up, and with them the very foundation of mutual obligation that, far more than any specific text, constitutes the basis for the continuing association of states in the voluntarist communitarian venture that is the U.N. Dworkin uses comparable imagery drawn not from political science but moral philosophy. Thus "the right of a political community to treat its members as having obligations in virtue of collective community decisions— is to be found not in the hard terrain of contracts or duties of justice or obligations of fair play that might hold among strangers . . . but in the more fertile ground of fraternity, community, and their attendant obligations. Political association . . . is in itself pregnant of obligation." This, he notes, invites the investigation of "what a bare political community must be like before it can claim to be a true community where communal obligations flourish."[418]

This, inevitably, is where this investigation must now lead: to the traces of community in a world of nations.

11

Adherence: Legitimacy and Normative Hierarchy

Do not take scepticism too seriously. . . . A true sceptic will be diffident of his philosophical doubts, as well as of his philosophical conviction; and will never refuse any innocent satisfaction, which offers itself, upon account of either of them.

R. Tuck*

In his book *The Concept of Law*, the Oxford legal philosopher Professor H. L. A. Hart compares the international system with the organization of a small, primitive tribe. He observes that "the rules for states resemble that simple form of social structure, consisting only of primary rules of obligation, which, when we find it among societies of individuals, we are accustomed to contrast with a developed legal system."[419]

Hart concedes that the international system does have many substantive "primary" rules, exemplified by the rights and duties typically enumerated in treaties or specified by the pedigree of customary usage. In his view, however, the system is primitive, if not illusory, because it lacks those crucial procedural "secondary" rules which permit a rule to change and adapt through legislation and the decision of courts. A related and even more serious disqualification, Hart alleges, is the international system's lack of "a unifying rule of recognition specifying 'sources' of law and pro-

* (Paraphrasing D. Hume), *Hobbes*, 116 (1989).

viding general criteria for the identification of its rules."[420] Thus he finds that the international community resembles a rudimentary social unit which, while having rules of obligation about such matters as land or kinship, has not yet developed a system of governance that allocates and regulates social roles or which, by an established process, facilitates the making, changing, application, and reinterpreting of the substantive rules.

In Hart's view, such rules as are to be found in the international system lack the quality of being validated by an infrastructure of rules about rules. We shall refer to this property as *adherence*, by which is meant the vertical nexus between a *primary rule of obligation*, which is the system's workhorse, and a hierarchy of secondary rules identifying the sources of rules and establishing normative standards that define how rules are to be made, interpreted, and applied. Primary rules, if they lack adherence to a system of validating secondary rules, are mere *ad hoc* reciprocal arrangements. They may well exert a pull to compliance, but a weaker one than is evinced by primary rules of obligation that are reinforced by a hierarchy of secondary rules which define the rule-system's "right process." Another way to say this is that a rule is more likely to obligate if it is made within the framework of an organized normative hierarchy, than if it is merely an *ad hoc* agreement between parties in a state of nature.

Hart's critique of the international system as small and primitive is still widely accepted and even those who think that the global system is in a more sophisticated state of development must concede that Hart's "misgivings" are not wholly unjustified. Small the international community surely is, with fewer than 200 "members," even including all states and major international organizations. Moreover, the recurrence of wars, other conflicts, and unremedied injustices still invites the appelation "primitive." Such misgivings, however understandable, result from misunderstanding. Of course, there *are* rule-making institutions in the system. One has but to visit a highly structured multinational negotiation such as the decade-long Law of the Sea Conference of the 1970s to see a kind of incipient legislature at work. The Security Council, the decision-making bodies of the World Bank, and, perhaps, the U.N. General Assembly and the International Law Commission[421] also somewhat resemble the cabinets, commissions and legislatures of national governments, even if the international organs are not as disciplined or highly empowered as their national counterparts. There *are* courts functioning in the international system: not only the International Court of Justice,[422] the European Community Court, and the regional Human Rights tribunals, but a very active network of quasi-judicial committees and comissions as well as arbitral tribunals such as the one established by the Algiers agreement ending the Iran hostage crisis, or as exemplified by the investment-dispute arbitrators operating under the auspices and procedures of the World Bank and the International Chamber of Commerce. All of these have been established by treaties and contracts providing for mandatory or consensual *ad hoc* third-party conflict resolution.[423] These agreements also usually establish the procedures and sources of rules to be used in deciding cases.[424]

Hart's exaggerated critique of the international system is deeply colored by Austinian positivism, which was more fashionable among legal scholars then than now. He looks for an effective police force and finding none, asks: "Can such rules as there are between nations be meaningfully and truthfully said ever to give rise to obligations?"[425]

The answer to that question, nowadays, is "yes." Indeed, Hart himself found that states think and act as if the rules do exert a strong pull to compliance, that "what these rules require is thought and spoken of as obligatory; there is general pressure for conformity to the rules; claims and admissions are based on them and their breach is held to justify not only insistent demands for compensation, but . . . counter-measures. When the rules are disregarded it is not on the footing that they are not binding; instead, efforts are made to conceal the facts."[426]

Observation of contemporary practice makes clear what, in Hart's time, was still ambiguous and radically conjectural. For example, when Libya sends its armed forces into neighboring Chad, as it does periodically, no right to do so is asserted. Rather, Libya denies that its troops are involved and says that the in-

vaders were disaffected Chadian forces.[427] Or, it may claim that
the territory invaded was actually Libyan by right of historic
title.[428] Surely it is significant that even so iconoclastic a regime
as that of Colonel Qaddafi has not risked an open disavowal of
the binding nature of the rules. As for the rest of the international
community, it tends to rally around the norms. The nearby
African states, with France and the U.S., repeatedly have come
to Chad's rescue. No one, not even the Soviet Union, has given
open support to the Libyan aggression.

That the rules display so strong a compliance pull may have
surprised Hart. It should encourage the current generation of
jurisprudential thinkers to question not Hart's still-helpful theory
of obligation but the current validity of his verdict on what is
no longer a "primitive" international system. In Hart's theory, the
highest level of obligation could operate only in respect of a rule
which is part of a normative hierarchy capped by an ultimate
system-validating rule. Such an ultimate rule of recognition defines a community organized by rules and validates norms which
obligate everyone in the community *because of their status as
members*. In other words, the rules' compliance pull is stronger
if the basis of the obligation is associational, rather than merely
contractual. Hart did not see the rules of the international system
as corresponding to such a hierarchic model. It is this conclusion
which needs to be reconsidered in the light of modern state
practice.

Before doing so, it may be useful to illustrate Hart's theory.
In his view, a simple rule ("cross on the green, stop on the red")
may arise as a discrete obligation entered into consensually by
an otherwise unassociated group of actors: for example, random
pedestrians and motorists. But that obligation's compliance pull
would be enhanced if the traffic rule has been made by a city
council organized in accordance with a state constitution which,
itself, is a valid exercise of powers allocated to the state by the
national constitution. Primary obligations such as those imposed
by the traffic rule may come into operation as mere reciprocal
arrangements, lacking adherence to a system of secondary rules
about how rules are to be made, interpreted, and applied. Such

ad hoc rules are not necessarily incapable of obligating parties which have agreed to abide by them. But rules which adhere to a hierarchy of secondary rules are of a higher order of obligation because they can exert a pull toward compliance even on parties which have not specifically agreed to comply. The basis of an obligation created by a primary rule which is reinforced by a rule hierarchy is not specific consent but *status.*

The international system has such status-based rules. This, however, is not widely understood. "Why are treaties binding?" is a question usually answered by the superficial assertion that "treaties are binding because states have agreed to be bound." This explanation has its counterpart in domestic law. Contracts, which are often regarded as analogous to treaties, are also said to be binding because the parties have agreed to be bound. But this characterization of treaties as primary rule-based obligations is misleading, as is the analogy to contract. If two persons enter into a contract, it is binding because the law has defined the requirements of a valid commitment and, if those are met, it is *the law* which imposes a binding obligation on the parties. Thus contractual obligation cannot be explained by the mere agreement of the parties.[429] Neither can the obligation of parties to a treaty be explained merely by their mutual consent. Hart, too, understood the fallacy of this explanation, which makes it odd that he should have thought the international system "primitive." The "view that a state may impose obligations on itself by promise, agreement, or treaty," he said, "is not . . . consistent with the theory that states are subject only to rules which they have thus imposed on themselves." Rather, "*rules* must already exist providing that a state is bound to do whatever it understakes by appropriate words to do."[430] Such rules about treaties are now actually found in a global text defining the law of treaties,[431] which declares that *pacta sunt servanda* ("treaties are binding").[432] But the binding force even of that statement cannot emanate solely from the agreement of the parties. It must come from some ultimate unwritten rule of recognition, the existence of which may be inferred from the conduct and belief (*opinio juris*) of states.

The inductive demonstration of the existence of such an ultimate rule, through observation of the state system, is fundamental
to an understanding of the nature of all obligaton between states.
All nations act in professed compliance with, and reliance on, the
notion that when a state enters into a treaty it has a duty to
comply, an obligation, moreover, which is superior to its sovereign
will. It must act in accordance with the obligations it has assumed: not only for as long as it is in agreement but until the
agreement is amended or terminated in strict compliance with
its textual requirements.

In a sense, this analysis has its origins in much earlier notions
of natural and divine law, which imposed obligations on states
because of the nature of man and our species' subservience to
codes of right reason implanted in human consciousness by a
divine creator.[433] In the last decades of the twentieth century, such
natural law, or neo-natural law, explanations for the existence of
an ultimate rule of recognition have become more an emanation
of personal taste than a requisite of rational inquiry. The belief
of states, governments, judges, and the public that such a rule
hierarchy exists, and their tendency to act on that belief, is a
sufficient, if contingent, proof of the thing believed.

It is easily demonstrable that the international community
believes, and acts on the belief, that a rule-hierarchy exists and
obligates states. The most recent instance of this is to be found
in an advisory opinion rendered by the International Court of
Justice on April 26, 1988. In it, the judges unanimously aver the
existence of an obligation deriving its pull to compliance not from
specific consent but from membership in a community. That
opinion was given at the request of the United Nations General
Assembly[434] after the U.S. Congress had enacted a law, later
signed under protest by President Reagan, requiring the closing of
the Observer Mission of the Palestine Liberation Organization.[435]
That law violated the U.S. Government's own interpretation of
its obligations under the U.N. Headquarters Agreement.[436] In
such a conflict between a treaty obligation and a national law,
the Court said, the treaty obligation is paramount. It confirmed
"the fundamental principle of international law that it prevails

over domestic law"[437] and, in support, cited its own earlier opinion that "in the relations between Powers who are contracting Parties to a treaty, the provisions of municipal law cannot prevail over those of a treaty."[438] The point was confirmed in a concurring opinion of the U.S. judge, Stephen M. Schwebel, who wrote that "a State cannot avoid its international responsibility by the enactment of domestic legislation which conflicts with its international obligations."[439] In other words, the sovereign will of states is subordinate to obligations that derive from their status as members of a community. This, by definition, cannot be deduced from specific consent and few, today, would seek to anchor the principle in the will of God or nature. Instead, we tend to a demystified behavioral explanation: it is so because it is generally believed to be so.

It would be wrong to derive from the foregoing discussion the idea that the rule *pacta sunt servanda* is an exhaustive rehearsal of the international community's ultimate rule of recognition. The other parts of the international community's ultimate rule can also be adduced inductively and demonstrated circumstantially by state belief and behavior. For example, there is widespread acceptance by states of the notion that time-and-practice-honored conduct—pedigreed custom—has the capacity to bind states, even when they prefer to act inconsistently with such a customary rule. The nations, by word and conduct, assert that there is an *obligation* to comply with custom which is analogous to the compliance pull exerted by a treaty. This was reaffirmed in 1986 by the International Court of Justice at the "merits" phase of the suit brought by Nicaragua against the United States. The majority opinion defined U.S. obligations almost entirely in terms of customary rules to most of which the U.S. never explicitly consented.[440] Indeed, a treaty ratified and implemented by most states may also, incidentally, create a prevalent pattern of behavior which, as "customary law" obligates states that have not accepted the treaty. For example, Professor Theodor Meron has concluded that non-signatories to universal human rights treaties may be obligated by the "customary character" of the norms in those treaties which bind "states that are not parties to the instrument in which the norm is stated."[441] This capacity of custom to bind non-acquiescent states is even more dramatic evidence that obligations are perceived to arise in the international community as an incident of a state's status as a member of the community.[442] In the words of Judge H. Mosler, states are subject by their status, rather than by consent, to the requisites of "public order," which he defines as "consisting of principles and rules the enforcement of which is of such vital importance to the international community as a whole that any unilateral action or any agreement which contravenes these principles can have no legal effect. The reason for this follows simply from logic: the law cannot recognize any act either of one member or of several members in concert, as being legally valid if it is directed against the very foundation of law."[443]

It thus appears that the international community's capstone is the rule or set of rules defining formal sources of *obligation*. This should not be confused with treaties which define *sources of law*, as, for example, is done by article 38 of the Statute of the International Court of Justice. That treaty provision, like a "choice of laws" clause in an international contract, is a secondary rule, or rule of recognition, which refers the parties, in effect, to specified parts of the law library. Article 38 tells us *what* rules may be applicable to a dispute. It does not tell us *why* those, or any other, rules should determine the outcome of a dispute. For the answer to that more fundamental question it is necessary to locate an altogether different kind of rule, a rule about the nature of obligation, an ultimate rule of recognition. The notion that treaties and generally accepted custom are binding is one example or aspect of such an ultimate rule, which asserts that obligation derives not from nations' consent but from their status as members of a community of rules. That community, reciprocally, is defined by its ultimate rule of recognition.

There are other parts of this ultimate rule of recognition which may also be adduced from the practice of states in complying with the rule *as an incident of their community-bestowed statehood*, rather than as a consequence of specific consent. Thus new states are deemed to be obliged to comply with the duties of statehood not because they agree to do so, but because they have satisfied requirements for the recognition of their right to membership in the community.[444] The obligations, so to speak, come with the rights. States may also "inherit" certain rights and duties from a "parent" state of which they were previously a part,[445] again not by virtue of consent but as a concomitant of status. Successor *governments*, too, inherit rights and obligations from their predecessors in a similar fashion.[446]

Thus there are various rights and obligations that derive from a tacit acceptance by the state and its government that they are part of a community which is composed of individual states whose interdependence is institutionalized and systematized by what Hart calls "secondary rules of recognition." As we have seen, these are rules which, at the textual level, define the processes of community rule-making and the rights and obligations which go "automatically" with statehood. But at a more profound level these rules define the source of all obligation, which derives from *status in the community*. This is further evidenced by another phenomenon to which reference was made in the preceding chapter: states frequently insist on the adherence of their peers to rules creating obligations not because they have a direct interest in a particular application of a particular substantive rule—not, in other words, because they themselves have a rule-based claim—but, rather, in pursuit of their more general interest in reinforcing, by reiteration and implementation, the validity of the rule itself. A state which has no current claim based on another state's obligation may nevertheless perceive itself to have a very important stake in the principle that the obligation be discharged and the relevant rule applied. This may be more true of weak than of strong states, since reliance on rules tends to be greater where there can be less reliance on power; but to some extent rule-consciousnss is always part of the political sense of every state.

For example, during the Argentine invasion of the British Falkland Islands, states which were normally closer to Argentine than to Britain, as well as states which had no direct interest in the outcome of the Falklands war, nevertheless sided with Britain. This was because they believed themselves, as members of the community of states, to have a stake in the validity of the

U.N. Charter and, particularly, in its prohibition of the use of force. Many states otherwise uninterested in the disposition of the remote Falkland Islands thought it important to their own long-term security to reinforce article 2(4) and the compliance-pull of the Charter as a whole.[447] They sided with Britain against Argentina out of concern that the Charter's legitimacy—and their own security, protected by that system of rules—would erode further, perhaps irretrievably, if Argentina were to succeed. They reacted rather as did the citizens of New York when a subway rider, Bernard Goetz, shot some rousting teenagers who appeared to threaten him. While sympathizing with his instinct, they were concerned, as subway riders, with the prospect, if Goetz were vindicated, of being caught in crossfire between hoodlums and vigilantes. Their sympathy for Goetz, in other words, was overruled by concern for the systemic effect on the community if his action went unreproved.

There are important differences in the degree or extent to which obligations arise in a developed national legal system and in the fledgling international community. But it is also demonstrable that there *are* obligations owed by states *which they widely recognize as concomitants of community membership and which are accurate predictors of actual state behavior.* There are rules which obligate not because they have been accepted by the individual sovereign state but because they come with membership in the community of peers. The members of that community relinquish their absolute sovereignty by the very fact of statehood. Sovereignty, in the international community, thus resides in a set of principles of universal application, such as those pertaining to the binding nature of treaties and of custom. These ultimate rules of recognition are sovereign in the sense that, while they are not coercively enforced, they are known to obligate (and also entitle) all states, with or without their specific consent. Moreover, these rules are not themselves sanctioned, as are most rules, by reference to other enabling or empowering norms. That is why they may be referred to as "ultimate."

The international community, it thus appears, is a more developed framework of rules and obligations than has sometimes been acknowledged by those whose expectations are shaped by the study of national legal systems. The global rule system, too, is characterized by a large number of primary rules which, for the most part, are not free-standing. Rather, those primary rules adhere to a hierarchy of secondary rules, culminating in an ultimate rule or set of rules of recognition, which legitimates the members of the community, but, in return, exerts a compliance pull powered less by nations' specific voluntary consent to that rule than by the obligation that goes with the status they have sought and achieved as recognized members of the community.

To summarize: The legitimacy of a rule determines, in whole or in part, the capacity of a rule to exert compliance pull upon states. In the voluntarist community, such compliance pull is usually evidenced by the agreement of states to act in accordance with the rule. In a mature voluntarist community, however, the capacity of rules to obligate does not derive only from the specific consent of the members but as a concomitant of the status of membership. This does not make the community less voluntarist, because compliance is not compelled by an Austinian super-government. But it does mean that there is a further aspect of a rule's legitimacy which is its validation by adherence to a rule hierarchy. A rule has greater legitimacy if it is validated by having been made in accordance with secondary rules about rule-making.

The capacity of these secondary rules to validate primary rules is further augmented by their adherence to, or validation by, an ultimate rule of recognition which defines the nature of obligation in the community of states. Specifically, a primary rule may be evidenced by the text of an agreement. A secondary rule may define how such agreements are to be negotiated, interpreted, and validated. The ultimate rule of recognition, however, tells us that agreements, once validated, are binding, whether or not states wish to abide by them. These three rule categories constitute a validating hierarchy each level of which legitimates the next. The legitimacy of the primary rule may be demonstrated by showing that it was entered into in accordance with the right process outlined in the secondary rules. The legitimacy of the secondary rules may be demonstrated by the specific or implied consent of states. The legitimacy of the ultimate rule of recognition, however, cannot be demonstrated by reference to any other validating rules or procedures, but only by the conduct of nations manifesting their belief in the ultimate rules' validity *as the irreducible prerequisites for an international concept of right process*. It can only be inferred, that is, from the nature of the international system as a community of states.

12

Community and Legitimacy

Only that precept is law which is instituted in general for all the
persons included within a given community.

Francisco Suarez (1548–1617)[448]

I learn to do a service to another, without bearing him any real
kindness; because I foresee, that he will return my service, in expectation of another of the same kind and in order to maintain
the same correspondence of good offices with me and with others.

D. Hume*

As we have seen, it is a commonly held view, vigorously cham-
pioned by John Austin, Hans Kelsen, and others, that law is "a
coercive order" which characteristically employs "that specific
social technique which consists in the attempt to bring about
the desired social conduct of men through the threat of a measure
of coercion which is to be taken in case of contrary, that is, legally
wrong, conduct." This belief-system holds that the coercive order
is a hallmark of a developed social community, which is also
marked by "the establishment of a special organ, a tribunal, competent to ascertain by a definite procedure the fact that a delict
has been committed and to order the sanction provided for by
the law; it consists also in the establishment of a special executive
organ competent to carry out the sanction ordered by the tribunal."[449] Kelsen sharply contrasts this model of a developed
community with systems of morals or other social orders that are

* "Of the Obligation of Promises," in A *Treatise of Human Nature* (bk. III,
sec. V), 573 (E. C. Mossner, ed., 1969).

non-coercive and depend upon voluntary compliance.[450] The international community is relegated to the latter category.

It is evident that Kelsen, like most legal philosophers, perceives an evolution in systemic relations between persons that is marked by upward progress from the primitive (non-coercive) to the highly developed (coercive). To the extent—usually rather marginal—that the international system is addressed at all, it is with a parallel evolution in mind: the states must eventually evolve from their present non-coercive primitivism to become a genuine, organized community in which "real" obligations are enforced by judges and a police force deployed by a supranational executive.

This prognosis, even if based on a correct charting of the evolution of national communities—a debatable proposition—is flatly wrong about the direction which development is likely to take in the community of states. The international system appears to be evolving a rather sophisticated normative structure without police enforcement. A sense of obligation pulls states in the direction of compliance with norms which, on the one hand, are not coercively mandated by a global sovereign, but, on the other hand, do not obligate solely on the basis of states' grace and favor. Though states' *compliance* with the rules may be voluntary, states' *obligation* to them is not. Nations, or those who govern them, recognize that the obligation to comply is owed by them to the community of states as the reciprocal of that community's validation of their nations' statehood.

Obligation thus is uniquely rooted in the notion of community. While obligation can arise in other ways—as by a mutual exchange of promises—it can also arise as a concomitant of status, but only after an association has reached an advanced stage of development. A "community" differs from a rabble, first, in that it is an organized system of interaction in accordance with rules, while a rabble typically involves unstructured, standardless interactions between actors whose conscious relationship to one another is limited to the circumstance of casual proximity. A rabble is a crowd whose members interact because they just happen to be in the same space at the same time. "Members" of a rabble do not regard themselves as members, anymore than persons on a crowded subway car regard themselves as "members" of an underground. They do not attempt to relate except through isolated, random interaction in which opportunistic displays of power and deference are acceptable modes of accommodation. In a primitive society, which is a social notch above a rabble, parties may comply with certain obligations assumed bilaterally, or even in compliance with rules voluntarily accepted. For example, some persons on a subway do yield their seats to the elderly or handicapped, even when no law requires it and there is little peer pressure to do so. Moreover, those who choose to give their seats do not expect ever to see the beneficiary again, or to benefit in future from their deference to others.

The difference between a rabble or even a primitive association and a developed community is that in the latter members accept specific reciprocal obligations as a concomitant of membership in that community, which is a structured, continuing association of interacting parties. Individuals in a rabble or primitive society do not ordinarily attempt to imagine the reality of those with whom they share a space, nor do they concern themselves with how they may be perceived by those others. There is no expectation that a single, limited transaction will establish a continuing, structured relationship, nor is each such interaction thought to occur within a framework in which the many have a stake, including even those not directly involved. It is the citizens of New York, not any specific carriage of subway riders, which feel that they have a stake in constraining violent conduct such as that of Bernard Goetz, to which reference was made in the preceding chapter.

A developed community—the citizenry of New York in our example—differs from other forms of association in that each party expects an ongoing relationship to persist for as long as he or she is affiliated with the community. In addition, there may be specific relationships between some members that exclude others, but even these will be governed by secondary rules of recognition— generalized, rational principles of distinction—which apply all the way to the outer limits of the rule's reach and in which all have an interest. The evolution of such rules of general application and the uncoerced compliance with those rules are significantly abetted by all community members' expectation that they are part of an ongoing relationship, that the other members, in effect, are not getting off at the next stop.

This expectation of continuity, indicative of a developed community, has important implications for the pull to compliance. It affects behavior of members of a mature community because it prompts them to believe that each transaction with other participants has, and is generally understood to have, resonance at two levels: that of a primary obligation and of a secondary obligation. If a member of a community contracts with another to sell a commodity at a fixed price on a date certain, the primary obligation is to buy and to sell the agreed item at the agreed date and price. This primary obligation is set in the terms of the contract and is owed by the contracting parties to each other. The secondary obligation is to carry out contractual obligations or to pay appropriate compensation if specific performance is impossible or socially undesirable. This obligation is based on the terms of those secondary rules by which the community has established the requirements and incidents of contracting. It is owed by both contracting parties not merely to each other but to the entire community. By complying with the contract, the parties do more than go through with a deal; they reinforce the validity of an important secondary rule of the community. Since all members of the community have a stake in the rule's validity, none can be indifferent to whether there is compliance or violation. This communitarian peer pressure is an important indicator of a rule's legitimacy and also is evidence of the existence of a community. Usually, the peer interest has far less to do with the primary rule than with the community's stake in the secondary rule.

This, indeed, is the most basic indicator of a rule's legitimacy: whether it is validated by community or, to put it another way, whether the rule is systemically based.

International *system* is a term which has been defined by Professor Stanley Hoffman to mean a "pattern of relations between the basic units of world politics which is characterized by the scope of the objectives pursued by those units and of the tasks performed among them, as well as by the means used in order to achieve those goals and perform those tasks."[451] Charles Hermann states that "a system is a set of actors (for example, nations, international organizations, and so on) interacting with one another in established patterns and through designated structures."[452] At the footing of the concept of system lies a notion of *reciprocity*, an awareness that what one actor does in a particular transaction is of more than passing interest because it will affect the behavior of the same, and also other, actors in a continuing line of similar—or even different—transactions.

Such reciprocity is central to the idea of system.[453] Reciprocity is widely regarded as a basic socializing principle. According to the sociologist Professor Alvin Gouldner, some concept of reciprocity invariably appears in social arenas that achieve a high level of continuous interaction.[454] Jean Piaget has identified a sense of reciprocity as the first inkling by a child of its part in a social contract.[455] Put another way, reciprocity evokes the obligatory nature of commitment. Eventually, as the system matures, reciprocity may become a multidirectional web, rather than a part of a purely bilateral set of transactions. For example, the fish which A buys from B may be purchased with an endorsed I.O.U. which A had received from C, a shoemaker, who agreed to make a free pair of shoes for A as payment to A for a delivery of leather. B may not need shoes, but may endorse C's note to D, a doctor, in payment for a medical service rendered to E, who has agreed to deliver fish nets to B. D may then present the note to C and receive a pair of custom-made shoes. The point, of course, is that this web of reciprocity creates a shared interest among A, B, C, D, and E that each perform in accordance with commitments made or implied. Although A, B, C, D, and E may be unaware of one another, they will be conscious of a beneficial skein of relationships which facilitates something more sophisticated than bilateral barter. They are in a "system" but do not yet constitute a mature "community."

This system, if it continues to facilitate and regulate interaction, eventually will become very important to the parties. As awareness of this importance impinges on the parties, they begin to form an early phase of community. Thus, if shoemaker C were to suffer an illness which prevents him from making the shoes to which D is entitled, A, B, and E may join to buy another pair of shoes for D in order to maintain the efficacy of the system, relying on C later to compensate them in some agreed fashion.[456] Gradually we see emerging out of these patterns of interactions reasonable expectations which become set in rules. If the rules are of a high level of legitimacy, they, in turn, will reinforce the tendency to conform to the established pattern of behavior: not because of an Austinian policeman's enforcement power but because of everyone's perception that the system must be kept going.

In the example of the shoemaker's I.O.U., the decision of A, B, and E to make good the promise to D on which C has defaulted may become—perhaps through repetitive practice and the passage of time—a fixed condition of joining the transactional skein. In other words, a cost of enjoying the convenience of doing business with endorsed bills like the I.O.U. drawn by C may be that, if the bill is not honored by the drawer, an obligation will attach to each of the endorsers to make a proportionate contribution that will cover the debt. Such an obligation need not be accepted consciously or specifically: it may simply be implicit or inherent in the status of an endorser. If so, a more sophisticated community has begun to evolve. The rule that an endorser may have to pay the debt of the failed drawer of the bill is another sort of rule, differing in kind from the one which says that the drawer of an I.O.U. owes a debt to the person to whom it is drawn. That latter, *primary* rule only defines the binary contractual rights of A and B, A and C, B and D, the parties to the I.O.U. The rule that makes an endorser of the I.O.U. a surety for an unpaid debt between two other parties is not binary. It may be a status-based obligation: so to speak, an obligation arising not out of a specific promise to another, but from an obligation *erga omnes* which is not specifically assumed but is inherent in the *status* of an endorser. It has now become a general cost of "doing business" with promissory notes. It is an obligation owed by virtue of a *rule of recognition* which takes its validity from status, rather than from explicit consent to the various subsequent transactions in which the bill may be used. The endorser merely agrees to join the system by an act of original volition, just as a state or government may be said to enter the international system by qualifying for recognition.

In this example, the secondary rules will define *first* what *is* a negotiable instrument (what is formally necessary to the creation of a valid instrument of this sort) and, *second*, what additional obligations are imposed on each endorser toward all other endorsers by virtue of joining the skein. These rules are implicit in the bilateral relations of A with B, A with C, or B with D, yet they do not rest upon these parties' specific consent but, instead, upon their decision to make use of the promissory note, the incidents of which have their roots in some larger framework than any particular binary obligation. Indeed, in due course all parties to all promissory notes within the community will have some degree of interest in sustaining the integrity of such notes in the event of default. They may institutionalize this interest by establishing a central claim fund by which bad debts are satisfied and to which every drawer or endorser pays a small fee as part of the transaction.

This, then, is evidence of a functional "community." Hart, publishing in 1961, would probably have been skeptical that the international system had evolved into what we have called a "community"—a term he does not employ—because he was unable to detect convincing examples of secondary rules of recognition, let alone an ultimate rule of recognition such as the Constitution of the United States which sets out the essential parameters which define and shape the community and from which no derogation is possible. A quarter of a century after Hart's seminal book, however, the verdict might well be different as evidence accumulates showing a community's gradually coming into being.

Community, in the sense in which it is here employed, does not seek to implicate any of the many theoretical—inductively or deductively derived—definitions developed by sociologists or anthropologists.[457] It is used here solely to denote a high level of sophistication in the *rule* structure within which a group of actors habitually interact. Analogies to tribes with ties of kinship, proximity and belief-system are helpful only metaphorically (as in "the global village") or else are downright misleading. We are speaking of a community of *states* and interstate institutions, not of persons. While persons may be in fixed communion at many different levels and by virtue of many different forces, states are more limited in the ways they can relate to one another. True, one may speak of a cultural "francophone community" linking France and its former colonies. However, the usual form of affiliation among states is by rules of conduct and rules that govern the making, interpretation, and application of obligating rules. It is this "rule community" which coming into existence already has the capacity to legitimate the primary rules made in accordance with its rules about rules.

The "community" of states has important secondary rules of recognition, "associative" obligations, in Dworkin's terms,[458] which obligate states because of their status as validated members of the international community. Only by stretching the term "consent" beyond its natural limits can such associative obligation be said to have been assumed consensually. Dworkin rightly points out that "associative" rules of obligation are of an interpretative mode,[459] defining what a member owes others in the community in general. Thus the obligation to honor treaties (*pacta sunt servanda*) is acquired associatively, not by consent, and is owed generally towards all (*erga omnes*). The obligation, moreover, cannot be extinguished by renouncing a consent which was never given, but only by extinguishing the statehood status which is the real basis of the obligation, or by a valid process that permits states' collectively to alter the terms of the ultimate rules of recognition. In this sense, the pull to obligation resembles that which medieval jurisprudence attributed to "eternal law"—that is, law which exists out of temporal context, has not been "made," and is not validated by reference to any other authority, but is binding indirectly by its being subsumed in "made" laws.[460]

According to Dworkin, a true community, as distinguished from a mere rabble, or even a system of merely random primary rules of obligation, is one in which the members "accept that they are governed by common principles, not just by rules hammered out in political compromise. . . . Members of a society of principle accept that their political rights and duties are not exhausted by the particular decisions their political institutions have reached, but depend, more generally, on the scheme of principles those decisions presuppose and endorse. So each member accepts that others have rights and that he has duties flowing from that scheme. . . ." Nor are these rights and duties "conditional on his wholehearted approval of that scheme; these obligations arise from the historical fact that his community has adopted that scheme . . . not the assumption that he would have chosen it were the choice entirely his."[461]

Moreover, the community "commands that no one be left out, that we are all in politics together for better or worse."[462] And its legitimating requirement of rule integrity "assumes that each person is as worthy as any other, that each must be treated with equal concern according to some coherent conception of what that means."[463]

Does that describe the social condition of the nations of the world in their interactive mode? The description does not assume justice, harmony or an absence of strife. According to Dworkin, an "association of principle is not automatically a just community; its conception of equal concern may be defective. . . ."[464] What a rule community, a community of principle, does is to validate behavior in accordance with rules and applications of rules that confirm principled coherence rather than acknowledging only the power of power. Also, a rule community operates in conformity not only with primary rules but also secondary ones—rules about rules—which are generated and applied by valid legislative and adjudicative institutions. Finally, a community accepts its most basic (ultimate) secondary rules of recognition not consensually, but as an inherent concomitant of membership status.

Each of these described conditions of community is observable today in the international arena of states. Since states, unlike citizens of a nation, cannot leave the community by emigrating to another, the community's ultimate rules of recognition—although changeable by the community acting collectively in accordance with the ultimate rules' procedures—apply to every state until the state or the community ceases to exist. This does not mean that any particular rule—a command—of the community of states *is legitimate*, because, as we have seen, a rule's degree of legitimacy is determined by a number of factors. It does mean that the system of states has developed, in more than rudimentary even if less than perfected form, those rules about rules and rule making that make it *possible* for a community to issue legitimate commands to, and impose valid obligations on, its members. It means that the conduct of members in what we have called a voluntarist association is not, after all, entirely voluntary. It also means that the legitimacy even of mere primary rules that obligate by consent can be tested by their coherence with, and validation by, the secondary rules of recognition and the general principles that connect primary rules in a mature community. In particular, it means that the standard for measuring legitimacy is sufficiently understandable that states can know the approximate degree of legitimacy of each command, the weight of obligation it imposes, and the strength of its pull to compliance.

The idea that the degree of legitimacy of rules and institutions is measurable itself can only be sustained if there is a community which agrees upon and applies that standard. In this sense, community is not only the essential ingredient in an ultimate rule of recognition, it is also the *sine qua non* of the entire enterprise of defining legitimacy. Conversely, if it can be demonstrated that rules' and institutions' legitimacy can be measured, that itself constitutes important evidence of community.

Legitimacy is to rules as the Greenwich Mean Longitude is to time, or as the Paris Metre Bar is to distance. It is a hypothetical *absolute*, contrived to facilitate the understanding of some *relative* factor—distance, for example, or time—within the boundaries of a stockade. That stockade is the circumference of a community. That those within recognize Mean Time and the Metre Bar is one of the evidences that nations of the world constitute a "community" with a common notion of time and of distance. The common assumption of a meter bar also permits the making of further logically deducible subsidiary assumptions, such as minutes or centimeters, as well as aggregate assumptions, such as months and kilometers. In a sense, these conditional absolutes—measures of time, distance, or legitimacy—share with ultimate rules of recognition the same debt to community status. Legitimacy is not a measure accepted by states, anymore than people any longer specifically "accept" the meter, or time. These simply exist as functions of living in a society which uses those measures. So, too, with the notion of legitimacy by which the compliance pull of rules is measured. And legitimacy, too, has its logical concomitants which help to make it applicable to the community but which cannot be verified except by the community's deference to them. These concomitants of legitimacy, its factors, have been the subject of our inquiry. The truth of all that we have purported to discover, however, is circumscribed by the condition of community. It is the community which invests legitimacy with meaning; it is in the community that legitimacy exerts its pull to rule-compliance. It is because states constitute a community that legitimacy has the power to influence their conduct.

The world has evolved as a community of rules, a stockade within which all states are to be found, bound together by a set of common, or at least compatible, assumptions. These assumptions have been evident for sometime. Victoria, in the sixteenth century, noted the emergence of a "law of nations" which "exists clearly enough" and derives from "a consensus of the greater part of the whole world . . ."[465]; and Grotius, too, based much of a work dating to 1604 on what he called "the consensus of all nations" or "common consent of mankind," which he traced back to Cicero's notion of human "right reason" and Heraclitus' "universal form of reason or understanding. . . ."[466] Whatever their origins and however subject to reinterpretation, these compatible assumptions of states are not now based explicitly on consent. They are in the form of rules and standards which obligate. To many rules, states have given specific consent. But consent is not required or applicable to those rules which tell us about the sources and nature *of obligation* itself.

In a sense, all rules obligate. Traditional international law teaches us that treaties and custom are the two best sources of binding obligation. But observation of the behavior of the international community indicates far greater variation than this observation indicates. An indeterminate new treaty may exert a less powerful pull to compliance than a venerable and clearly understood custom. A clearly determinate treaty or custom may be rendered incoherent by a countervailing General Assembly resolution or by inconsistent state conduct, as we saw in our study of self-determination in Chapter 10. The force of a rule's compliance pull cannot be gauged solely or primarily by examining its source. The community of states, lacking enforcement powers, has come up with its own meter bar to measure the pull to compliance.

Legitimacy is the standard by which the community measures rules' capacity to obligate. It has been our contention, throughout, that, just as one can measure distance, one can measure legitimacy, although, as with distance, one can only measure it by a standard which is an assumption having validity solely in the context of the community which relies on it. For the community of states, this basic measure is legitimacy. Once the power of legitimacy is understood, its component factors—determinacy, symbolic validation, coherence, and adherence—can be worked out deductively.

None of this directly involves the idea of law, because the international community is not organized as, or even in a manner analogous to, a state, certainly not one with an Austinian sovereign and gendarmerie. On the other hand, it is perfectly possible to call the international system of rules "law"—and, for that matter, the international community could be called an anarchist-utopian superstate—but this is neither necessary nor particularly helpful. It is a functioning community with a concept of *obligation*. This phenomenon of obligation is observable *externally* (most countries obey many rules much of the time) by our Martian on a spaceship, and also *internally* by a global psychiatrist observing the behavior, motives, and, yes, the guilty consciences of those who guide the conduct of states. Internal observers can testify that when rules are obeyed, it is because countries *think* an obligation exists, and they say so; and when obligations are disobeyed, countries tell furtive lies about the facts to cover their discomfort and avert the community's censure. Quite often, when rules are violated by a state, conscientious citizens demonstrate in the streets against their own country's scoff-rule conduct. Thus is manifest the internal perspective on the phenomenon of obligation.

While all primary and secondary rules of the global rule community are capable of generating a sense of obligation by virtue of their legitimacy, some are more legitimate and thus obligate more than others. This study has proposed a taxonomy of legitimacy to explain why this should be so.

To the extent such a taxonomy is not merely descriptive but also, potentially, prescriptive, it points the way to better rule making. It permits a prediction as to whether a proposed rule is likely to exert a significant compliance pull and suggests ways to augment its capacity to obligate. It indicates ways to validate rules symbolically, to make their intent more transparent, to garner authority for the rule by connecting it to accepted principles justifying other rules, and to add weight to an obligation by demonstrating the rule's compliance with a hierarchy of rules about rules. This means that the community of nations is capable, potentially, of better governing and realizing itself. In Theodor Meron's felicitous phrase, "the 'ought' merges with the 'is,' the *lex ferenda* with the *lex lata*" in fulfillment of the community's "teleological desire."[467] It is not necessary, fortunately, to await the millennium of Austinian-type world government before the community of nations can proceed with constructing—even one day perfecting—a system of rules and institutions that will exhibit a powerful pull to compliance and a self-enforcing degree of legitimacy.

13

Postlude:

Why Not Justice?

Mon ami, si vous demeuriez de ce côté je serais un assassin et
celà serait injuste de vous tuer de la sorte; mais puisque vous
demeurez de l'autre côté, je suis un brave et celà est juste.
                                                    Blaise Pascal*

. . . ethical grounds into which enter considerations of propriety,
magnanimity, wisdom, public duty, in short, of policy . . . are
matters with which municipal courts have nothing to do.
              Lord Alverston in *West Rand Central Gold Mining
                     Company v. Rex* [1905] 2 K.B. 391, 401.

There are two reasons for not including justice among the factors
making for legitimacy. One is *operational*, the other *theoretical*.

The *operational* reason is that justice can only be said to be
done to persons, not to such collective entities as states. Of course,
it is possible to say that the Treaty of Versailles did an "injustice"
to Germany at the end of the First World War. To the extent
that all Germans suffered from the inflation, unemployment and
social unravelling which followed the treaty's imposition of huge
reparations and their concomitant deprivations, the statement may
be useful as metaphorical shorthand for the wrongs imposed on
the people. Even so, the reifying metaphor of a suffering Germany
is misleading, if only because some Germans prospered and prof-

* "La Justice et la raison des effets," in *Pensées*, Article V.

208

ited at the same time others were being severely deprived. An aggregate concept of justice and injustice thus distorts reality. The real injustice of Versailles can only be accounted in units of suffering by individuals, not by some imaginary suffering of that inanimate aggregation known as "the state."

Since one can only talk metaphorically of justice among states, it is difficult to say anything meaningful or true about the justice of the international rule system. At its present stage of development, most systemic rules command not persons but states, allocating duties and benefits on an aggregate basis. To say that the rules operate justly among nations, however, is to say little about the rules' actual impact on those who matter: the individuals who, unlike states, are capable of pleasure and pain. That this is an inevitable barrier to assessing the *justice* of the international rule system, however, does not affect our ability to measure quite accurately and usefully the *legitimacy* of those rules. It does suggest, however, the need not to muddle the separate ideas of legitimacy and justice.

The second, or *theoretical,* reason for refusing to include justice among the indicators of a rule's legitimacy is that the concepts of justice and legitimacy are related but conceptually distinct. This is demonstrably so even in national legal systems, where justice is more readily measured precisely because most rules address persons, or in those portions of the international system—human rights is the best example—where the rules also address individuals, and, thus, can be tested for justice without encountering the previously discussed operational difficulty.

The conceptual differences between legitimacy and justice are essential to an understanding of each. As a matter of jurisprudential theory, any given rule or institution—national or international—may have a high level of legitimacy *and yet be quite unjust.* Or it may be very just *and yet be distinctly illegitimate.* Justice and legitimacy do have something in common. Both tend to pull toward non-coerced compliance. They frequently interact synergistically. Nevertheless, they are discrete phenomena; neither is a dependent variable of the other. Precisely because of this somewhat confusing, overlapping synergy, some understanding of the nature of justice is essential to comprehend the distinct power of legitimacy in the international system.

Both the operational and theoretical reasons for treating legitimacy and justice as discrete phenomena will be discussed in this chapter. Before proceeding further, however, it may be helpful to recapitulate the purpose and limits of our inquiry. We have sought to identify legitimacy's power: its capacity to pull those addressed by commands—primarily states—toward uncoerced compliance. This is of peculiar importance in the rule system of states because otherwise, without legitimate rules, there could be no normative system and the community would not have the means to meet, co-operatively, the contemporary challenges of nuclear arms, ozone depletion, desertification, hunger, and virulent disease. The community would also be incapable of promoting systematic development, commerce, science, culture, and transportation. Nevertheless, it is surely true that compliance with rules is not the sole or ultimate goal of any decent social structure, including the global one. If, as may happen in any society, the rules are unjust, reflecting the society's imperfect social values, there may even be a good case for non-compliance. In the international system, however, the first task for now, is to build a rule system of such manifest legitimacy as to engender a broad base of uncoerced habitual *compliance.* Lexically, the task of ensuring the *justice* of that rule system is the second, not the first order of business on the urgent, but still largely unfinished, global agenda.

With that caveat, let us now examine further the *operational* problems and prospects of justice as it relates to the international rule system. To reiterate, these operational problems derive from the fact that justice can only be said to be done to persons, not to collectivities or corporate fictions, unless, as rarely happens, a rule has precisely the same effect on all individuals in the collective or corporate entity. Or, unless one is speaking, as often happens, metaphorically.

Even as to persons, however, the notion of justice became

significantly more difficult to pin down after the divine order began to be disestablished and replaced by moral skepticism. Before the emergence of humanism in sixteenth and seventeenth century western Europe, in the system of Western natural law, with a Christian God as the ultimate source of all commands, the problem of law's justice did not arise, or, at least, it was not perceived as a problem so long as God spoke through one tradition and a single church-state hierarchy. It is only more recently, with the emergence of a positivist rule system and social pluralism such as we find in America and, especially since the breakdown of empire and the decolonization of the global community, that the problem of justice in a pluralist system has become difficult. When different belief systems contend, what can one say about the justice of rules?

The United States, with its many cultures and centers of power, is an approximate analog to the international community. A brief look at the way in which the uniquely American legal philosophy of John Rawls has tried to deal with the problem of justice in the context of our moral-pluralist society thus may help to clarify thinking about justice in the global community and advance an understanding of the formidable operations problems inherent in devising a theoretically and practically acceptable global measure of justice.

Modern American theories of justice, particularly that of Rawls, the leading thinker in the field, have been shaped by the positivist and pluralist assumptions of American constitutionalism. Like the Constitution itself, the American philosophers have been attracted to notions of social contract first developed by Europeans. However, contract theory, originally, did not claim to be a theory of justice—in any event not in the sense in which we use that word today—but of social order. The evolution occurred gradually and without much notice. Beginning with Hobbes's *The Leviathan*,[468] social contract doctrine has been refined by Locke's *The Second Treatise of Civil Government*,[469] Rousseau's *The Social Contract*,[470] and Kant's *The Foundations of the Metaphysics of Morals*.[471] Professor Rawls, in his principal work, *A Theory of Justice*, has brought Locke, Rousseau, and Kant together to infuse the social contract tradition into modern American justice theory.[472]

Locke, like Hobbes, maintained that we are by our nature free, equal—in the sense of autonomous—and independent beings.[473] Consequently, it follows that persons can only be deprived of their estates and liberty, and subjected to the political control of another, if, and to the extent that, each agrees to empower such authority. We do this, Locke said, "by agreeing . . . to join and unite into a community for [our] comfortable, safe, and peaceable living one amongst another, in a secure enjoyment of [our] properties and a greater security against any that are not of it."[474] The theory of social contract thus reinforces the power of rules and the obligation to obey constituted authority, sweeping aside any lingering belief in the divine right of kings or the natural (God-given) authority of laws and substituting a volitional act of freely determined association for the greater good of all. All this, although conceived as explanation of the nation, is quite relevant to the notion of community as it applies to the international system. Its relevance to legitimacy, as we noted in Chapter 12, is apparent. Its relation to justice, however, is less so.

The community formed by the consent of each individual, according to Locke, acts as one body, obeying the will and determination of the majority.[475] Each person, in consenting to join an association of politics, is thereby obliged to submit to the "determination of the majority, and to be concluded by it." Were it otherwise, the original social compact would be meaningless, and we would "be left free and under no other ties than [those existing] before in the state of Nature."[476] Moreover, where the majority cannot make a determination or draw a conclusion, it cannot act as one body, and therefore dissolves.[477]

Writing nearly a century later, Rousseau validated the social compact as "a form of association which defends and protects with all common forces the person and goods of each associate. . . ." The compact calls for "the total alienation of each associate, together with all of his rights, to the entire community."[478] Properly understood, Rousseau believed, the social contract does not depreciate the value of an associate's person and property, but rather appreciates them. Associates in the social union,[479] by giving themselves and their belongings to the community, actually give all this back to themselves, in somewhat altered form. What they acquire are precisely the same rights that they yield to others. They thereby gain an equivalent for everything that they lose. In addition, they gain an augmented collective force for the preservation of what they have.[480] This, too, is relevant to any analysis of legitimacy, not least as it operates in the international community of states. It is also relevant to justice.

Rousseau understood the first virtue of the social contract to be its capacity to organize a collective defense of liberty and order. Second, the social contract also establishes a community with potential for doing justice. Rousseau explained that associates have obligations both to themselves and to every member of the union. These obligations civilize and socialize the members. As they move "from the state of nature to the civil state . . . duty takes the place of [their] physical impulses. . . ."[481] Notions of justice replace instinct as guides to their conduct, thereby giving their actions the morality that had been wanting in the state of nature. "[They are] forced to act on different principles, and to consult [their] reason before listening to [their] inclinations."[482]

Kant, too, observed that the individual, in a social contract, tends to act in accordance with general principles which are intuitively recognized and not self-contradictory: that is, are understood as a "categorical imperative."[483] Examples include the keeping of promises or the telling of truth. In other words, each individual will "act according to that maxim which you can at the same time will to be a universal law."[484] The categorical imperative therefore enables the freedom of each person's will to exist together with the freedom of others according to mutually recognized *coherent* principles.

In all of this, it is apparent that social contract theory came to rely on a rationale in which justice and legitimacy are mingled, rather than clearly distinguished. Citizens should want to obey the rules, the writers contend, because of the evident benefits derived from membership in the community and because the rules will be fair to all in a free association of equals, working in a principled manner by treating likes alike. Only rarely is there recognition of the potential for conflict between the operation of the social contract as a means of ensuring order and security and its regard for individuated liberty and fairness in allocating obligations and rights. Little is made of the capacity of a majority of free and equal citizens to use the law to oppress minorities. Since universal suffrage had not yet appeared, its capacity for populist oppression of dissenting minorities could not have been contemplated, although a premonition of it can be seen in Hobbes profound fear of parliamentarianism.

To be sure, Kant placed great emphasis, as did his contemporary Rousseau, on human dignity and equality. For him, rational beings exist as ends in themselves, and not merely as the means to an end.[485] The systematic union of individuals by common, positivist secular laws is called a "kingdom of ends" because these laws have in view the relation of these beings to one another as ends.[486] In this realm "everything has either value or dignity. Whatever has a value can be replaced by . . . [its] equivalent."[487] Because persons are ends, and may not be used merely as means, they are above all price, and have no equivalent. They therefore possess dignity.[488] In this can be seen emerging a sort of secular morality, a concept of associational justice as dignity.

Nevertheless, it remained for Rawls specifically to build a modern theory of *justice* on these contractarian notions of Locke, Rousseau, and Kant, adapting the idea of the social compact to formulate moral principles.[489] Rawls's project was to devise a formula for measuring the presence or absence of justice in the basic rule structure of a society in which the social compact operates as it should. While Rawls does not seek to advance any particular form of government, his theory is intended to facilitate justice, understood as fairness. His attention is directed almost entirely to the rules and institutions of a closed social system strongly resembling the liberal secular United States. But because even that model has its serious defects—the failure of the Constitution to abolish slavery or to enfranchise blacks, women and the unpropertied class provides the most obvious examples—Rawls uses an idealized social contract model, rather than demonstrate his principles by reference to any system in actual existence. More precisely, he defines justice not in terms of a particular kind of association capable of producing a designated social good, but as one based on an ideal rule of procedure, of decision. Rawls's principles of justice are whatever "free and rational persons concerned to further their own interests would accept in an initial position of equality as defining the fundamental terms of their association."[490] It is the *Process* by which principles of justice are defined which assumes pivotal importance. What the principles produce in the way of "goods" is not irrelevant, but secondary.

Crucial to this process-oriented concept of justice is an idealized social contract infused with the notion of an initial situation of equality among the associates. Rawls refers to it as the "original position," a purely metaphoric construct. Meeting in this original position to devise principles of justice, the parties to the social compact are unaware of their social or class status. They choose principles of justice behind a *veil of ignorance,* by which is meant that they would make their choice lacking specific knowledge of who they are in the real world, in ignorance of their relative strengths, vulnerabilities, and weaknesses. "This [veil of ignorance] assures that no one is advantaged or disadvantaged in the choice of principles by the outcome of natural chance or the contingency of social circumstances. Since all are similarly situated and no one is able to design principles to favor his particular condition, the principles of justice are the result of a fair agreement or bargain."[491]

The veil of ignorance is the essential element of the original position since it implements the element of fairness that is essential to Rawls's theory. But there are three other components of the original position which also need to be understood before seeking to apply Rawlsian notions of justice—the most relevant available model—to the international system: the *circumstances of justice, formal constraints on the concept of right,* and *rationality of the parties.*

Circumstances of justice[492] refers to the background conditions which make social co-operation necessary in the original position. From an objective standpoint, there must exist a condition of *moderate scarcity*. By this Rawls means that parties must be in a situation of mutual co-existence with numerous claims to limited resources. In a Garden of Eden, the notion of justice would be irrelevant and the need to develop its principles behind a veil of ignorance would be a *non sequitur*. Subjectively, parties must possess their own life plans, which Rawls refers to as *conceptions of the good*, and these conceptions must consequently come into continuous conflict, each person being primarily interested in promoting his or her own well-being. Only in these circumstances is a notion of distributional justice relevant. As Rawls points out, "circumstances of justice obtain whenever . . . persons put forward conflicting claims to the division of social advantages under conditions of moderate scarcity."[493]

Formal constraints of the concept of right[494] are procedural limitations which Rawls believes must operate in the original position if principles of justice are to be negotiated successfully. The first constraint is that all principles of justice agreed upon must be *general* in form: "it must be possible to formulate them without the use of what would be intuitively recognized as proper names, or rigged definite descriptions."[495] Second, they must be *universal*, holding for everyone by virtue of their being moral persons.[496] Third, there must be *publicity*. Everyone in the community must be able to know what principles have been accepted. Fourth, there must be a process by which conflicting claims arising in respect of the application of an agreed general principle can be *ordered* through a process independent of such factors as the parties' social position, or intimidation and coercion. Fifth, the system of principles established in the initial position must be *final* in that "[t]here are no higher standards to which arguments in support of claims can be addressed."[497] In sum, Rawls states, "a conception of right is a set of principles, general in form and universal in application, that is to be publicly recognized as a final court of appeal for ordering the conflicting claims of moral persons."[498]

Rationality of the parties[499] is assumed in discussion of the original position. As explained by Rawls, "[a] rational person is thought to have a coherent set of preferences between the options open to him. He ranks these options according to how well they further his purposes; he follows the plan which will satisfy more of his desires rather than less, and which has the greater chance of being successfully executed."[500] Consequently, the principles of justice are derived through a process that seeks to maximize the self-interest of each participant in the social compact, given their limited information about the community and their role in it. In other words, the parties are deemed to have in their heads a map of the sort of society to which they want to belong even though they do not know what their role in it will be. They are assumed to intend to pursue the building of such a society in a rational manner by negotiating applicable general principles to govern that society's operations. Stated another way, "persons in the original position try to acknowledge principles which advance their system of ends as far as possible. They do this by attempting to win for themselves the highest index of primary social goods, since this enables them to promote their conception of the good most effectively whatever it turns out to be."[501]

This, in outline, is Rawls's process for determining the community's principles of justice, presented as a ritual in which participants negotiate the social compact behind a veil of ignorance, which guarantees that they will choose neutral principles because they lack biasing knowledge of their role, circumstances, talents, and infirmities in "real" life. They bargain in socio-economic conditions of moderate scarcity and have conflicting claims to limited resources that reflect their various conceptions of the social good.

What choices will such negotiators make? Where will their preferences overlap to form general principles? Rawls believes that under the posited conditions, parties acting rationally and in compliance with the formal constraints of the concept of right will agree on two principles for ordering the basic institutional structure of society. The first, the *Principle of Liberty*, would state that "Each person is to have an equal right to the most extensive basic liberty compatible with a similar liberty for others."[502] The second, the *Principle of Equality*, would state that "Social and economic inequalities are to be arranged so that they are both (a) to the greatest benefit of the least advantaged and (b) attached to offices and positions open to all under conditions of fair equality of opportunity."[503]

Moreover, these two principles would emerge in "lexical order." Rawls explains that "[t]his is an order which requires us to satisfy the first principle in the ordering before we can move to the second. . . . [T]he basic structure of society is to arrange the inequalities of wealth and authority in ways consistent with the equal liberties required by the preceding principle."[504]

As we have noted, Rawls speaks, essentially, to justice in the national community, to which he refers as "a special case of the problem of justice."[505] By this he means that his notions of how principles of justice are negotiated behind the veil of ignorance assumes that the negotiators are drawing up rules "for the basic structure of [a] society conceived . . . as a closed system isolated from other societies."[506] Thus, his principles are not necessarily applicable to a multinational gathering of negotiators, and Rawls admits that "the law of nations may require different principles arrived at in a somewhat different way."[507] Nevertheless, after describing the principles for domestic justice (the basic institutional structure for an ideal society of persons),[508] Rawls does briefly consider the problem of justice in the international arena.[509]

He begins by reinterpreting his concept of the original position as follows:

> [O]ne may extend the interpretation of the original position and think of the parties as representatives of different nations who must choose together the fundamental principles to adjudicate conflicting claims among states. Following out the conception of the initial situation, I assume that these representatives are deprived of various kinds of information. While they know that they represent different nations each living under the normal circumstances of human life, they know nothing about the particular circumstances of their own society. . . . Once again the contracting parties, in this case, representatives of states, are allowed only enough knowledge to make a rational

choice to protect their interests but not so much that the more fortunate among them can take advantage of their special situation. This original position is fair between nations; it nullifies the contingencies and biases of historical fate. Justice between states is determined by the principles that would be chosen in the original position so interpreted.[510]

Rawls does not argue for any specific international principles, but, instead, presumes that states would agree to principles that are already familiar to us. Citing Professor Brierly,[511] he does suggest what some of these are likely to be. The first might be that states are endowed with certain fundamental equal rights, ones which are analogous to the equal rights of citizens under a constitutional government. Starting here, Rawls finds it possible to deduce some other principles to which states would agree in the original position, including those that approximate "liberty." Thus, in addition to the notion of equality, states might agree to the principles of *non-intervention* and *self-determination*.

We will use these two hypothetical principles to test the applicability of Rawls's notion of justice to the international community, using them to examine whether *any* general principles of justice arrived at in the prescribed manner could serve as a reliable yardstick with which to measure justice in the global rule system.

To make this examination, we will assume that representatives of the world's states have gathered to try to agree on an applicable principle of justice without knowing which nations they represent, but aware of an actual crisis to which a just rule could be applied if one could be negotiated to everyone's satisfaction. The first crisis implicates the principle of *non-intervention* and the second the principle of *self-determination*, the two which Rawls himself thought likely to result from the operation of his model.

Scenario #1 (non-intervention): Suppose control of the sovereign state of Malarkey, with a population of 7 million, had been seized from a democratic but corrupt government by an army coup headed by a paranoid colonel who instituted a reign of terror against the middle class, professionals, civil servants, and anyone with more than an elementary education. In the first twelve months, a million civilians had been executed summarily, half a million were arbitrarily imprisoned or had disappeared. The economy was destroyed and two million starving refugees fled to neighboring states. The foreign ministers of the nations have gathered to discuss what, if anything should be done. Should they intervene collectively to stop the killing? Should neighboring states intervene to stanch the flow of refugees across their borders? Or should Malarkey be left alone to resolve its own problems? Is it possible for states' representatives, in the original position, negotiating behind the veil of ignorance, to arrive at an applicable principle of justice to guide their actions? What might such a principle look like?

As noted in the previous section, Rawls has addressed this problem briefly. Using his veil of ignorance metaphor, he has pictured *representatives of states*, unaware of which nations they represent, arriving at a general principle of *non-intervention*.

In his conception of the international original position, Rawls postulates a world of separate and equal states, sovereign and autonomous entities, analogous to those persons Kant defined as ends in themselves.[512] Representatives of these nations, negotiating behind the veil of ignorance, naturally would arrive at a principle of justice which recognized a fundamental *equality* between "independent peoples organized as states,"[513] because *that is what the negotiators represent*. Using Rawls's model, one would also expect the negotiators to agree on this principle of non-intervention as justice for the further good reason that, being ignorant of whether "their" states are powerful or weak, threatened or threatening, they would seek first to preserve their governments' autonomy in a world of gross power disparity.

Non-intervention as a principle of justice, however, requires that the foreign ministers, meeting against the backdrop of the Malarkey case, *do nothing*. But that cannot be right. Doing nothing looks suspiciously like the Hobbesian understanding of the state of nature. For Hobbes, the state of nature is populated by persons who are equal and autonomous. In it, he said, *no* moral principles can govern.[514] If nations exist in the state of nature, then, similarly, no moral rules apply to them because "in states, and commonwealths not dependent on one another, every commonwealth . . . has an absolute liberty to do what it shall judge . . . most conducing to [its] benefit."[515] Hobbes would neither require states to intervene nor to abstain from intervention, so long as the state of nature prevails in their domain. Each nation would act solely on self-interest, not on principle. Professor Charles Beitz characterizes this not as justice but as "international moral skepticism,"[516] although Professor Antonio Cassese has noted that the desire of states to be seen as autonomous and equal has become more prevalent than ever, with a hundred new nations jealously guarding their hard-won sovereign prerogatives.[517]

While the state of nature may, indeed, describe one tendency in contemporary Realpolitik, it would be exceedingly odd if that were to coincide with an ideal of justice. Such coincidence between what the negotiators in the original position agree upon, and Hobbes's state of nature, should warn us that something must be wrong with the model producing that result.

According to such an idiosyncratic account of justice, no state would ever be justified in intervening in the internal affairs of any other. The agreement reached behind the veil of ignorance would require states to leave Malarkey alone to sort out its own problems. Applying such a principle, justice would have been served when the world left Hitler free to kill the Jews of Germany and Field Marshal Idi Amin and Pol Pot free to decimate the populations of Uganda and Cambodia. Before these recent developments, John Stuart Mill could still plausibly extol the virtue of non-intervention on the ground that leaving nations alone to deal with their own problems of misgovernment builds their moral character.[518] With today's hindsight, that seems rather unfeeling or jejune.

Intuitively, we know these to be untenable results. The principle of non-intervention cannot lead both to Hobbes's brutish state of nature and also to Rawls's community of just principles. That the principle of non-intervention compels non-interference in Malarkey should stir doubts not only about Rawls's proposed principle, but about the process by which it was reached: the metaphorical negotiation of representatives of *governments* behind the veil of ignorance. Perhaps this is simply the wrong way to think about principles of justice in the international community.

We have already observed that a negotiation between governments inevitably would favor a principle of non-intervention because it liberates governments, within their own borders, to do largely as they please. This might seem *just* to governments, but does not necessarily do justice to their citizens. Nevertheless, it is important to note that the principle treats governments equally, and undoubtedly meets the moral expectations of many who govern. Governments do share the belief that they have a moral right to govern without interference from "outside." Second, the representatives of governments, negotiating principles of justice, are also likely to choose non-intervention because, not knowing which governments they represent, the weak or the powerful, it would be rational for them to agree on a principle which best protects an autonomy professed by all. The negotiators, acting rationally, would suspect that a principle *permitting* intervention, even if limited to particularly egregious regimes, could easily be abused by the powerful, who would be tempted to see it as a license to intervene in the affairs of the weak for their own parochial purposes. Third, governments concerned with maintaining the delicate balance on which rests the aspiration for world peace, would favor a rule which precludes the use of force in ways that could lead to unpredictable and unmanageable consequences.

Thus rational governmental representatives would agree upon an absolute principle of non-intervention; and they would agree because the negotiators would have the shared moral perspective of *governments*. It is the special self-interest of governments—all governments—to protect their authority against external intervention, and to prefer order above other virtues. It is this shared governmental perspective which would shape the international principle of justice if we proceed to define it by the metaphorical process developed by Rawls. The result, however, is not a principle which yields justice for the people of Malarkey.

That false result, alone, does not render inoperable the veil of ignorance as a useful way to think about justice. But it does invalidate the assumption that one can think about principles of international justice by imagining a negotiation between representatives of *states*. The metaphor would become more useful if one were to substitute as the metaphorical negotiators all *persons*, or *representatives* of all persons *who are not engaged in governing states*. The characteristics of such non-governmental persons would provide us with clues as to what principles those individuals would probably agree upon. They would choose principles advancing *personal*—not governmental—autonomy and equality. They would imagine the possibility that, emerging from behind the veil, they might find that they were prisoners of conscience, disappeared persons, or torture victims of their own governments. Presumably they would balance those personal concerns with their concerns for national security and independence.

This difference in the perspective of governments and citizens is fully born out by examining contemporary state practice. Real nations, not behind Rawls's veil but, rather, practicing actual multilateral diplomacy, tend to prefer to act in accordance with a principle which elevates non-intervention above such humanitarian concerns as are evident in the Malarkey case. For this reason, when contemplating military intervention, the United Nations usually has preferred not to differentiate between just and unjust reasons to intervene. Instead, the nations have favored treating all states as autonomous entities entitled to be left alone, and doing so on grounds of maintaining international peace and order, rather than advancing justice. At least in their public posture, nations seem almost to agree with Hobbes that, in the world "nothing can be unjust. The notions of right and wrong, justice and injustice have no place."[519] While Hobbes thus avoids endorsing any rule, such reticence does not infect article 2(4) of the U.N. Charter,[520] which categorically proscribes the "threat" or use of force against the territorial integrity or political independence" of any nation, without distinguishing between Malarkey and Denmark. Moreover, the Charter pointedly prohibits the international community "to intervene in matters which are essentially within the domestic jurisdiction of any state" (article 2(7)). The U.N. Declarations on Principles of International Law Concerning Friendly Relations and Co-operation Among States and on Inadmissibility of Intervention[521]—both relatively recent formulations of global normative consensus—also give high priority to the principle of nonintervention.

What the texts suggest, the behavior of states confirms. Despite ample, credible reports of government-sanctioned genocide in Cambodia, the nations did not act,[522] choosing, instead, to deplore the Vietnamese military intervention which ended the tenure of the offending regime.[523] Governments reacted out of concern for national autonomy, and fear of the destabilizing effect of any recourse to military force, not concern for justice. They seem to have preferred to rally around a rule perceived as advancing not justice but orderliness and to bar violence against governments rather than against *persons*.

Similarly, in 1971, the U.N. called on India to withdraw its troops and observe a cease-fire after its army had joined Bengali insurgents to end Pakistan's bloody repression in the territory that became the state of Bangladesh.[524] Both the Vietnamese and Indian humanitarian interventions undeniably believed what, in any defensible conception of justice, must surely be recogizable intuitively as injustice. Yet the U.N.—the community of states—unblinkingly chose to reaffirm the norm of non-intervention in circumstances that must make justice weep.

Regrettably, yet understandably, states seem reluctant to distinguish between interventions that may be said to advance human rights—as in the cases of Cambodia or Bangladesh—and interventions, such as those of the Soviets in Afghanistan[525] and the U.S. in Nicaragua,[526] which—arguably—do not. Where regimes have slaughtered tens of thousands of their own citizens, as in Cambodia, Uganda, and Burundi, the U.N. has remained mute and passive. It is, after all, a community of *governments*.

This preference of those who govern for order over justice is exemplified by Abraham Lincoln's letter to Horace Greeley of August 22, 1862, more than a year after the commencement of the Civil War:

My paramount object in this struggle is to save the Union, and is not either to save or to destroy slavery. If I could save the Union without freeing any slave, I would do it; and if I could save it by freeing all the slaves, I would do it; and if I could do it by freeing some and leaving others alone, I would also do that.

So, too, in the international system. Even the most enlightened of those who govern first seek to preserve an orderly, predictable state system. Only to the extent order can be advanced by justice will justice be done. This leaves the international system some leeway to make, or interpret, rules in consonance with their intuitive notions of justice. In confronting a case of extreme injustice, it may even bend the rules a little. For example, Tanzania was not criticized by the members of the U.N. for its invasion of Uganda, which toppled Idi Amin at last. India, while told to withdraw its troops, was not actually condemned for invading East Pakistan (Bangladesh). France escaped uncensured when its troops ousted Emperor Bokassa of the Central African Empire after he had begun to murder large numbers of children. Israel was not penalized, or even seriously reprimanded, for its invasion of Uganda to liberate hostages hijacked to Entebbe.[527] Still, in the eyes of most states, just and unjust interventions tend to be lumped together as posing manifestly unacceptable risks to states' autonomy and safety.[528]

That is the *governmental* perspective. In defense of Rawls's model, it should be noted that his negotiators, although representing the regimes of the world, could be expected to have a different perspective because they would reach issues of international justice only *after* agreeing on the principles of justice applicable to their domestic systems of governance. They would represent only *just* governments.

This might produce quite a different negotiating dynamic. Professor David Richards has concluded that such *just* negotiators, "where there is a grave violation of equal liberty within institutions . . . will view war . . . [as] a justified means in stopping this. . . . [They] are concerned not with the well-being of institutions . . . but with the well-being of persons; and thus, it is perfectly natural that the contractors may approve the destruction of a certain nation, if it severely frustrates the interests of its populace."[529]

This version of Rawls's model permits us to imagine rules of justice for a world of *just* states. Unfortunately, this is a formidable barrier to theoretical speculation, requiring us—counter-intuitively—to imagine two things at once: just nations making a just world. It does not much help in the task of defining principles of justice for the real world. On the other hand, any version of the Rawls model which shifts the perspective to that of non-governing persons will encounter much the same problem of unreality. What would be the relevance of the principles arrived at from that perspective? Very few secular rules of the international system apply to individuals, while almost all apply to states. This makes it virtually inevitable that these rules, made by and for governments, would not be congruent with principles of justice devised by the governed, or by an assemblage of perfectly just governments.

To put it another way, if we were to apply a measure of justice derived from the perspective of *persons*, the international rule system is likely to appear more unjust than almost any nation's legal system, precisely because the structure of the international system is that of a concert of rulers rather than a parliament of humanity. The priorities and sensibilities of rulers, not the people's shared (or intersecting) notions of justice, usually frame the contents of the rules and also have the most say in determining their compliance pull.

Scenario #2 (self-determination): Imagine a sovereign state of Euphoria with a population consisting of two different ethnic groups: the *Sucrose* and the *Lactose* peoples. The former inhabit the northern region, the latter the south. Sucrose people make up 60 percent and Lactose 40 percent of the population. For generations, the Sucrose have dominated the Lactose. By virtue of their numerical superiority, the Sucrose have dominated Euphoria's elected parliament and used this majority to impose various restrictions on the Lactose minority. Lactose citizens are restricted to 20 percent of jobs in the public sector of the economy, 20 percent of the land, and that in the inclement southern mountains of the country, and 20 percent of places in the public schools and universities. Legislation enacted ten years ago by the parliament has imposed a stiff poll tax on Euphoria's voters which effectively disenfranchises most Lactose citizens, who are poor. Sucrose has been made the sole official language of the nation. The effect of all this has been to create a Lactose secessionist movement, with a political wing which campaigns peacefully for a Lactose homeland, and an underground army, which fights for the same objectives.

The political and military struggle in Euphoria has been under way for a decade, since the enactment of the poll tax. It has disrupted life not only in Euphoria, but also in the neighboring states, where thousands of refugees from Euphoria's civil strife—both Sucrose and Lactose—are now camped. The war is also causing severe economic, social, and political dislocation throughout Euphoria. The world's foreign ministers are meeting to try, in Rawls's original position, to devise a principle of justice relevant to this crisis. Do the Sucrose people have a moral right to secede and should such a right be recognized by the international community?

As we have seen, Rawls did briefly address this problem, too. Behind the veil of ignorance, he suggested, rational state representatives would agree upon a right of *self-determination* as a general principle of justice. In this he could be right only if the nations whose representatives were negotiating the applicable principle of justice were themselves models of justice.

Professor Beitz has observed that the concept of self-determination can be regarded as the "positive" aspect of state autonomy.[530] While the principle of non-intervention protects the rights of states already independent, self-determination protects the independence option of nations under foreign control. Non-intervention is conservative, tending to preserve the international status quo. Self-determination, however, is dynamic in that it sanctions change in the structure of the international order. It is apparent that the two principles, rather than invariably supporting one another, actually may sometimes conflict.

As we noted in some detail in Chapter 10, the idea that national or ethnic groups are entitled to "self-determination" began to be applied in the settlement of post-World War I European land claims. After World War II, the principle of self-determination was expanded to include colonial possession in Africa, Asia, and the Americas. It was spelled out in the U.N. Charter which obliges the colonial powers to "develop self-government, to take due account of the political aspirations of the peoples, and to assist them in the progressive development of their free political institutions. . . ."[531] Between 1947 and 1977, nearly one billion people benefited from this right.

However, while the European application of the principle of self-determination in the 1920s had encouraged the breakup of multi-ethnic nations like Austro-Hungary and the Ottoman empire and led to wholesale rearrangement of boundaries as various groups elected to shift allegiance, the principle operated differently in Africa and Asia in the period following World War II. In the latter, self-determination was defined in almost every instance as a right exercisable collectively by all the inhabitants of an existing colony within the colony's sacrosanct borders. Many of these colonies, however, had been created quite arbitrarily by the imperial powers, lumping together disparate races, cultures, and religions. Applied in this way, self-determination did not advance but actually frustrated the ambitions of various tribes and other groups. The resultant denials of self-determination—for example by Nigeria to the secessionist Ibo tribal state of Biafra[532]—was vigorously defended on grounds not of fairness but of order and legitimacy. The application of the principle to permit tribal secession, it was argued, would create chaos throughout Africa and end in an economically and politically devastating balkanization. Besides, each new multi-tribal nation was itself legitimate: usually it had come into being by a recognized, well-established process with determinate procedural rules and had been validated by pedigreed institutions such as the United Nations, the parliament of the colonial power, and by the political process of the colony itself.

As we saw in Chapter 10, the new states of the third world, drafting the U.N. Declaration on Granting of Independence to Colonial Countries and Peoples,[533] had proclaimed the principle that "[a]ll persons have the right to self-determination" but had also carefully added the order-and-legitimacy-based caveat that "[a]ny attempt aimed at the partial or total disruption of the national unity and the territorial integrity of a country is incompatible with the purposes and principles of the United Nations."[534] This contradiction was reinforced, rather than resolved, in subsequent General Assembly iterations.[535] Soon powerful African and Asian states, themselves only recently freed from alien rule, felt free to send military aid to sister governments forcibly repressing disaffected minorities seeking to secede. Most remarkable is the recent spectacle of India providing troops to suppress the secessionist movement in Sri Lanka mounted by Tamils of Indian origin. There are other such paradoxes. Nigeria sought and received military assistance from its former colonial masters, the British, to extinguish secessionist Biafra. Zimbabwe, having only recently gained control of the country from its white settlers[536] vigorously used a large white-led militia to suppress secessionism among the Ndebele tribe in its western region.[537] As for the United Nations, it actually dispatched a large multinational military force led by Irish and Swedish troops to prevent a populist tribal secession in the Katanga province of newly independent Zaire.[538]

Against this background of state practice can be set Rawls's belief that self-determination is a general principle of justice at which representatives of nations would arrive in a negotiation behind the veil of ignorance. If this were so, the meeting of foreign ministers, addressing the problems of Euphoria, would formulate a principle of justice that would recognize the right of the Lactose people to choose independence. By validating the Lactose cause, the community of nations would give it reinforcement even without recourse to military intervention. It would probably justify states, individually or collectively, helping the Lactose to achieve justice.

However, we know that this is not the principle upon which the Foreign Ministers would agree. States—that is, governments, *all* governments—would hesitate to adopt so dynamic and centrifugal a principle. Like Lincoln, they would give priority to preserving the union—*any* union. As governments, they would favor cohesion, unity, and order. We know this because such postcolonial secessionist movements as those in Biafra and Kashmir have met with almost no support from any governments. This tells

us something about governments: that it is generally in their nature to abhor secession. It would follow that a negotiation in the
original position, among persons who knew that they represented
governments, even if not which, would very quickly agree on a
principle not of self-determination but of something else: that
sovereign, equal *states* have a right to "territorial integrity." In
plainer words, they have the same "right" the U.S. exercised when
it crushed the Confederacy. Such a principle of justice would have
almost nothing to do with justice as *people* might understand it,
but everything to do with the way governments naturally think.

It is highly unlikely that government negotiators would agree
on the Wilsonian principle that every discrete ethnic group is entitled to self-determination "on demand" and regardless of circumstances. Even Wilson compromised the principle in such cases as
the Rhineland.[539] In its purest form, the principle has been cham-
pioned by John Stuart Mill, who wrote: "Where the sentiment of
nationality exists in any force, there is a *prima facie* case for unit-
ing all the members of the nationality under the same government,
and a government to themselves apart."[540] In practice, however,
few, if any, genuine representatives of governments, even behind
the veil of ignorance, would subscribe to a principle of justice defined with so little regard for the national security, economic well-
being, and stability of nations.

If, on the other hand, Rawls's negotiators were representatives
of people, rather than governments, they would be able—indeed
might even be compelled by prudence—to imagine themselves as the
Lactose people, or other oppressed disentitled minorities around
the globe, and all might therefore choose a principle which sought
to respond to the most basic concerns of victims. For example,
they might agree that minorities should be given as much liberty
to secede as was compatible with the rights of the non-seceding
others to live within secure, defensible boundaries and with a viable economy. Or, as we proposed in Chapter 10, they might argee
that justice entitles minorities *persistently denied equal rights* to
separate from the oppressing state and form their own nation.
They might also concede that neighboring peoples have a right to
help victims achieve separation where such intervention *is the*

only, or the fastest, least costly and painful, way to realize that just result. Some similar principle of justice might also have been reached if one had imagined a negotiation among the foreign ministers of all states which, as a precondition, had already satisfied all the conditions of justice in the organization of their national societies. As suggested in Chapter 10, even existing governments might be imagined as moving toward enunciating a new, coherent concept of self-determination which is both legitimate and also just: but they have not yet done so, which is why the concept is in danger of falling into desuetude.

In the real world, nations have not reached the state of perfect domestic justice, and the interests of governments often do not accord with the justice-based claims of its citizens. Thus the international system, based on rules made among states to suit the overlapping priorities of governments, cannot be expected consistently to generate real principles of justice. In reality, only *individuals* have the capacity to enjoy or suffer, be happy, or sad, satisfied or hungry. A rule or principle can only be fair *to a nation* if the nation itself distributes to its citizens in a just fashion all the aggregate benefits derived from the application of the rule or principle. In most collectives it cannot be presumed that this will happen. Thus, when we speak of justice between states we usually speak not literally but metaphorically.

This metaphoric quality of justice among states can be demonstrated by a simple example. State Alpha, ruled by a ruthless dictator, is attacked by state Beta, also ruled by a dictator. Alpha manages to defeat Beta, which sues for peace. The price of peace is the payment of five billion dollars in compensation by the government of Beta to the dictator of Alpha. Beta's government raises the money by a head tax on each citizen. Alpha's ruler deposits the payment in his Swiss bank account. In a metaphoric sense, the payment of reparations by Beta to Alpha seems to satisfy the sense of justice, since Beta did, indeed, attack Alpha without provocation. In reality, however, the injustice of this outcome is demonstrated by the answer to the question: who pays and who receives payment?

The metaphorical use of justice to describe a fair arrangement between states may be appropriate if it reflects the identity of citizens' interest in specific instances. For example, all citizens of Russia and the U.S. may be said to benefit alike when Soviet and American governments obey the just—and, as it happens, very legitimate—rule against initiating nuclear aggression. In that instance, it is possible to say that the rule is just because all persons benefit as equals. But the 1988 free trade agreement between Canada and the United States, while it imposes the same terms of commerce on both nations, is only metaphorically just to all Americans and all Canadians. In actual operation, it benefits some citizens of each nation more than others. This may be the result of a deliberate decision to promote not justice but efficiency. Whatever that treaty's rationale, its justice cannot be demonstrated by comparing the aggregate gains and losses of each country, but only by examining the fairness of the way those collective benefits and costs are allocated among all individuals. Since few institutions and rules of the international system address individuals—human rights constitute one important exception—their justice in the literal, as opposed to metaphorical, sense is not on the negotiators' agenda. Moreover, if the legitimacy of these institutions and rules were conditioned on their justice, most would be found sadly wanting. That is the gist of the operational reason for not including justice among the indicators of legitimacy.

An especially dramatic example of this is the set of rules by which the system determines and recognizes nationality. These rules are certainly legitimate. They are determinate (the ground rules are quite clearly fixed), symbolically validated by long usage, coherent and reinforced by adherence to a hierarchy of rules about rules. But there is nothing about the rules of nationality which is just in the sense of being fair to persons. On the contrary, the rules governing bestowal and recognition of nationality severely distort individual life chances by their deference to place of birth and parentage. The egregious unfairness these rules promote, however, but little undermines states' perception of their legitimacy.

The rules applicable among states cannot be expected to embody principles of justice because the notion of *states*, itself, is an arbitrary and unfair suspension of personal equality. It embodies a difference principle no student of justice would accept.

Rawls himself conceded that his justice principles "apply only within the borders of a nation-state."[541] His Harvard colleague, Robert Keohane, contends that "states cannot be considered independent subjects of moral theory; a justification of the morality of states . . . must ultimately be made in terms of the rights and interests of individual human beings."[542] The evolution of a system of global justice, therefore, must await, and go hand in hand with, the system's transformation from one based on states to one based on the primacy of world government and global citizenship. Universal *individual* rights may be an historic imperative whose day will come; but it is not yet fully upon us.

In summary, the system of states, which is the basic contemporary circumstance of the international community, vastly complicates the task of discerning applicable principles of justice. The best model is the one devised by John Rawls; but when it is translated from the national to the international political context, it yields odd, counter-instinctive results. It can be applied, if at all, only by replacing the foreign ministers Rawls would summon to negotiate in the original position with an entirely different set of non-governmental representatives, or with negotiators representing not states as we know them, but infinitely more graceful regimes. The difficulty in using Rawls's model of negotiating foreign ministers merely illustrates the difficulty in applying the test of justice to rules devised by, and for, states. It also leads to a more *theoretical* examination of the differences between justice and legitimacy as evidenced by their different teleological design.

The tendency we have observed, so evident in early social contractarian writing, to move without notice from the justice concept to the legitimacy concept, as if they were the same, or as if one contained the other, is due in part to wishful thinking. We would *like* the rules to be both legitimate and just and therefore are inclined, in hortatory writing, to pretend that they are *neither* when they are not *both*. More often, the confusion is due to a certain similarity in their effects. Justice, like legitimacy, pulls toward rule-compliance. Indeed, some rules exert a particularly strong compliance pull precisely because they are perceived as both just and legitimate. One example is the previously discussed rule that nations should act in accordance with solemn treaty commitments, even when it is inconvenient to do so and they have the power to choose to do otherwise. This rule—*pacta sunt servanda*—as it happens, exerts a strong pull towards compliance powered *both by its justice and its legitimacy*. The *justice*-based claim, nevertheless, is different from the *legitimacy*-based one, even though both claims happen to use identical rule-text to pull toward compliance. That difference is of sufficient theoretical importance to warrant more detailed consideration. It is important, for our purposes, because the task of distinguishing between the two concepts helps us understand the nature and function—as well as the limits of the power—of legitimacy in the international community.

The legitimacy-based claim of *pacta sunt servanda* derives from a *secular* political community's preference for, and dependence on, order and predictability. The identical-appearing justice-based claim, in contrast, derives from the belief of a community of *shared moral values*—what Rawls calls a common concept of right—that fairness requires the honoring of commitments. Justice always has a moral basis, even though morality encompasses far more than justice. In a community of moral values, promises are sacred because trust and reciprocity are believed to be instrumental in advancing not *order*, but *fairness*.

The example illustrates that a secular rule and a moral rule may cover similar ground, yet derive from a very different set of teleological imperatives. That "promises should be kept" happens to be a rule both of a secular and of a moral order. Both the legitimacy of the secular rule and the justice of the moral rule may exert a similar, powerful pull toward uncoerced compliance. Nevertheless, two different and independent energies empower that pull, reflecting the duality of each person's distinct secular and moral being.

The secular rule appeals to our need for orderly procedures and predictable outcomes. It should be recalled that the perception of an institution's, or a rule's, legitimacy was defined, in Chapter 1, as deriving from a generally held belief that the institution or rule has come into being and operates in accordance with generally accepted principles of right process. These elements of right process, which are the subject of this book, define the legitimacy of rules, institutions, and, ultimately, the political or secular community itself. Determinacy, symbolic validation, coherence, and adherence are the building blocks of this right process.

Justice, however, is quite another matter. The moral rule appeals to our awareness that the allocation of finite resources in society must take into account the equality with which all persons are endowed by virtue of their common membership a moral community. That and other agreed principles of justice, if implemented by rules and rule making or rule-applying institutions, creates a just society. The perception of an institution's, or a rule's, justice thus may be said to derive from the belief that it operates in accordance with certain principles of fairness and decency shared by all members of a moral order who hold common or overlapping fundamental moral values.

Membership of a particular moral community may, but need not, be co-extant with that of a secular political one. The tiny Asian mountain nation of Bhutan may encompass both sociopolitical and religious communities composed of all the people of that nation. They may not even recognize such a split in their allegiance. Most Western nations, however, encompass various coexisting communities of shared moral values. These cut across, and come together in, shifting political alliances. They engage in a sort of continuing mixed moral-political discourse that constitutes civil war by other means. As for the world, while it may be taking shape as a secular political community, it has barely begun to coalesce into a moral community with universally shared or overlapping values and concepts of justice, and is unlikely to do so in the foreseeable future. At best, it somewhat resembles the secular liberal democracies to the extent it accommodates differing moral values within one functioning secular community. Unlike the liberal democracies, however, the global secular system does this less by compromising, than by *de-emphasizing* the importance of, diverse precepts of right. Iranian Shiite fundamentalists, Irish Catholics,

Orthodox Israelis, Indian Hindu secularists, American Episcopalians, and West African Animists may share a world of states and secular rules, but not a common system of values, a globalized understanding of fairness, or a shared canon of justice principles. They may agree that armed aggression is too dangerous to permit, yet disagree about the rights of workers, women, homosexuals, the unborn, blasphemous or pornographic writers, and usurous bankers. Compromise on such matters remains elusive. The co-existence of radically different concepts of right within an emergent global secular system often is made possible by emphasizing the manifest *legitimacy* of secular rules while deliberately postponing to another day considerations of justice.

In recognizing such lexical priority of legitimacy over justice, the global community is only different in degree from the secular democracies. For example, in the U.S., there may be agreement as to the legitimacy of a secular rule found in the text of the Constitution, a decision of the Supreme Court, or a law written by Congress, even when it pertains to a value-charged issue such as abortion, providing the rule was made, or the command issued, in accordance with generally accepted principles of right process. But alongside, there will persist a lively, continuing (if generally civilized) disagreement as to the morality, justice, and fairness of an admittedly legitimate rule or command. Most persons, at least in Western nations, nowadays hold views of a rule's legitimacy and its justice, and they hold these views concurrently but separately. Sometimes justice and legitimacy may appear to coincide, thereby mutually reinforcing a command's compliance pull; at other times and in other instances, not.

If such a bifurcation—the separation of justice and legitimacy— is essential to any Western secular state in which diverse moral value systems must co-exist, it is a far greater imperative for a *global* secular rule community. The justice of even the most basic secular rules will be assessed differently by the various moral value systems which co-exist, however uneasily, within a still-fragile secular global community. That community would have few rules, if the validity of each rule depended on shared perceptions of its justice. In building a secular community, it is often useful to focus on shared principles without examining too closely the reasons why members agree, lest the agreement evaporate. For example, David Hume thought that the obligation to keep promises was a key building block in the construction of a community, but characterized that obligation as purely a secular invention. He insisted that "promises have no natural obligation, and are mere artificial contrivances for the convenience and advantage of society . . . built entirely on public interest and convenience."[543] Hugo Grotius, too, subscribed to the principle, but thought that *pacta sunt servanda* is sanctioned by rules of nature: that "nothing else is so congruous with natural equity and the good faith of mankind, as is the observance of agreements which have been accepted among the various parties." Hume and Grotius might both have been able to accept Cicero's proposition that "good faith [keeping promises] is the foundation of justice,"[544] providing they did not examine too closely their understanding of "justice."

The duty to obey treaties can be accepted either as a convenient social contrivance or as a principle derived from God or nature. It is possible to believe that an obligation assumed by a promise has a moral weight determined by its justice or that its gravity derives from the legitimacy of the formal process of commitment. From this it does not follow, however, that the two pulls to compliance are dependent, or that they are the same. A treaty which is just, either metaphorically or literally, is not necessarily a legitimate one. For example, a treaty between two states barring the use of nuclear weapons is no less just if it has been extorted by one party from the other by force; yet that may make the agreement both illegitimate and invalid. The converse is equally demonstrable. A rule might well be legitimate, yet unjust. For example, a principle dividing equally the water resources of a river shared by two nations could be perfectly legitimate if it is determinate, entered into in accordance with the long-recognized rules about rule-making, and if it is coherent with generally used principles of resource allocation. Yet the rule's equal division of river resources may be unjust if the population of one of the two nations is ten times greater than that of the other.[545]

Both secular and moral values appear to reinforce the notion of *pacta sunt servanda,* at least in the *abstract.* Nevertheless, many rules or commands do not speak in tones of such mellifluous confluence between justice and legitimacy. A treaty may be the locus of a lively dispute between those who wish to see it obeyed because it is legitimate even though unjust and others who wish to see it repealed or even violated because it is unjust although legitimate. Indeed, the survival of a secular community depends upon its willingness to accommodate divergent views as to the justice of its legitimate secular rules and institutions. Survival also depends upon the willingness of those who think a rule unjust nevertheless to recognize *provisionally* the validating power of its legitimacy, even while the moral factions dispute its justice.

In a secular community which accommodates diverse communities of moral principle, the secular rules usually find a way to accommodate a notion of conscientious objection, or of civil disobedience, thereby making allowance for the deep moral commitment to justice of those who cannot bend their consciences beyond a breaking point. Such accommodation between justice and legitimacy is equally—perhaps *more*—necessary to the survival of a secular community of states. Sometimes this takes the form of a deliberate, if implicit, agreement to water down the determinacy of rules in order to avoid bringing the moral issues to the fore. In 1979, for example, the international rule system opened for ratification a secular set of rules defining the universal rights of women, but it also permitted a few states with large populations professing religious orthodoxy—such as Democratic Yemen, Egypt, Iraq, Jordan, Tunisia, and Turkey—to ratify those rules subject to the caveat that they understand the rules as not requiring anything that would violate those nations' Islamic precepts.[546] Almost one hundred nations have now ratified this set of new rules, despite, or because of, the element of ambiguity thus introduced.

Such accommodation, in both national and international communities, must begin with an appreciation of the separation between legitimacy and justice. The citizens and governments of most, but not all, national communities have little difficulty making this distinction. The moral rule that it is "meet, right and our bounden duty" to rescue a drowning person even at great risk to our own life may be mandatory in the Christian moral order, yet not be required by the secular legal system of a Christian state. It may be unjust that the secular rules do not command us to be Good Samaritans, but that does not invalidate them. Most citizens of the United States or of Britain understand that their secular order is a system of mutual obligation that proceeds from the notion of social contract. To be binding, such contract must have been entered wittingly at some point in time, but while it is desirable that it be just, it need not be, nor is it expected always to yield justice. Britain has a legitimate royal family, but that institution makes no claim based on justice. Neither does the rule that foreign-born American citizens are ineligible for the Presidency. Rather, the social contract and its canon embodies the secular community's response to commonly perceived dangers of chaos, disorder, or other overweening threats to its security and material progress. That is the basis of their claim on the citizen's acquiescence. The Crown, in Britain, stands for orderly process, not social justice or notions of equal entitlement. The secular order generates personal rights to be safe and autonomous and, within limits, to acquire and hold property. As to some, or all, of these rights, common moral values may coincide with a shared sense of the rules' legitimacy. But such synergy is a happenstance. Turn to the tax laws, the definition of the right to privacy and much else, and the synergy of legitimacy and justice soon runs out.

If legitimacy promises order in return for compliance, the principles and rules of justice are a moral community's response to perceptions of distributive unfairness, inequality, or lack of compassionate grace. The principles of justice hold out the promise of fairness in return for compliance. Because justice, too, pulls to compliance, it may be said to promise the same ultimate prize as is sought by legitimacy: an orderly, compliant society. In this sense, justice may be said to promote a higher form of order. But justice is still different from its symbiotic cousin. The principles of justice and legitimacy, in most nations, of course do bleed into each other. Justice, it may be said, redeems the social contract, in somewhat the way the New Deal is said to have saved capitalism, and the notion of market-oriented *perestroika* may yet save Soviet socialism. But the secular order and the moral order are not merely two tendencies within a single system, in the way socialism and capitalism have merged in Scandinavian social democracy. They are two separate systems: with different rules, validations, loyalty systems, and pulls to compliance. In the post-Enlightenment West, most persons perceive themselves to be members of both a moral and a secular order, but can readily distinguish between them even while trying to serve both and reconcile the differences.

Yet, it should be recalled, this awareness of separation and spirit of accommodation was not always prevalent in the West and is not evident in parts of the world even today. Machiavelli has written of Numa Pompilius, who, succeeding Romulus as the head of the Roman state, that he "turned to religion as the instrument necessary above all others for the maintenance of a civilized state. . . . It was religion which facilitated whatever enterprise the senate and the great men of Rome designed to undertake. . . . [I]ts citizens were more afraid of breaking an oath than of breaking the law. . . ."[547] While "Romulus did not find it necessary to appeal to divine authority" in governing Rome, "to Numa it was so necessary that he pretended to have private conferences with a nymph who advised him about the advice he should give the people. This was because he wanted to introduce new institutions to which the city was unaccustomed, and doubted whether his own authority would suffice."[548] Since Numa's day, there has been no shortage of rulers who have erased the distinction between moral and secular orders so as to be perceived as validated by both. Even today, it is an unceasing battle, even in established liberal democracies, to keep the two orders from being perceived as one.

Such bifurcated allegiance—or, rather, its open acknowledgment and accommodation—is a fairly recent social phenomenon, one which is marked by the shift in legal philosophy from the idea of "natural" law—in which secular and divine rules *must* coincide for either to be valid—to positivism in which the legal system is freely acknowledged to be secular, not divine. Rulers may not seek to validate their commands by cavorting with nymphs. Strict positivism, as Hume's dogmatic secular views on contractual obligation illustrates, was anything but conciliatory to ideas of natural justice and certainly did not strive to accommodate or reconcile the secular with the moral orders. In the early days of communist control, the jurisprudential thought of Soviet legal scholars denied the very existence of a concept of justice because it "itself emanates from the exchange relation and has no meaning apart from it."[549] Only after Western positivism and socialism had undergone the shattering experience of Nazi laws did their jurisprudence begin to question the sufficiency of the secular rules as the sufficient and complete codex of a society's values and obligations.[550]

This has not—how could it?—led back to the easy but false comfort of a natural law-based jurisprudence. Instead, it has caused positivists to recognize the symbiosis, as well as the tensions between justice and legitimacy, two distinct forces pulling to compliance in separate, if sometimes intersecting, canons. Thus understood, the tension between legitimacy and justice remains both empirically demonstrable and useful to the study of compliance with the rules of both secular and moral systems. No one in contemporary America, for example, understands the rule that traffic may cross an intersection on the green light but not on the red as anything but a utility, a mechanism for creating secular order, not a moral one for doing justice. This is not a *rationally*, but a *pragmatically* dictated, understanding. It could have been otherwise, for example, if a faction regarded the color green as weighted with religious implications. But, fortunately, this has not happened. The red and green traffic light exerts its compliance pull even against an occasional claim that it is unfair or unnatural: as, for example, if the light were to impose equally long waiting periods on two intersecting streets, one of which is much more heavily traveled than the other. In exactly this sense, many secular rules in the international system neither claim nor display attributes of fairness or justice. The debate on their fairness is simply suspended by general agreement. They are valued merely because they introduce the certainty and order which facilitates necessary community-sanctioned activity. They carry little moral gravity, and any they do carry is suspended by common sense, for the sake of order and security.

To be sure—and as we have just observed—it could reasonably

be argued that the realization of orderly certainty is itself the highest principle of justice. It should be noted, however, that this is not the same as the proposition that perfect justice would promote perfect order. Rather, this further proposition asserts that order *itself* is the highest form of justice. It is not, however, a proposition acceptable to most legal philosophers. They would argue, instead, that justice sometimes requires disorder to confound injustice. As Held, Morgenbesser, and Nagel have observed, "unjust arrangements induce and possibly sometimes justify violence. . . ."[551] The stylized violence of civil disobedience, or in the international community the refusal to adhere to a blatantly unjust rule, demonstrates the power of justice to confront and, sometimes, to overcome the compliance pull of a norm that is legitimate but unjust. Legitimacy thus may be defeated by the pull toward noncompliance that injustice can muster. Legitimacy recognizes this blocking power of justice, and, with that in mind, secular authorities sooner or later ameliorate blatantly unjust rules: perhaps more out of respect for order and stability than for love of justice.

None of that bleeding of justice into legitimacy makes them the same, however. Even when secular rules operate in symbiotic tandem with moral ones, both pulling toward compliance with identical or similar rules, they remain steadfastly different in the teleology of their compliance pull. The legitimate rule pulls toward compliance because those addressed perceive themselves as perpetually interacting parties engaged in a secular community with rules and rule-based institutions within which the rule-induced benefits of safety, order, and predictability promote the aggregate well-being of the community. The just rule gets its capacity to pull toward compliance from the agreement of the parties of a moral order on principles governing the fair allocation of finite resources among individuals. Obviously, rules of the secular state, or of the secular community of states, exert their most powerful pull toward voluntary compliance when they are generally perceived to be both *legitimate* and *just*, and a legitimate rule may pull less powerfully toward compliance when it is seen to be unjust. Nevertheless, this does not make justice another dependent variable of legitimacy.

Sometimes, legitimate rules are most able to pull toward compliance when there is no coincidence with the mandate of justice. This occurs in two demonstrable circumstances. The *first* exists when a secular rule is generally perceived by the moral community to be justice-neutral—neither particularly just nor significantly unjust; the ordinary traffic light might be an example—and, *second,* when a secular community's perceptions of the requisites of justice are so deeply fragmented that the only acceptable secular rule would have to be the one which least offends, but cannot satisfy, all the diverse notions of justice entertained by the several moral communities comprising the secular one. In these two instances, and perhaps in others, the pull-power of a secular rule is not dependent upon the rule also being perceived as just by the moral order, but merely as *necessary* to defend the integrity, and keep order in, the secular community. In these instances, the rational moral order suspends judgment, or mutes it, in order to promote the survival of the secular community. It is precisely in these circumstances, for example, that the legitimate secular rule which permits the most powerful and richest states certain privileges in the Security Council and World Bank may be accepted provisionally by all in the international community as a sort of contingent principle also of fairness. This willingness to recognize conditionally the justice of the rule—or to suspend attack on its imperfect justice—is derived from the knowledge that, in a culturally fragmented international community, fairness will often be in the eye—the value system—of the beholder, but that the good of all is advanced by rules that make for an orderly deployment of power. In other words, if a secular community wishes to survive, the various moral communities comprising it must sometimes provisionally defer, to the extent of accepting, however tentatively, the contingent or imperfect justice of at least those secular rules absolutely necessary to the political community's survival. This deference is owed, even in the face of an instinctive preference for some other rule more likely to promote a particular notion of justice, because to persist would probably evoke a greater injustice: the disintegration of the secular community or the crippling of its capacity to maintain peace and deliver essential services.

Such conditional acceptance of the justice of rules necessary

to a secular community's survival is not the same as accepting predictability and certitude as the highest justice, which we previously
found to be incongruent with most philosophical inquiry into the
nature of justice. For example, it is undeniably congruent with
contingent, if not absolute, justice, for the U.S. not to have sent
its armed forces to support the liberal Czech regime which was
crushed by foreign invaders in 1968. This is so *not* because stability
itself is a principle of justice but because the consequence of a
destabilizing intervention might have been to set off an accidental
world war. If legitimacy must understand the value of justice as
an ally in legitimacy's quest for predictability and stability, justice
must likewise understand the importance of legitimacy as a tool
in preserving a socio-political framework within which justice eventually can be done. While stability and predictability are not, in
themselves, values dear to the heart of those interested in justice,
global survival surely is.

For this reason, secular rules validated by their legitimacy often
are also allies of justice when they merely serve to bridge the gap
between dissonant, strongly held moral principles. For example,
imagine a secular community of 100 persons composed of 10 religious communities having 10 adherents each. Everyone might
agree, as a moral value, that the community should have an established state religion. There might even be general agreement, in
principle, that the nation and its rulers should be recognized to
operate under some form of divine guidance or inspiration, or that
they are capable of doing so. Yet no group, in this scenario, is
willing to accept the establishment of another group's religion or
interpretation of divine guidance. In such circumstances, a secular
social contract among all 100 persons which simply prohibits the
establishment of any religion, is likely to exercise a powerful pull
toward compliance based on general recognition of its *legitimacy*,
even though none of the parties would regard the rule as reflecting
the most morally desirable principle. However, its justice might
be accepted conditionally by the 100 persons because they valued
survival above other justice-based claims: if, in other words, they
did not wish to repeat the experience of the 100 years' war. It
could then be said that each of the ten groups would accept as

better, in relative terms, the adoption of the secular rule which is least morally offensive to their idea of justice. That assumes, however, a degree of rationality on the part of each justice claimant. John Rawls's theory of justice as fairness depends on the assumption that there is to be found in the community just such a body of overlapping consensus, as well as a capacity for rational instrumental choice.[552] Indeed, he would assert that, in the 10-religion community, a rule prohibiting the establishment of any religion would be recognized not merely as legitimate but also as *just*.

Even so, what we would then have is no more than another happy confluence of legitimacy and justice, married by reason. When principles of justice and the secular rule system are not synchronized, the legitimacy of the secular rule often still exercises a powerful pull toward compliance, one which the countervailing pull of justice may challenge but does not invariably defeat. A law that is legitimate but does not meet Rawls's test of justice may nonetheless exercise considerable compliance pull if it has a high degree of legitimacy. In Britain, for example, the Church of England, which counts as adherents approximately 2 percent of the population, nevertheless remains the established church, by virtue of acts of Parliament which are validated both by the formal legislative process and by the venerable monarchial traditions which are thought to preserve order, continuity, and stability and of which the rule of church establishment is an enduring, even endearing, yet obsolete and certainly unjust, component. Few in Britain would defend the fairness of this arrangement, although Anglicanism may well be everyone else's second-favorite religion because of its current tendency to be broadly accommodating to dissent and countervailing beliefs. Similarly, in the international community, the rules determining persons' nationality, or those granting diplomatic immunity, retain their high level of legitimacy even though neither could be said to advance justice. On the contrary, it is surely unfair that birth should determine nationality or that diplomats should not have to account like everyone else for the wrongs they may commit. These rules' compliance pull derives from their manifest importance to the secular system of orderly, predictable interaction between states, which the rules promote even at some acknowledged cost to the principle which demands that the holder of the scales of justice be blind. When rules are justice neutral, or even perceived to be unjust, this does not necessarily diminish the perception of their legitimacy.

The secular and the moral communities overlap, it would seem, and, often, both address similar issues, sometimes even in the same terms; but they have quite different teleological aims, and so offer different rationales for securing their members' compliance with rules. The secular community's survival, however, depends upon the existence of rules which are complied with because of their manifest *legitimacy*. That gives legitimacy a claim to priority which justice does not have. Put another way, it remains rather idealistic to expect justice of the rules and institutions that operate among *states*. It is perfectly realistic, however, to demand of them a high degree of legitimacy.

That is for now.

As the firm outlines of world order become readily apparent, and as that order increasingly focuses on the individual's place in global society, a keener understanding of the theory, function, and power of justice must surely move to the top of the agenda.

Notes

1. H. Grotius, *The Law of War and Peace* 3 (L. Loomis trans., 1949).

2. W. E. Connolly, "Introduction: Legitimacy and Modernity," in *Legitimacy and the State* 5 (W. E. Connolly ed., 1984).

3. H. L. A. Hart, in *The Concept of Law* (1961), which treats international law as an integral part of the teleological issue and devotes the final chapter (ch. 10) to it. *See also* Schachter, *Towards a Theory of International Obligation*, 8 Va. J. Int'l L. 300 (1968). More typically, international law is confined to some four pages in John Rawls's seminal *A Theory of Justice* (1971).

4. Reisman, *International Lawmaking: A Process of Communication*, in Proceedings, Am. Soc. Int'l L. 101 (1981). He adds: "Since John Austin, lawmaking or the process of prescribing norms has not been a major concern of jurisprudence in the English-speaking world. . . ." *supra*. This is certainly true of international law.

5. See the discussion of *politike koinonia* in Aristotle's political Greek city-state, the *polis*, in the first book of the *Politics*. An excellent analysis is to be found in Reidel, "Transcendental Politics? Political Legitimacy and the Concept of Civil Society in Kant," 48 Social Research 588 (1981). The "central obligation associated with political communities . . . is that of general fidelity to law. . . ." So the question is: "What must politics be like for a bare political society to become a true fraternal mode of association?"

6. R. Dworkin, *Law's Empire* 208 (1986).

7. Reidel, *supra* note 5, at 595–96. For a summary of the "contractarianism" of Hobbes, Rousseau, Kant, Hume, and Locke *see* J. Keane, *Public Life and Late Capitalism: Toward a Socialist Theory of Democracy* 227–29 (1984).

8. Ricoeur, "The Political Paradox," in *Legitimacy and the State* (W. E. Connolly ed., 1984).

9. J. Perez de Cuellar, "The United Nations and the United States," Address at the Fiftieth Anniversary Celebration, The Dickey Endowment, Dartmouth College 14 (May 10, 1988) (mimeo).

10. *See* M. Gluckman, *The Ideas in Barotse Jurisprudence* 38–39, 130–33 (1965); J. Comaroff and S. Roberts, *Rules and Process: The Cultural Logic of Dispute in an African Context* 70–84 (1981).

11. Natural law is defined by Bentham as a device "for prevailing upon the reader to accept the author's sentiment or opinion as a reason for itself." It is "an obscure phantom, which, in the imagination of those who go in chase of it, points sometimes to manners, sometimes to laws, sometimes to what the law is, sometimes to what it ought to be." J. Bentham, *Principles of Morals and Legislation*, ch. II, para. XIV (1879).

12. J. Austin, *The Province of Jurisprudence Determined* 201 (ed. 1954). *See also* Janis, *Jeremy Bentham and the Fashioning of "International Law,"* 78 Am. J. Int'l L. 404 (1984).

13. Marx views law as an expression of the *will* of those persons comprising the capitalist class; what shall be law is determined by their common interest masquerading as the general will. K. Marx & F. Engels, *The German Ideology* 357–58 (S. Ryazanskaya trans., 1964).

14. Holmes saw that the development of legal principles flows from policy considerations determined by judges. O. W. Holmes, Jr., *The Common Law* 35–36 (1881).

15. Unger's power-hierarchy analysis holds that as a society becomes less "closed" in its hierarchic determination, people begin to question the legitimacy of any basis for ordering. People become conscious of the effect of power distribution in shaping "accepted ideas about right conduct." Moral skepticism follows. "People lose confidence in their own judgments and they lose hope of discovering criteria for common judgments." R. M. Unger, *Law in Modern Society: Towards a Criticism of Social Theory* 170–76 (1976).

16. Bentham is often cited as the inventor of the term "international law" and justified this by arguing that it was "sufficiently analogous" to municipal law. J. Bentham, *Principles of Morals and Legislation*, ch. XVII, para. XXV, n.1 (1879).

17. Austin regarded commands issued by a "political superior," with the coupling of coercive power—the "enforcer of obedience," as "inseparably connected" elements of law and therefore dismissed international law as mere "positive morality." J. Austin, *Province of Jurisprudence Determined* (Lecture I) 9–33 (Berlin, Hampshire and Wollheim eds., 1965).

18. *See* Schachter, *supra* note 3, and the sources cited therein.

19. Rawls, *supra note 3*, at 377–91.

20. R. M. Unger, "False Necessity: Anti-Necessitarian Social Theory in the Service of Radical Democracy" (pt. 1), in *Politics: A Work in Constructive Social Theory* 32–40 (1987).

21. Foucault rejects all notions of dominance, whether embodied in theories of sovereignty (divine rule, autocracy, "public rights," and so forth) or embraced in "mechanisms of discipline," including, for example, "power that is tied to scientific knowledge." He visualizes, instead, a new form of "right" which is anti-disciplinarian and divorced from concepts of sovereignty. M. Foucault, *Power/Knowledge: Selected Interviews and Other Writings* 106–8 (C. Gordon ed., 1980). *See also* M. Foucault, *The Order of Things* (1970), wherein he charges that the modern "disciplinary society" presses the individual to "inscribe in himself the power relation and become the principle of his own subjection." *Id.* at 203.

22. R. Nozik, *Anarchy, State and Utopia* 26–28 (1974).

23. International Convention on the Elimination of All Forms of Racial Discrimination, March 7, 1966, 660 U.N.T.S. 195. Entered into force Jan. 4, 1969. As of Dec. 31, 1979, fully 105 states had ratified this treaty.

24. *See* Declaration on the Protection of All Persons From Being Subjected to Torture and Other Cruel, Inhuman or Degrading Treatment or Punishment, G.A. Res. 3452, 30 U.N. GAOR Supp. (No. 34) at 91, U.N. Doc. A/10408 (1975).

25. International Covenant on Economic, Social and Cultural Rights, Dec. 19, 1966. Entered into force Jan. 3, 1976. International Covenant on Civil and Political Rights, Dec. 19, 1966. Entered into force March 23, 1976. Both Covenants were adopted by the U.N. General Assembly: G.A. Res. 2200A, 21 U.N. GAOR Supp. (No. 16) at 49, U.N. Doc. A/16546 (1966).

26. N. Machiavelli, *The Prince* 71 (L. de Alvarez, rev. ed., 1981).

27. "Legitimacy means that there are good arguments for a political order's claim to be recognized as right and just; a legitimate order deserves recognition. Legitimacy means a political order's worthiness to be recognized. This definition highlights the fact that legitimacy is a contestable validity claim; the stability of the order of domination (also) depends on its (at least) de facto recognition. Thus, historically as well as analytically, the concept is used above all in situations in which the legitimacy of an order is disputed, in which, as we say, legitimation problems arise. One side denies, the other asserts legitimacy. This is a *process*. . . ." J. Habermas, *Communication and the Evolution of Society* 178–79 (T. McCarthy trans., 1979).

28. Habermas holds that a rational society is capable of devising accepted criteria of legitimacy and of holding its public authority to account in applying those criteria to governance. Connolly, *supra* note 2, at 14.

29. Weber postulates the validity of an order in terms of its being regarded by the obeying public "as in some way obligatory or exemplary" for its members because, at least, in part, it defines "a model" which is "binding" and to which the actions of others "will in fact conform. . . ." At least, in part, this legitimacy is perceived as adhering to the authority issuing an order, as opposed to the qualities of legitimacy which inhere in an order itself. This distinction between *an* order (command) and *the* order (authority) is easily overlooked but fundamental. 1 M. Weber, *Economy and Society: An Outline of Interpretive Sociology* 31 (G. Roth & C. Wittich eds., 1968). For a critique see Hyde, *The Concept of Legitimacy in the Sociology of Law*, 1983 Wisc. L. Rev. 379 and M. Ciacci, "Legitimacy and the Problems of Governance," in *Legitimacy/ Légitimité* 20 (A. Moulakis ed., 1986).

30. "What are accepted as reasons and have the power to produce consensus . . . depends on the *level of justification* required in a given situation." Habermas, *supra* note 27, at 183.

31. *Id.* at 185.

32. *Id.* at 188.

33. Hyde, for example, believes that the concept of legitimacy should be abandoned and replaced by investigation of "rational grounds for action." Hyde, *supra* note 29, at 380.

34. *Id.* at 411–17, 422–25.

35. *See, for example*, L. Oppenheim, 1 *International Law* (H. Lauterpacht, 8th ed., 1955).

36. I. Kant, "Perpetual Peace" in Kant's *Political Writings* 113–14 (H. Reiss ed., H. Nisbet trans., 1970).

37. Transcript for May 31, 1787. J. Madison, *The Debates in the Federal Convention of 1787 which Framed the Constitution of the United States of America* 37 (G. Hunt and J. B. Scott eds., 1987).

38. A. Koch, *Jefferson and Madison* 71 (1950).

39. *Id.* at 64.

40. J. Taylor, *Construction Construed and Constitution Vindicated* 234–35 (De Capo ed., 1970).

41. J. R. Brierly, *The Outlook for International Law* 13 (1944) (quoting Sir Alfred Zimmern).

42. A. D'Amato, "Is International Law Really Law?" in *International Law: Process and Prospect* 1–26 (1987).

43. *Id.* at 10.

44. Even so, Nazi Germany did not take the position that all rules of the international system were inapplicable to it. See, for example, an account of the German agreement to return to Switzerland a refugee, Herr Jacob-Solomon, kidnapped on Swiss territory by German agents. The Nazi regime called the incident "regrettable" and claimed to have disciplined its functionary. *See* Preuss, *Settlement of the Jacob Kidnapping Case (Switzerland-Germany)*, 30 Am. J. Int'l L. 123 (1936).

45. Declaration on Principles of International Law Concerning Friendly Relations and Co-operation Among States in Accordance with the Charter of the United Nations, G.A. Res. 2625, 25 U.N. GAOR Supp. (No. 28) at 121, U.N. Doc. A/8028 (1970). This declaration proclaims the "principle that States shall refrain in their international relations from the threat or use of force against the territorial integrity or political independence of any State, or in any manner inconsistent with the purposes of the United Nations." *Id.*

46. Definition of Aggression, G.A. Res. 3314, 29 U.N. GAOR Supp. (No. 31) at 142, U.N. Doc. A/9631 (1974).

47. International Covenant on Civil and Political Rights, *adopted* Dec. 16, 1966, 999 U.N.T.S. 171; International Covenant on Economic, Social and Cultural Rights, *adopted* Dec. 16, 1966, 993 U.N.T.S. 3.

48. It is possible, of course, to think of international law as "enforced" by powerful states with interests to protect and agendas to pursue, which provide a law with the requisite "control intention" when it serves their policy concerns to do so. *See* Reisman, *supra* note 4, at 110–20. If that is what law means in the international context, however, it is difficult to see why it should not be called what it is: the policy-preference for the time being of dominant actors in the system. Moreover, this would not account for most actual compliance behavior today.

49. *Id.* at 107.

50. *Id.*

51. Hart, *supra* note 3, at 209.

52. M. Arnold, "On Dover Beach," in *The Poetical Works of Matthew Arnold* 401, 402 (1942).

53. L. Henkin, *How Nations Behave* (1968).

54. Vienna Convention on the Law of Treaties, *done* May 23, 1969, U.N. Doc. A/Conf.39/11, 1969, *reprinted in* 8 Int'l Legal Mat. 679 (1969). Arts. 59 and 60 deal with the consequences of a "material breach" of a treaty by a party on the rights of other parties. U.N. Doc. A/Conf.39/27, 1969.

55. As to the effect of "a material breach" of obligations in bilat-

eral and multilateral treaties on the other party or parties see Vienna Convention on the Law of Treaties, 1969, *id.* at art. 60(2).

56. International Convention on Load Lines, *done* Apr. 5, 1966, 18 U.S.T. 1857, T.I.A.S. No. 6331, 640 U.N.T.S. 133. Entered into force 1968. This treaty was in force for 108 states in 1987.

57. Treaty on the Execution of Penal Sentences, Nov. 25, 1976, United States-Mexico, 28 U.S.T. 7399, T.I.A.S. No. 8718.

58. General Treaty for the Renunciation of War as an Instrument of National Policy of Aug. 27, 1928, T.S. No. 796, 46 Stat. 2343, 94 L.N.T.S. 59.

59. Statute of the International Court of Justice, arts. 4, 5, 59 Stat. 1055, T.S. No. 993.

60. Treaty on Principles Governing the Activities of States in the Exploration and Use of Outer Space, Including the Moon and Other Celestial Bodies, Jan. 27, 1967, 18 U.S.T. 2410, T.I.A.S. No. 6347, 610 U.N.T.S. 205.

61. European Convention on the Suppression of Terrorism, *done* Nov. 10, 1976, Europ. T.S. No. 90.

62. Protocol Additional to the Geneva Conventions of 12 August 1949, and Relating to the Protection of Victims of International Armed Conflicts (Protocol I), *opened for signature* Dec. 12, 1977, 16 Int'l Legal Mat. 1391 (1977); Protocol Additional to the Geneva Conventions of August 12, 1949 and Relating to the Protection of Victims of Non-International Armed Conflicts (Protocol II), *opened for signature* Dec. 12, 1977, 16 Int'l Legal Mat. 1442 (1977).

63. Meron, *The Geneva Conventions as Customary Law*, 81 Am. J. Int'l L. 348 (1987).

64. Vienna Convention on the Law of Treaties, *supra* note 54.

65. S. F. Moore, *Law as Process* 3 (1978).

66. Convention on the Continental Shelf, April 29, 1958, 15 U.S.T. 471, T.I.A.S. No. 5578, 499 U.N.T.S. 311.

67. *Quoted in* S. Padover, *The Complete Jefferson* 138 (1943).

68. *See* 31 Cong. Rec. 3984 (1898). Congress now seems to accept that this power, if such it was, has lapsed.

69. *United States v. Pink*, 315 U.S. 203, 230 (1942) (stating that "No such obstacle can be placed in the way of relations between this country and another nation, unless the historic conception of the powers and responsibilities of the President in the conduct of foreign affairs is to be drastically revised." (Citations omitted.)); *United States v. Belmont*, 301 U.S. 324, 330 (1937) (stating "That the negotiations, acceptance of the assignment and agreements and understandings in respect thereof were within the competence of the President may not be doubted."); *Goldwater v. Carter*, 444 U.S. 996 (1979)

(directing District Court to dismiss complaint filed by several legislators who had argued that the President's termination of the mutual defense treaty with Taiwan, as part of the exchange of recognition with communist China, was unconstitutional).

70. 92 Cong. Rec. (Senate) 10694 (1946).

71. *Id.* at 10684, 10691.

72. *Switzerland v. U.S.,* 1959 I.C.J. 101 (Dissenting op. of Lauterpacht, J.).

73. Military and Paramilitary Activities in and against Nicaragua (*Nicar. v. U.S.*), 1984 I.C.J. 392 (Judgment of Nov. 26).

74. Military and Paramilitary Activities in and against Nicaragua (*Nicar. v. U.S.*), 1986 I.C.J. 14 (Judgment of June 27).

75. *Brown v. Board of Education of Topeka,* 347 U.S. 483 (1954).

76. *Plessy v. Ferguson,* 163 U.S. 537 (1896).

77. L. Wittgenstein, *Philosophical Investigations* 81, para. 201 (G. E. Anscombe trans., 1953).

78. Kennedy, *Towards a Critical Phenomenology of Judging,* 36 J. Legal Educ. 518 (1986).

79. Vienna Convention on Diplomatic Relations, *done* Apr. 18, 1961, arts. 31, 37, 23 U.S.T. 3227, T.I.A.S. No. 7502, 500 U.N.T.S. 95.

80. The Department of State, on August 5, 1978, submitted its views on a "bill to make certain members of foreign diplomatic missions and consular posts in the United States subject to the criminal jurisdiction of the United States with respect to crimes of violence." The Department (Ambassador Selwa Roosevelt) "could not support the proposed legislation because it would be detrimental to United States interests abroad." If enacted, the law "would place the United States in violation of its international obligations and would surely invite more harmful reciprocal actions." *See* 87 Dep't St. Bull. 29 (Oct. 1979).

81. H. C. Foreign Affairs Committee, First Report, The Abuse of Diplomatic Immunities and Privileges, Report with Annex; Together with the Proceedings of the Committee; Minutes of Evidence Taken on 20 June and 18 July in the Last Session of Parliament, and Appendices (Dec. 12, 1984). *See also* Higgins, Editorial Comment, 79 Am. J. Int'l L. 641 (1985).

82. G.A. Res. 3314, *supra* note 46.

83. *See* Vienna Convention on Diplomatic Relations, *supra* note 79, at arts. 27, 28.

84. *See* Vienna Convention on the Law of Treaties, *supra* note 54, at arts. 6, 55.

85. United Nations Convention on the Law of the Sea, *done* Dec.

10, 1982, U.N. Doc. A/Conf. 62/122, Corr. 1–11, *reprinted in* 21 Int'l Legal Mat. 1261 (1982).

86. Convention on Offenses and Certain Other Acts Committed on Board Aircraft, *done* Sept. 14, 1963, 20 U.S.T. 2941, T.I.A.S. No. 6768, 704 U.N.T.S. 219.

87. Universal Copyright Convention, *done* July 24, 1971, 25 U.S.T. 1341, T.I.A.S. No. 7868 (revised version of 216 U.N.T.S. 132).

88. As to compensation for expropriated property, there is agreement in principle, but disagreement as to the measure of compensation. *See, for example,* Charter of Economic Rights and Duties of States of Dec. 12, 1974, art. 2(2)(c), G.A. Res. 3281, 29 U.N. GAOR Supp. (No. 31) at 50, U.N. Doc. A/9631 (1974). *See also* General Assembly Resolution on Permanent Sovereignty Over Natural Resources, G.A. Res. 1803, 17 U.N. GAOR Supp. (No. 17) at 15, U.N. Doc. A/5344/Add. 1, A/L.R12/Rev.2 (1962). Art. 4 of the latter states in part concerning expropriation: "In such cases the owner shall be paid appropriate compensation, in accordance with the rules in force in the State taking such measures in the exercise of its sovereignty and in accordance with international law." *But see* General Assembly Resolution on Permanent Sovereignty Over Natural Resources, G.A. Res. 3171, 28 U.N. GAOR (2033rd plen. mtg.), U.N. Doc. A/9400 (1973), *reprinted in* 14 United Nations Resolutions 422–23 (D. J. Djonovich ed., 1978). Art. 3 "affirms" that: ". . . each State is entitled to determine the amount of possible compensation and the mode of payment, and that any disputes which might arise should be settled in accordance with the national legislation of each State carrying out such measures."

89. For discussion of "just" and "unjust" wars see Grotius, *supra* note 1, and references *infra* note 132.

90. United Nations Convention on the Law of the Sea, *supra* note 84, at art. 83(1).

91. North Sea Continental Shelf Cases (*W. Ger. v. Den. & Neth.*), 1969 I.C.J. 54 (Judgment of Feb. 20).

92. *See* Continental Shelf (*Tunisia v. Libyan Arab Jamahiriya*), 1982 I.C.J. 18, 35 (Judgment of Feb. 24).

93. Continental Shelf (*Malta v. Libyan Arab Jamahiriya*), 1985 I.C.J. 13, 44 (Judgment).

94. L. Henkin, R. C. Pugh, O. Schachter, H. Smit, *International Law* 1247 (1987); Fisheries Case (*U.K. v. Nor.*), 1951 I.C.J. 116, 147 (Judgment of Dec. 18).

95. Convention on the Continental Shelf, *done* April 29, 1958, art. 1, 15 U.S.T. 471, T.I.A.S. No. 5578, 499 U.N.T.S. 311.

96. United Nations Convention on the Law of the Sea, *supra* note 85, at arts. 12, 57, 76.

97. As of December 31, 1984, 75 states were parties to the Convention on the Continental Shelf, *supra* note 95. Multilateral Treaties Deposited with the Secretary-General, U.N. Doc. ST/LEG/SER.E (1985).

98. A. Cassese, *International Law in a Divided World* 398 (1986).

99. An example is the refusal of the General Assembly to validate Morocco's forcible occupation of the Western Sahara. G.A. Res. 3458(A), 30 U.N. GAOR (2435th plen. mtg.), U.N. Doc. GA/5438 (1975), *reprinted in* 15 United Nations Resolutions 556–57 (D. J. Djonovich ed., 1984).

100. The United States has refused to validate Morocco's occupation of the Western Sahara. *Subcommittee on African Affairs of the House Committee on Foreign Affairs*, 95th Cong., 2nd Sess. (1979) (statement of Harold H. Saunders, Assistant Secretary for Near Eastern and South Asian Affairs), *reprinted in* 79 Dep't St. Bull. 53 (Oct. 1979). It has also refused to validate Israel's annexation of East Jerusalem. *Reagan Calls Bill to Move Embassy in Israel "Unwise,"* Wall Street J., March 30, 1984, at 4, col. 4; Dutton, *"Jerusalem Bill": A Loser*, N.Y. Times, July 30, 1984, at A21, col. 1.

101. The Western Sahara's occupation by Morocco has been rejected by the Organization of African Unity. *Co-operation between the United Nations and the Organization of African Unity*, 1982 U.N.Y.B. 329, 330; *Western Sahara Question, id.* at 1350. For an account of the OAU's efforts to seat the Polisario Front *see* Hodges, *The Western Sahara*, 32 Int'l Commission Jurists Rec. 25, 30–31 (1984).

102. Supplementary Treaty Concerning the Extradition Treaty, June 25, 1985, U.S.-U.K., 24 Int'l Legal Mat. 1105.

103. The District Court in *Matter of Doherty*, 599 F. Supp. 270 (S.D.N.Y. 1984), *declaratory judgment denied, U.S. v. Doherty*, 615 F. Supp. 755 (S.D.N.Y. 1985), *aff'd* 786 F.2d 491 (2d Cir. 1986), held that the political offense exception prohibited the extradition of a member of the Provisional Irish Republican Army. 599 F. Supp. at 277. The political offense exception was first articulated in a United States court in *In re Ezeta*, 62 F. 972 (N.D. Cal. 1894). It was later addressed by the Supreme Court in *Ornelas v. Ruiz*, 161 U.S. 502, 16 S. Ct. 689 (1896).

104. 85 Dep't St. Bull. 58–59 (Dec. 1985).

105. Pyle, *Defining Terrorism*, 64 Foreign Pol'y 63, 75 (1986).

106. Sofaer, *Terrorism and the Law*, 64 Foreign Aff. 901 (1986).

107. According to art. 12 of the Hostages Convention, to the

extent the 1949 Geneva Conventions and/or the 1977 Geneva Protocols are applicable to hostage taking, *and* to the extent the Conventions/Protocols require the prosecution or extradition of the hostage taker, the Conventions/Protocols govern instead of the Hostages Convention. International Convention Against the Taking of Hostages, G.A. Res. 34/146, 34 U.N. GAOR, Supp. (No. 46) at 245, U.N. Doc. A/34/46 (1979), *reprinted in* 18 Int'l Legal Mat. 1457 (1979). (The United States deposited its ratification of the Hostages Convention on Dec. 7, 1984 and the Convention entered into force for the U.S. on Jan. 6, 1985. Concomitant domestic legislation was passed. 18 U.S.C.A. sec. 1203 (West Supp. 1986).) Geneva Convention I for the Amelioration of the Condition of the Wounded and Sick of Armed Forces in the Field, 6 U.S.T. 3114, T.I.A.S. No. 3362, 75 U.N.T.S. 31; Convention II for the Amelioration of the Condition of the Wounded, Sick and Shipwrecked of Armed Forces at Sea, 6 U.S.T. 3217, T.I.A.S. No. 3363, 75 U.N.T.S. 85; Convention III Relative to the Treatment of Prisoners of War, 6 U.S.T. 3316, T.I.A.S. No. 3364, 75 U.N.T.S. 135; Convention IV Relative to the Protection of Civilian Persons in Time of War, 6 U.S.T. 3516, T.I.A.S. No. 3365, 75 U.N.T.S. 287, all signed on Aug. 12, 1949; Protocols to the 1949 Geneva Conventions, U.N. Doc. A/32/144, Annexes I & II (1977), *reprinted in* 72 Am. J. Int'l L. 457 (1978). In other words, if the coverage of the Hostages Convention and the Geneva Conventions/Protocols coincide, the latter controls, but in no event are the standards of the Hostages Convention evaded. *See generally* Verwey, *The International Hostages Convention and National Liberation Movements*, 75 Am. J. Int'l L. 69 (1981).

Under the coverage of the Hostages Convention and its Geneva Conventions/Protocols subset, the Hostages Convention would directly govern most instances of terrorist hostage-taking. If the terrorist action takes place during a non-international armed conflict, that act violates common art. 3 of the Geneva Conventions. However, that violation does not constitute a "grave breach" of the Conventions and consequently does not give rise to an obligation to prosecute or extradite. Therefore, as the obligations incurred under the Geneva Conventions fall short of the standards the Hostages Convention imposes, the latter controls. If a terrorist takes a hostage during an international armed conflict, that act, if against civilians, violates art. 34 of the fourth Geneva Convention and constitutes an explicit art. 147 "grave breach" of that Convention, giving rise to a prosecute-or-extradite obligation. To this extent, the Geneva Convention rather than the Hostages Convention directly controls.

It is unlikely, however, that a terrorist group would be engaged in an international armed conflict.

Implementation of Protocol I via art. 1(4) is predicated on both target state ratification and insurgent group acceptance of Protocol I (the latter achieved by filing a unilateral declaration with the Red Cross pursuant to art. 96). While fifty-five states have accepted Protocol I, the two paradigmatic target states, Israel and South Africa, have not ratified the Protocol (for that matter neither has Afghanistan or Kampuchea). Int'l Comm. Red Cross, *Annual Report, 1985*, 93–96 (1986). No insurgent group has successfully filed an art. 96 declaration. Aldrich, *Progressive Development of the Laws of War: A Reply to Criticism of the 1977 Geneva Protocol I*, 26 Va. J. Int'l L. 702–3 (1986). *Cf.* U.N. Doc. A/35/710 (Annex) (1980) (African National Congress acceptance of "general principles of humanitarian law applicable in armed conflicts"). Following the Israeli invasion of Lebanon, the P.L.O. attempted to file an art. 96(3) declaration but the Swiss government, as depository, rebuffed that maneuver on the ground that the target state, Israel, had not ratified Protocol I. Telephone interview with Jean-Jacques Surbeck, I.C.R.C. liaison to the U.N. (April 3, 1987). Furthermore, as the target state would be administering the Protocol, it would be loathe to agree with the assessment that it was a racist, colonialist, or alien regime, and would act accordingly. For these reasons, the Red Cross Legal Advisor has termed the controversy surrounding art. 1(4) "mainly academic." Gasser, *A Brief Analysis of the 1977 Geneva Protocols*, 19 Akron L. Rev. 529 (1986). The head of the U.S. delegation to the conference that adopted the 1977 Protocols bluntly calls the clause a "dead letter." Aldrich, *supra*, at 703. An additional prerequisite for Protocol implementation is that the armed forces involved be ruled under a system of command of a party and be subject to an internal disciplinary system. Protocol I, *infra* note 109, art. 43(1). Few insurgent groups and fewer "terrorists" would meet that standard.

Sofaer accepts that art. 12 of the Hostages Convention does not "create a legal gap in coverage" but complains that its language gives national liberation movements and terrorism a "rhetorical and political victory." Sofarer, *supra* note 106, at 916. That assessment is wrong; the twenty-nine countries that have ratified the Hostages Convention have accepted a straightforward rule with which Sofaer should have little difficulty. His criticism aims at what was widely regarded as a victory for the West. As the State Department emphasized at the time, art. 12 "ensures that all those who violate the Hostages Convention will be subject to prosecution or extradition under either the

Convention itself or the Geneva Conventions/Protocols of 1977." Letter from Anthony Quainton, Director of the Office for Combatting Terrorism, to Israel Singer, Executive Director of the North American Branch of the World Jewish Congress (Dec. 11, 1979), *reprinted in* 74 Am. J. Int'l L. 420 (1980). An American participant in the negotiations enthusiastically reported that art. 12 "underline[s] the application of the prohibition against the taking of hostages as to liberation movements." Rosenstock, *International Convention Against the Taking of Hostages: Another International Community Step Against Terrorism*, 9 Den. J. Int'l L. & Pol'y 169 (1980).

108. As Sofaer correctly notes, international conventions define piracy to encompass only "illegal acts of violence, detention or any acts of depredation, committed for *private ends*." Sofaer, *supra* note 106, at 910–12; *referring to* art. 15 of the 1958 Geneva Convention on the High Seas, 13 U.S.T. 2312, T.I.A.S. No. 5200, 450 U.N.T.S. 82 (emphasis added); *see also* art. 101 of the United Nations Convention on the Law of the Sea, *supra* note 85. Sofaer is wrong, however, to use this as "yet another" example of third world irresponsibility or to imply that pirate-terrorism necessarily escapes international law. The exclusion dates to a 1932 Harvard Research Draft, composed long before the third world's emergence. *See* Draft Convention on Piracy, 26 Am. J. Int'l L. 768–69 (Supp. 1932). Its provision is variously attributed to an anachronistic "Long John Silver" model of piracy; to a desire to altogether avoid nineteenth-century distinctions between the legal attacks of belligerents and the pirate attacks of insurgents by definitionally excluding all "public" piracy; and to a perception that the flag state of the captured vessel could adequately handle the matter by applying its own municipal law. Note, *Towards a New Definition of Piracy: The Achile Lauro Incident*, 26 Virg. J. Int'l L. 723, 731–32, 738 (1986); Draft Convention on Piracy, *supra*, at 786. Moreover, a broader piracy *jure gestum* arguably survives these conventions and continues to supplement the conventions in condemning politically motivated attacks by parties to a civil conflict when made against neutrals. *See The Magellan Pirates*, 164 Eng. Rep. 47 (1853); Oppenheim, *supra* note 35, at 612. Applying this broader definition to the 1985 seizure of the Italian liner *Achile Lauro* by the Palestine Liberation Front, Gerald McGinvey concludes its captors were pirates. McGinvey, *The Achile Lauro Affair—Implications for International Law*, 52 Tenn. L. Rev. 691, 700 (1985); Halberstam, *Terrorism on the High Seas: the Achile Lauro Piracy and the IMO Convention on Maritime Safety*, 82 Am. J. Int'l L. 269 (1988). *But see* Note, *supra*, 26 Virg. J. Int'l L. at 744. United States law, which

criminalizes "piracy as defined by the law of nations," might well refer to this broader customary standard. 18 U.S.C.A. sec. 1651 (1984). The Department of Justice, in its arrest warrants against the *Achile Lauro* captors, however, stated that the seizure was in pursuit of "private ends," preferring to use the narrower treaty language in charging the Palestinians with piracy. 24 Int'l Legal Mat. 1553, 1556–57 (1985). The Justice Department apparently did not share Sofaer's misgivings.

109. Protocol I to the Geneva Convention, U.N. Doc. A/32/144, Annex I (1977), *reprinted in* 72 Am. J. Int'l L. 457 (1978) [hereinafter: Protocol I].

110. G.A. Res. 40/61, 40 General Assembly (Agenda Item 129), U.N. Doc. A/RES/40/61 (1985), *reprinted in* 25 Int'l Legal Mat. 239 (1986).

111. Sofaer, *supra* note 106, at 922.

112. *See supra* note 107.

113. *Legal Consequences for States of the Continued Presence of South Africa in Namibia (South West Africa) Notwithstanding Security Council Resolution 276 (1970)*, 1971 I.C.J. 16 (Advisory Opinion of June 21); *Western Sahara*, 1975 I.C.J. 12 (Advisory Opinion of Oct. 16).

114. Sofaer, *supra* note 106, at 906.

115. 86 Dep't St. Bull. 23 (Sept. 1986).

116. Protocol I, *supra* note 109, art. 1(4). The Protocol achieves this extension of coverage by appellating these internal wars "international armed conflicts." Article 1(4) definitionally expands "international armed conflicts" to include "armed conflicts in which peoples are fighting against colonial domination and alien occupation and against racist regimes in the exercise of their right of self-determination."

117. Sofaer, *supra* note 106, at 913.

118. 23 Weekly Comp. Pres. Doc. 91, 92 (Jan. 29, 1987).

119. Sofaer, *supra* note 106, at 912.

120. *Id*. at 922.

121. N.Y. Times, Jan. 9, 1987, at C3, col. 2.

122. *Regina v. Dudley and Stephens*, 14 Q.B.D. 273 (1884). See also *U.S. v. Holmes*, 26 Fed. Cas. 360, 1 Wall Jr. 1 (1842).

123. Model Penal Code sec. 3.02 (1985). The provision reads: "(1) Conduct that the actor believes to be necessary to himself or to another is justifiable, provided that: (a) the harm or evil sought to be avoided by such conduct is greater than that sought to be prevented by the law defining the offense charged. . . ." *See also* T. Franck, *The Structure of Impartiality* 52–56 (1968).

124. G. B. Kerferd, *The Sophistic Movement* 59–67 (1981).

125. D. Swann and M. Flanders, "At the Drop of a Hat" (1957). For Broadway premiere *see* N.Y. Times, Oct. 9, 1959, at 22, col. 4.

126. *See* Franck, *Who Killed Article* 2(4)?, 64 Am. J. Int'l L. 809, 820–22 (1970).

127. M. Lachs, *The Development of General Trends of International Law in Our Time*, 169 Recueil des Cours 1980(IV), 163 (1984). For a serious effort to construct a textured sophist rule on the use of force in the nuclear age *see* Schachter, *In Defense of International Rules on the Use of Force*, 53 Chicago L. Rev. 113 (1986).

128. Address by Ambassador Kirkpatrick, National Press Club (May 30, 1985). The Reagan Doctrine is not the only twentieth-century attempt to revive the just war doctrine. The Soviet Union has long maintained that "[j]ust wars . . . are not wars of conquest but wars of liberation, waged to defend the people from foreign attack and from attempts to enslave them, or to liberate the people from capitalist slavery, or, lastly, to liberate colonies and dependent countries from the yoke of imperialism." Commission of the Central Committee of the C.P.S.U., *History of the Communist Party of the Soviet Union (Bolsheviks)* 167–68 (1939). The modern Non-Aligned Movement has also upheld the just war doctrine, one result being the provisions of Protocol I, discussed *supra* note 116 and accompanying text. This position was dramatically put forth in a 1973 General Assembly resolution: "colonial peoples have the inherent right to struggle by all necessary means at their disposal against colonial Powers and alien domination in exercise of their right of self-determination." G.A. Res. 3103, 28 U.N. GAOR Supp. (No. 30) at 142, U.N. Doc. A/9030 (1973). *See also* G.A. Res. 2105, 20 U.N. GAOR Supp. (No. 14) at 3, U.N. Doc. A/6104 (1965). For a case study, *see* Dugard, *SWAPO: The Jus ad Bellum and The Jus in Bello*, 93 S. Africa L.J. 144 (1976).

129. F. Russell, *The Just War in the Middle Ages* 12 (1975).

130. *Id.* at 18–20.

131. T. Aquinas, *Summa Theologica, secunda secundae*, Q. 40 (art. 1) (T. Heath trans., 1972).

132. *See* Grotius, *supra* note 1; Edwards, *The Law of War in the Thought of Hugo Grotius*, 19 J. Pub. L. 371 (1970). Grotius expressly contemplated a third state intervening to protect the natural law rights of the citizens of another state. *See* Book II, Chapter XXV of Grotius, *supra*, entitled "On the Causes of Undertaking War on Behalf of Others."

133. Kirkpatrick, *supra* note 128.

134. It may strike some as passing odd to see Pyle intellectually

ranged on the side of Aquinas and Ronald Reagan, while Judge Sofaer, with Porfiry, firmly opposes the effort to reintroduce the muddle between pitying those who are driven to violence and making their acts legal. At this early stage of our analysis, however, the consistency of the adversaries is only of marginal interest. Our first objective must be to understand the basic jurisprudential theories that underpin Porfiry's proposition and Pyle's counter-proposition.

135. Even during the Middle Ages papal neutrality was questioned. This skepticism finds expression in the demand that combatants, including those serving in a nominally just war, serve penance for inflicting injury on the enemy. Russell, *supra* note 129, at 32.

136. *Id.* at 34–35; Shaw, *Revival of the Just War Doctrine?*, 3 Auckland L. Rev. 163 (1977).

137. Muldoon, *The Remonstrance of the Irish Princes and the Canon Law Tradition of the Just War*, 32 Am. J. Legal Hist. 309, 312 (1978). Muldoon chronicles the unsuccessful Irish attempts to persuade the Pope to revoke his bill authorizing English invasion of Ireland. The need to strengthen England as a political counterweight to France determined the papal position. *Id.* at 323. Muldoon concludes: the "Irish were the first in what proved to be a long line of people on the edges of European society who looked to the papacy for justice against their conquerors. Like all the others, the Irish were doomed to frustration." *Id.* at 325. *See also* M. Walzer, *Just and Unjust Wars* (1977).

138. For analysis of Vattel's views and their effect *see* Brierly, *supra* note 41, at 26–29.

139. Pyle, *supra* note 105, at 78.

140. Vienna Convention on the Law of Treaties, *done* May 23, 1969, art. 26, U.N. Doc. A/Conf. 39/29 (1969). Entered into force Jan. 27, 1980.

141. U.N. General Assembly Documents (A/8768–8799), U.N. Doc. A/8791, A/8791/Add.1 (1972).

142. *See, for example*, Ad Hoc Committee on International Terrorism (1973–77), Observations of States Submitted in Accordance with General Assembly Resolution 3034 (XXVII), U.N. Doc. A/AC.160/1, A/AC.160/1/Add.1, A/AC.160/1/Add.2 (1973).

143. Ad Hoc Committee on International Terrorism (1973–77). U.N. Doc. A/AC.160/3/Add.2 at 3 (1977).

144. Ad Hoc Committee on International Terrorism (1973–77). U.N. Doc. A/AC.160/2 at 7 (1977). However, Ambassador Oakley has reported a new Soviet "awareness that distinctions must be made between so-called liberation movements and groups whose objectives

and operations are primarily directed toward producing terror, and whose targets are often unrelated to their putative 'liberation' goals." Oakley, *International Terrorism*, 65 Foreign Aff. 628 (1987).

145. *See* T. Franck, *Judging the World Court* 53–76 (1986).

146. *See* D. F. Vagts, *Dispute-Resolution Mechanisms in International Business*, 203 Recueil des Cours 62–70, 80–84 (1987–III).

147. International Convention Against the Taking of Hostages, *supra* note 107. The negotiations for the Hostage Convention reveal the opposition that an idiot rule, even one for a compartmentalized activity, faces. Attempts at a reformulation of the Convention ranged in sophistication. Several delegations suggested the Convention should only protect "innocent" hostages. *See, for example*, U.N. Doc. A/32/39 (1977) at 38 (statement of Egypt); at 40 (statement of Guinea, using Ian Smith as an illustrative guilty hostage). The Tanzanian delegate proposed an exculpatory clause and provided an umpire: "For the purposes of the Convention, the term 'taking of hostages' shall not include any act or acts carried out in the process of national liberation against colonial rule, racist and foreign regimes, by liberation movements recognized by the United Nations or regional organizations." U.N. Doc. A/AC.188/L.5 (1977). The Pakistani delegate wished to condition invocation of the Hostages Convention against national liberation movements on the target state's acceptance of both the Geneva Conventions and the 1977 Protocols. U.N. Doc. A/C.6/34/SR.62 at 2 (1979). *See* Implementation of Protocol I via art. 1(4), *supra* note 107. In response, the French delegate argued: "[The] taking of hostages was an act which must be condemned absolutely and which no circumstances or grounds could justify, regardless of the nobility of the cause for which it might have been committed." U.N. Doc. A/33/39 (1978) at 64. The French position ultimately prevailed. *See supra* note 107.

148. Convention on the Prevention and Punishment of Crimes Against International Protected Persons, including Diplomatic Agents, Dec. 14, 1973, 28 U.S.T. 1975, T.I.A.S. No. 8532, 1035 U.N.T.S. 167. *See also* Convention to Prevent and Punish Acts of Terrorism, Feb. 2, 1971, 27 U.S.T. 3949, T.I.A.S. No. 8413. The latter, an OAS version of the International Protected Persons Convention, specifically condemns all physical attacks on diplomats, "regardless of motive" (Art. 2). This protection afforded diplomats can be analogized to the eleventh-century Peace of God doctrine which declared certain classes, especially the clergy, exempt from all violence. Russell, *supra* note 129, at 34.

149. Tokyo Convention on Offenses and Certain Other Acts Committed on Board Aircraft, Sept. 14, 1963, 20 U.S.T. 2941, T.I.A.S.

No. 6768, 704 U.N.T.S. 219; Hague Convention for the Suppression of Unlawful Seizure of Aircraft, Dec. 16, 1970, 22 U.S.T. 1641, T.I.A.S. No. 7192, 860 U.N.T.S. 105; Montreal Convention for the Suppression of Unlawful Acts Against the Safety of Civil Aviation, Sept. 23, 1971, 24 U.S.T. 564, T.I.A.S. No. 7570, 974 U.N.T.S. 174.

150. This scenario most notably occurred when an East German hijacked a Polish airliner to West Berlin. As an outgrowth of the historical and jurisdictional freak that is Berlin, the hijacker was charged with crimes under West German law but prosecuted by the United States and tried in an American court. The U.S. ambassador to West Germany appointed a New Jersey federal district judge, the Hon. Herbert Stern, to preside at the trial. *See* H. Stern, *Judgment in Berlin* (1984). Judge Stern, applying U.S. constitutional law, determined that the defendant was entitled to a jury trial (despite the anomaly that juries generally do not exist under German law). *United States v. Tiede*, 86 F.R.D. 227 (U.S. Ct. Berlin 1979). Impaneling a jury of West Berliners to judge an East German "refugee" raised the specter that the jury would refuse to convict the defendant in the American tradition of jury nullification. *See* Lowenfeld, *Hijacking, Freedom, and the "American Way,"* 83 Mich. L. Rev. 1000, 1005 (1985). In other words, the jury would in effect graft a sophist clause upon the idiot law of the Hague Convention. In the end, the jury did acquit the defendant of hijacking but convicted him of hostage-taking. Stern, *supra*, at 350. Judge Stern, affronted throughout the trial by the American prosecutor's stance that the U.S. Constitution was inapplicable to West Berlin and skeptical that parole (which he thought appropriate) would be granted, sentenced the hostage-taker to time served (nine months) and released him from custody. *Id.* at 369–70.

151. Hague Convention, *supra* note 149, arts. 7, 8.

152. Memorandum of Understanding on Hijacking of Aircraft and Vessels and Other Offenses, Feb. 15, 1973, United States-Cuba, 24 U.S.T. 737, T.I.A.S. No. 7579 [hereinafter: Cuban Accord].

153. 1975 Dig. U.S. Prac. Int'l L. 184 (1976). Unfortunately, the accord was short-lived. In October 1976, Fidel Castro formally denounced the accord in retaliation for alleged C.I.A. involvement in the crash of a Cuban airliner. 1976 Dig. U.S. Prac. Int'l L. 400 (1977). The United States "categorically denied any U.S. responsibility for the crash." *Id.*

154. 78 Dep't St. Bull. 5 (Sept. 1978) [hereinafter: Bonn Declaration].

155. *Id.* This language tracks art. 7 and art. 9(2) of the Hague Convention, *supra* note 149. The Bonn Declaration in effect grafts an enforcement mechanism upon the norms embodied in the Hague

Convention. However, imposition of sanctions under the Bonn Declaration is not premised on violation of the Hague Convention. Accordingly, sanctions might be taken against a state that had refused to sign the Hague Convention, not on the basis of the duty to prosecute or extradite (assuming, as is likely, that that is not a duty under customary international law), but on the basis that the support of international terrorism violates international law. *See* Levitt, *International Counter-Terrorism Cooperation: The Summit Seven and Air Terrorism*, 20 Vand. J. Transnat'l L. 259, 282–83 (1987). *See also* Chamberlain, *Collective Suspension of Air Services with States which Harbour Hijackers*, 32 Int'l & Comp. L.Q. 616, 628–32 (1983); Busuttil, *The Bonn Declaration on International Terrorism: A Non-Binding International Agreement on Aircraft Hijacking*, 31 Int'l & Comp. L.Q. 474 (1982).

156. S.C. Res. 461, 34 U.N. SCOR (Resolutions and Decisions 1979) at 24, U.N. Doc. S/13711/Rev. 1 (1979).

157. *United States Diplomatic and Consular Staff in Tehran* (*U.S. v. Iran*), 1980 I.C.J. 3 (Judgment of May 24).

158. 85 Dep't St. Bull. 58, 61 (Dec. 1985). *But see* Note, *Extradition in an Era of Terrorism: The Need to Abolish the Political Offense Exception*, 61 N.Y.U. L. Rev. 655, 684–86 (1986) (criticizing such agreements for creating an unnecessary, and possibly politically inflammatory, double standard).

159. *See also* European Convention on the Suppression of Terrorism, Jan. 27, 1977, Europ. T.S. No. 90, *reprinted in* 15 Int'l Legal Mat. 1272 (1976). Upon signing, the French delegation noted: "It is also clear that such a high degree of solidarity as is provided for in the Council of Europe Convention can only apply between States sharing the same ideals of freedom and democracy." 16 Int'l Legal Mat. 1329 (1977). Nevertheless, art. 13 of the Convention allows for far-reaching reservations. *See* Wood, *The European Convention on the Suppression of Terrorism*, 1981 Y.B. Eur. L. 307 (F. G. Jacobs ed., 1982).

160. Reisman, *supra* note 4, at 110.

161. Ciacci, *supra* note 29, at 22–23.

162. 91 Cong. Rec. (Senate) 7957 (1945).

163. For an excellent survey of various writings on the subject of ritual in society, *see* H. J. Wechsler, *Offerings of Jade and Silk* 20–31 (1985) [hereinafter: *Offerings*].

164. *Id.* at 24.

165. *Id.* at 24–25.

166. *Id.* at 26.

167. *Id.* at 30.

168. Kurtz, *Strategies of Legitimation and the Aztec State* 23 Ethnology 301, 306 (1984) [hereinafter: *Aztec*].

169. Moore, *supra* note 65, at 149.

170. M. Cranston, "From Legitimism to Legitimacy," in *Legitimacy/Légitimité* 37 (A. Moulakis ed., 1986).

171. Comaroff and Roberts, *supra* note 10, at 70–71.

172. *Aztec, supra* note 168, at 306.

173. *Id.* at 308.

174. *Offerings, supra* note 163, at 12–15.

175. *Id.* at 21.

176. *Aztec, supra* note 168, at 309.

177. *Id.* at 306.

178. Greene shows that even though a priest may fall into a secularized lifestyle, he retains his spiritual powers. A "whisky" priest is "a damned man putting God into the mouths of men" due to his authority to perform communion. *See* G. Greene, *The Power and the Glory* 83 (1940).

179. *Offerings, supra* note 163, at 10.

180. When presenting bills for royal assent, the Speaker of the House of Commons pays homage to the Crown with the formula: "Be it enacted by the Queen's most Excellent Majesty, by and with the advice and consent of the Lords Spiritual and Temporal, and Commons, in this present Parliament assembled, and by the authority of the same, as follows . . ." O. Phillips, *A First Book of English Law* 118–19 (7th ed., 1977). The Crown's right to refuse assent to bills which have properly passed through both Houses of Parliament is "practically obsolete." A. Dicey, *Introduction to the Study of the Law of the Constitution* 114 (9th ed., 1939). In fact, when the Unionists posited in 1913 that the reference to assent restored a real right of veto, the theory was criticized as "obviously absurd" and was said to have troubled the King. E. Ridges, *Constitutional Law* 106 (8th ed., 1950).

181. When a bill is presented to the Crown for assent, it bears an endorsement signed by the Speaker of the House certifying that the provisions of the Parliament Act have been complied with. The Parliament Act, 1 and 2 Geo. V. Cap. 13, 1911, Sec. 2(2), reproduced in *Select Statutes, Cases and Documents* 350, 352 (C. Robertson ed., 1935).

182. For a full discussion of this ritual as it applies to the enactment of both public and private bills by the House of Commons and House of Lords, *see* S. A. deSmith, *Constitutional and Administrative Law* 265–71 (3d ed., 1977).

183. The calling of banns is the public and official announcement

of persons who intend to marry and is meant to discover whether the parties are free to marry and whether any impediment to their lawful and valid marriage may exist. The tradition that no marriage was to be celebrated until after a triple publication of the church's bann originated in the eighth century and was extended over all Christendom by Pope Innocent III in 1215. *Encyclopedic Dictionary of Religion* 357 (1979).

184. *Offerings, supra* note 163, at 27.

185. *Id.*

186. *Id.* at 25.

187. *Id.* at 30.

188. *Aztec, supra* note 168, at 308.

189. *See* G.A. Res. 2029, 20 U.N. GAOR Supp. No. 14 at 20, U.N. Doc. A/6111 (1965).

190. Articles of Agreement of the International Bank for Reconstruction and Development, *entered into force* Dec. 27, 1945, 60 Stat. 1440, T.I.A.S. 1502, 3 Bevans 1390, 2 U.N.T.S. 134.

191. Constitution of the World Health Organization, *entered into force* Apr. 7, 1948, 62 Stat. 2679, T.I.A.S. 1808, 14 U.N.T.S. 185, as amended by World Health Assembly Resolution 1243 (1960), 11 U.S.T. 2553, T.I.A.S. 4643, 377 U.N.T.S. 380.

192. Constitution of the U.N. Food and Agricultural Organization, *entered into force* Oct. 16, 1945, 12 U.S.T. 980, T.I.A.S. 4803.

193. The United Nations International Children's Emergency Fund was founded by G.A. Res. 57, 1 U.N. GAOR (56th plen. mtg.) at 90 (1946).

194. *Aztec, supra* note 168, at 310.

195. *See* J. Dinneen, *The Purple Shamrock* (1949), which details the life of the Hon. James Michael Curley, four-time mayor of Boston. *See also* E. O'Connor, *The Last Hurrah* (1956), which, although fictional, is said to be based on Curley's life and career.

196. C. Krinsky, *St. Petersburg-on-the-Hudson: The Albany Mall*, citing Fortune, June 1971 at 92, in M. Barasch and L. Sandler, *Art the Ape of Nature* 771, 778 (1981).

197. The General Assembly adopted and authorized the use of the United Nations flag on October 20, 1947. *See* G.A. Res. 167, 2 U.N. GAOR (96th plen. mtg.) at 338–39, U.N. Doc. A/414 (1947).

198. The Secretary-General authorized, with the "support" of the Security Council, the flying of the United Nations flag on ships which would evacuate armed elements of the P.L.O. from Tripoli. *See* 38 U.N. SCOR (Resolutions and Decisions) at 5–6, U.N. Doc. S/16194, S/16195 (1983).

199. The United Nations Postal Administration was established

on January 1, 1951. *See* G.A. Res. 454, 5 U.N. GAOR Supp. (No. 20) at 57–58, U.N. Doc. A/1775 (1950).

200. The estimated 1986–87 net revenue from the sale of postage stamps is $8,667,700. *See First Report on Proposed Programme Budget for the Biennium 1986–1987*, Advisory Committee on Administrative and Budgetary Questions, 40 U.N. GAOR Supp. (No. 7) at 209, U.N. Doc. A/40/7 (1985).

201. The origin of the United Nations Military Observer Group in India and Pakistan (UNMOGIP) is found in a resolution of the U.N. Commission for India and Pakistan. *See* 3 U.N. SCOR Supp. (Nov. 1948) at 32, U.N. Doc S/1100, para. 75 (1948). The Security Council subsequently authorized its operation. *See* S.C. Res. 91, 6 U.N. SCOR (Resolutions and Decisions 1951) at 3, U.N. Doc. S/2017/Rev. 1, para. 7 (1951).

202. The Security Council established the U.N. Disengagement Observer Force (UNDOF) for the Golan Heights on May 31, 1974. *See* S.C. Res. 350, 29 U.N. SCOR (Resolutions and Decisions 1974) at 4, S/11305/Rev. 1 (1974).

203. The United Nations Force in Cyprus (UNFICYP) was formed by the Security Council on March 4, 1964. *See* S.C. Res. 186, 19 U.N. SCOR (Resolutions and Decisions 1964) at 2–4, U.N. Doc. S/5575 (1964).

204. The United Nations Interim Force in Lebanon (UNIFIL) was created by the Security Council on March 19, 1978. *See* S.C. Res. 425, 33 U.N. SCOR (Resolutions and Decisions 1978) at 5, U.N. Doc. S/12611 (1978).

205. S.C. Res. 619, 43 U.N. SCOR (Resolutions and Decisions 1988) at 11, U.N. Doc. S/20097 (1988) implementing U.N. Doc. S/20093 (1988).

206. For a discussion of the non-coercive role of U.N. peacekeeping forces *see* B. Urquhart, *A Life in Peace and War* 287–88, 342–43 (1987).

207. *See* Convention on the Privileges and Immunities of the United Nations, *adopted* by the General Assembly Feb. 13, 1946, 21 U.S.T. 1418, T.I.A.S. No. 6900, 1 U.N.T.S. 15. It entered into force for the U.S. on April 29, 1970. *See also* Agreement regarding the Headquarters of the United Nations, June 26, 1947, United States–United Nations, 61 Stat. 3416, T.I.A.S. No. 1676, 11 U.N.T.S. 11. This entered into force on November 21, 1947. *See further* Convention on the Privileges and Immunities of the Specialized Agencies, *approved* by the General Assembly Nov. 21, 1947, 33 U.N.T.S. 261.

208. In order to rectify the inequalities it perceived in its original system of compensation, the U.N. subjected U.N. salaries to a tax

assessed at a rate comparable to the employee's national income tax liability. G.A. Res. 239(III), 3 U.N. GAOR (159th plen. mtg.) at 100 (1948), as amended by G.A. Res. 359(IV), 4 U.N. GAOR (276th plen. mtg.) at 57 (1949).

209. *McCulloch v. Maryland*, 4 Wheat. 316, 347 (1819).

210. The origins of ambassadorial styles, privileges, duties, and immunities are explored in A. Gentili, "De Legationibus Libri Tres" (vols. 1–2), in 2 *Classics of International Law* (J. B. Scott ed., 1924). Gentili traces the origins to established usage described by, among others, Virgil (*id.* at 5), Livy (*id.*), Tacitus (*id.* at 18), Plutarch (*id.* at 23), and Cicero (*id.* at 58).

211. *See* M. J. McCaffree and P. Innis, *Protocol, the Complete Book of Diplomatic, Official and Social Usage* 87–104 (1985).

212. Legal Status of Eastern Greenland, *infra* note 241.

213. Gentili, *supra* note 210, at 186.

214. For a discussion of the Iranian hostage incident *see* Gross, *The Case Concerning United States Diplomatic and Consular Staff in Tehran: Phase of Provisional Remedies*, 74 Am. J. Int'l L. 395 (1980). For an analysis of the Libyan violations *see* Higgins, *The Abuse of Diplomatic Privileges and Immunities: Recent United Kingdom Experience*, 79 Am. J. Int'l L. 641 (1985).

215. S.C. Res. 457, 34 U.N. SCOR (Resolutions and Decisions 1979) at 23, U.N. Doc. S/13677 (1979) (adopted unanimously).

216. *See* United States Diplomatic and Consular Staff in Tehran (*U.S. v. Iran*), 1979 I.C.J. 7 (Provisional Measures Order of Dec. 15); 1980 I.C.J. 3 (Judgment of May 24); 1981 I.C.J. 45 (Order of May 12).

217. *See, for example,* "France Breaks Iran Ties and Isolates Embassy," N.Y. Times, July 18, 1987, at 1, which followed the Iranian embassy in Paris's grant of sanctuary to a non-diplomat wanted for questioning in connection with terrorist activities.

218. *See* Higgins, *UK Foreign Affairs Committee Report on the Abuse of Diplomatic Immunities and Privileges: Government Response and Report*, 80 Am. J. Int'l L. 135 (1986).

219. In the *Steamship Pesaro* case, the U.S. Supreme Court refused to recognize the difference between ships held and used by a government for a public purpose and ships used by the government in trade. "[The latter] are public ships in the same sense that war ships are. We know of no international usage which regards the maintenance and advancement of the economic welfare of a people in time of peace as any less a public purpose than the maintenance and training of a naval force." *Berizzi Bros. Co. v. S.S. Pesaro*, 271 U.S. 562, 574

(1926). The Court expounded upon this doctrine in *The Navemar*, holding "[a]dmittedly a vessel of a friendly government in its possession and service is a public vessel, even though engaged in the carriage of merchandise for hire. . . ." *Compania Espanola de Navigacion Maritime, S.A. v. Navemar*, 303 U.S. 68, 74–76 (1938).

220. The U.S. officially promulgated this policy in 1952, when the Department of State, by means of the "Tate Letter," declared its adherence to the "restrictive theory" of sovereign immunity. Under this theory, immunity would be recognized with regard to sovereign or public acts (*jure imperii*), but not with respect to private acts (*jure gestionis*). Letter by Jack Tate, Acting Legal Adviser to Philip Perlman, Acting Attorney General, May 19, 1952, *reprinted in* 6 *Digest of International Law*, Dep't St. Pub. No. 8350 (1968). For current European treatment of immunity, *see The European Convention on State Immunity and Additional Protocol, reprinted in* 11 Int'l Legal Mat. 470 (1972).

221. Foreign Sovereign Immunities Act of October 21, 1976, 90 Stat. 2891. *See also* Higgins, *Recent Developments in the Law of Sovereign Immunity in the United Kingdom*, 71 Am. J. Int'l L. 423 (1977).

222. *Offerings, supra* note 163, at 35.

223. McCaffree and Innis, *supra* note 211, at 103.

224. A. B. Bozeman, *Politics and Culture in International History* 309 (1960).

225. *Id.*

226. *See, for example*, Agreement regarding the Headquarters of the United Nations, art. 15, *supra* note 207. *See also* Vienna Convention on Diplomatic Relations, art. 11, *supra* note 79.

227. *See* Vienna Convention, *id.* at art. 9.

228. A resolution disapproving the U.S. action as a violation of diplomatic rights and privileges was passed in a meeting of the Organization of American States on November 18, 1988. N.Y. Times, Nov. 19, 1988, at 28.

229. Grotius, *supra* note 1.

230. Declaration on Principles of International Law concerning Friendly Relations and Co-operation among States in Accordance with the Charter of the United Nations, G.A. Res. 2625, 25 U.N. GAOR Supp. (No. 28) at 121, U.N. Doc. A/8082 (1970).

231. The Peace of Westphalia refers to a series of treaties that terminated both the Eighty Years' War between Spain and the Netherlands and the war between the German Empire and the united forces of France and Sweden. *See* Treaty of Peace, Jan. 30, 1648,

Spain-Netherlands, 1 Consolidated T.S. 70 (French trans.), Treaty of
Peace, Oct. 24, 1648, Sweden-Germany, *id.* at 198. Treaty of Peace,
Oct. 24, 1648, France-Germany, *id.* at 319.

232. The Treaty of Fez (1912) is an example of the hegemony
France once enjoyed in the Mediterranean. The International Court
of Justice noted that Articles V and VI of that agreement were broad
enough to give France complete control over Morocco's foreign affairs.
See Rights of Nationals of the United States of America in Morocco
(*Fr. v. U.S.*), 1952 I.C.J. 176, 193.

233. France and Spain had established a regime of capitulations
in their former dominions in Morocco. For a description of this regime
see *id.* at 194–95.

234. In the United Kingdom, a protectorate is defined as a territory, outside of Her Majesty's dominions, for whose international relations the Crown is responsible. The British government may also have
acquired some variable measure of jurisdiction over the protectorate's
domestic matters, but the protectorate did not thereby become part
of "Her Majesty's dominions" i.e. it was not formally a colony. 6
Halsbury's Laws of England sec. 806 (4th ed., 1974).

235. The Statute of Westminster (1931) "regularized" the independence of dominions in international affairs. The Statute provided
that no Act of Parliament would extend, or be deemed to extend, to
a dominion unless the dominion requested or consented to such extension. 6 *Halsbury's Laws of England* sec. 834 (4th ed., 1974). Therefore
any treaty Britain entered into would have no binding effect in its
dominions except if the dominions desired the treaty's application.

236. Pre-independent India was one of the original parties to the
Covenant of the League of Nations, *see* 1 League of Nations O.J. 11
(1920), and the Charter of the United Nations, *see* 1946–47
U.N.Y.B. 3 (1947).

237. For a discussion of Soviet strategy, *see* T. Franck, *Nation
Against Nation* 21 (1985).

238. The Charter prescribes that each state shall have one vote,
and that voting shall be by simple majority except on important matters requiring a two-thirds majority. *See* art. 18, Charter of the United
Nations, 59 Stat. 1031, T.S. 993, 3 Bevans 1153 (1945).

239. *See* art. 27, *id.*

240. I. Brown, "Thucydides and the Peloponesian War" (ms.,
1987).

241. For example, a pledged word commits powerful as well as
weak governments. There is widespread recognition by states, antedat-
ing the U.N. Charter, that a commitment equally obligates powerful,

as also weaker nations. *See* Legal Status of Eastern Greenland (*Den. v. Nor.*), 1933 P.C.I.J. (ser. A/B) No. 53, at 22 (April 5).

242. For documentation relevant to U.N. policy on membership and credentials, *see* T. Franck and M. Glennon, *Foreign Relations and National Security Law* 459–63, 508–24 (1987).

243. Reparation for Injuries Suffered in the Service of the United Nations, 1949 I.C.J. 174 (Judgment of April 11).

244. *See* L. J. Beck, *The Method of Descartes* 14–30 (1952); G. Berkeley, "A Treatise Concerning the Principles of Human Knowledge," in *Essays, Principles, Dialogues* 99 (M. W. Calkins ed., 1929).

245. *See, for example*, Letter dated 8 March 1950, Trygve Lie, Legal Aspects of the Problem of Representation in the United Nations, 5 U.N. SCOR Supp. (Jan.–May 1, 1950) at 18–22, U.N. Doc. S/1466 (1950).

246. The vote was 104 to 11, with 10 abstentions. G.A. Res. 2793, 26 U.N. GAOR Supp (No. 29) at 3, U.N. Doc. A/L.647/ Rev.1 (1971), *reprinted in* 13 *United Nations Resolutions* 359 (D. J. Djonovich ed., 1976).

247. *See* Aufricht, *Principles and Practices of Recognition by International Organizations*, 43 Am. J. Int'l L. 679, 683–85 (1949). For more information about the Universal Postal Union, *see* G. A. Codding, *The Universal Postal Union* (1964).

248. Letter of A. C. Botto de Barros to Thomas M. Franck, 15 Dec. 1987.

249. The resolution calls on governments "not to interrupt or hinder postal traffic as . . . in the event of dispute, conflict or war" and authorizes the Director-General of the International Bureau of UPU "to take what initiatives he considers advisable to facilitate, while respecting national sovereignties, the maintenance or re-establishment of postal exchange between parties to a dispute, conflict or war. . . ." Resolution C37, Lausanne Congress of 1974.

250. *See* G.A. Res. 3212, 29 U.N. GAOR Supp. (No. 31) at 3, U.N. Doc. A/L.739/Add.1 (1974), and S.C. Res. 353, 29 U.N. SCOR (Resolutions and Decisions 1974) at 7, U.N. Doc. S/PV.1781 (1974), and S.C. Res. 367, 30 U.N. SCOR (Resolutions and Decisions 1975) at 1, U.N. Doc. S/PV.1820 (1975).

251. After the secession of Bangladesh (formerly East Pakistan) from Pakistan, the World Bank held Pakistan responsible for all loans previously made. The country that signs a loan remains responsible for the loan, unless the country ceases to exist as a viable, recognized entity. In the case of Pakistan, special arrangements were eventually made, pursuant to which Bangladesh assumed some of the loans. Tele-

phone interview with David Goldberg, World Bank Legal Department (Nov. 23, 1987). *See also* J. Gold, *Membership and Nonmembership* 60–66, 284–85 n.1, 294, 470 (1974).

252. Admission was achieved by S.C. Res. 351, 29 U.N. SCOR (Resolutions and Decisions 1974) at 15, U.N. and G.A. Res. 3203, 29 U.N. GAOR Supp. (No. 31) at 2, U.N. Doc. A/L.728/Add.1 (1974).

253. G.A. Res. 2793, 26 U.N. GAOR Supp. (No. 29) at 3, U.N. Doc. A/L.647/Rev.1 (1971). The resolution called on India and Pakistan to withdraw from "the territory of the other" in circumstances in which only India was violating this injunction.

254. Admission of a State to the United Nations, 1948 I.C.J. 57 (Advisory Opinion of May 28).

255. *Id.* at 62, 63.

256. Letter dated 8 March 1950, Trygve Lie, *supra* note 245.

257. *Id.* at 21.

258. Statement by the Legal Counsel submitted to the President of the General Assembly at its Request. 1970 U.N. Juridical Y.B. 169 (1972).

259. 3 U.N. SCOR (294th mtg.) at 16 (1948).

260. For a discussion, *see* G. Hackworth, 1 *Digest of International Law* 161–387 (1940); M. Whiteman, 2 *Digest of International Law* 1–753 (1963).

261. *See* (for Australia) Starkes, *The New Australian Policy of Recognition of Foreign Governments*, 62 Austl. L.J. 390 (1988). For the British and U.S. practice, *see* Franck and Glennon, *supra* note 242, at 524. *See also* Peterson, *Recognition of Governments Should Not be Abolished*, 77 Am. J. Int'l L. 31 (1983); L. Galloway, *Recognizing Foreign Governments, The Practice of the United States* (1978); Warbrick, *The New British Policy on Recognition of Governments*, 30 Int'l & Comp. L.Q. 568 (1981); Dixon, *Recent Developments in United Kingdom Practice Concerning the Recognition of States and Governments*, 22 The Int'l Lawyer 555 (1988). *See further Restatement (Third) of the Foreign Relations Law of the United States*, sec. 202 (1986).

262. Cranston, *supra* note 170, at 39–40.

263. *Id.* at 41.

264. State Department Memorandum: U.S. Policy on Nonrecognition of Communist China, 39 Dep't St. Bull. 385 (Sept. 1958).

265. M. Whiteman, 2 *Digest of International Law* 111 (1963).

266. G.A. Res. 3207, 29 U.N. GAOR (2248th plen. mtg.) at 259, 277, U.N. Doc. A/L.731/Rev.1 (1974) (resolution on South Africa). Most recently, Oman, acting on behalf of 20 Arab states, proposed an amendment to exclude the credentials of Israel from General As-

sembly approval. The General Assembly voted not to act with regard to this amendment. *Credentials Committee Reports Adopted,* 24 UN Chronicle 16 (1987).

267. Credentials of Representatives to the Forty-first Session of the General Assembly: First Report of the Credentials Committee, 41 U.N. General Assembly (Agenda Item 3) para. 12, U.N. Doc. A/41/727 (prov. ed. 1986). "The representative of the United States of America stated that the credentials of the representatives of Democratic Kampuchea were in order, fulfilled the requirements of rule 27 of the rules of procedure, had already been 'accepted by the General Assembly in the past and should be accepted at the current session. The suggested alternative was a regime brought to power by a foreign military invasion and that was clearly not representative in any way, shape or form of the Kampuchean people." *Id.*

268. For the view that one Bantustan is entitled to recognition and U.N. membership by application of the "who's in charge" test, *see* Heydt, *Non-recognition of the Independence of Transkei,* 10 Case W. Res. J. Int'l L. 167 (1978).

269. Ijalaye, *Was Biafra at Any Time a State in International Law?,* 65 Am. J. Int'l L. 551 (1971).

270. U Thant discreetly arranged a meeting between the U.S. and North Vietnamese authorities and so informed Ambassador Adlai Stevenson. President Lyndon Johnson, however, did not act on this initiative. Correspondence with Sir Brian Urquhart, January 27, 1989.

271. Urquhart, *supra* note 206, at 266.

272. 5 U.N. SCOR (506th mtg.) at 5, (507th mtg.) at 1 (1950).

273. The Secretary-General conducted a series of talks with Chou En-lai "in the name of the United Nations" (*see* G.A. Res. 906, 9 U.N. GAOR Supp. (No. 21) at 56, U.N. Doc. A/2890 (1954)) in order to discuss the release of four U.S. fighter pilots shot down near the Yalu River between October 1952 and January 1953, while they were flying missions for the U.N. Command during the Korean War. *See* 2 Public Papers of the Secretaries-General of the United Nations: Dag Hammarskjold (1953–56), at 415–59 (1972), for details of the Secretary-General's mission.

274. *Lehigh Valley R.R. Co. v. Russia,* 21 F.2d 396, 401, *cert. denied* 275 U.S. 571, 48 S.Ct. 159 (1927).

275. *Guaranty Trust Co. v. United States,* 304 U.S. 126, 137–38 (1938).

276. *Id.* at 138.

277. *In re Luks' Estate,* 45 Misc.2d 72, at 75; 256 N.Y.S.2d 194, at 197 (Sur. Ct. N.Y. 1965). For the recent status of the three republics' delegations in Washington, D.C., *see* 3 *Missions with Noth-*

ing But a Cause Fight for Independence from Soviets, N.Y. Times, June 6, 1989, at B7.

278. 262 N.Y. 220, 186 N.E. 679 (1933).

279. *Id.* at 224, 186 N.E. at 681.

280. *Id.* at 227, 186 N.E. at 682.

281. *Id.* at 228, 186 N.E. at 683.

282. 13 A.D.2d 36, 213 N.Y.S.2d 417 (1961).

283. *Id.* at 38, 213 N.Y.S.2d at 419.

284. *Id.* at 39, 213 N.Y.S.2d at 420.

285. *Id.* at 42, 213 N.Y.S.2d at 422.

286. *Id.*

287. *Morgan Guaranty Trust Co. v. Republic of Palau*, 639 F. Supp. 706, 713 (S.D.N.Y. 1986).

288. *Id.* at 714. *See similarly Iran-Handicraft and Carpet v. Marjan International Corp.*, 655 F. Supp. 1275 (S.D.N.Y. 1987); *but see contra, Republic of Panama v. Republic National Bank of New York*, 681 F. Supp. 1066 (S.D.N.Y. 1988).

289. Credentials of Representatives to the Forty-first Session of the General Assembly: First Report of the Credentials Committee, 41 U.N. General Assembly (Agenda Item 3), U.N. Doc. A/41/727 (prov. ed. 1986) (accepting the credentials of Israel). In response to attempts to expel Israel, H. E. Amb. Benjamin Netanyahu, Israeli representative to the United Nations, stated, "Without adherence to the principle of universality, this body would be totally deprived of any moral authority. It would have all the moral authority of a Warsaw Pact gathering or an Islamic Conference gathering." 40 U.N. General Assembly (37th plen. mtg.) at 29–30, U.N. Doc. A/40/PV.37 (prov. ed., 1985).

290. The U.N. has acted "against" use of its symbols by unauthorized private persons or societies, so as to ensure that its flag and emblem will be able to exert the maximum compliance pull when flown over a demilitarized zone or worn on the sleeve of a truce observer. The seal and emblem are to be protected by member states through legislation. G.A. Res. of Dec. 7, 1946. *See also* Report of the Secretary-General to the Sixth Committee on the Official Seal and Emblem of the United Nations, considered at its 21st and 25th meetings on Nov. 20 and 30, 1946.

291. Credentials of Representatives to the Forty-first Session of the General Assembly, G.A. Res. 41/7A, 41 U.N. GAOR Supp. (No. 53) at 18, U.N. Doc. A/41/727 (1986); G.A. Res. 41/7B, 41 U.N. GAOR Supp. (No. 53) at 18, U.N. Doc. A/41/727/Add.1 (1986).

292. Aristotle, 5 *Nichomachean Ethics* (ch. 1), 1129.

293. R. Dworkin, *supra* note 6, at 178–84.

294. M. Whiteman, 1 *Digest of International Law* 917–20 (1936).

295. For a discussion, *see* Oppenheim, *supra* note 35, at 134–37. See also *Bank of Ethiopia v. National Bank of Egypt and Liguori*, ch. 513 (1937); and *Haile Selassie v. Cable and Wireless Ltd.* (No. 2), ch. 182 (1939).

296. Whiteman, *supra* note 294, at 917.

297. *Id.* at 918 (quoting French authority).

298. *See* Franck, *supra* note 237, at 216–18.

299. Dworkin, *supra* note 6, at 176–224.

300. *Id.* at 190–92.

301. *World Debt Tables*, External Debt of Developing Countries, 1985–86, published by the World Bank (1986) at xi.

302. *See* A. Riding, *Brazil to Suspend Interest Payment to Foreign Banks*, N.Y. Times, Feb. 21, 1987, at 1, col. 1; *Concern Renewed over Latin Debt, id.*, Feb. 22, 1987, at 11, col. 1.

303. *Resolving the Debt Crisis*, America, March 22, 1986, at 217. Gilprin, *Brazil Situation Spurs Action on Others' Debts*, N.Y. Times, Feb. 28, 1987, at 39, col. 1, at 42, col. 1.

304. *Latin American Nations Unite on Debt Question*, N.Y. Times, Oct. 18, 1986, at 4, col. 6; Henry, *Dance of Debt Isn't Over Yet*, U.S. News & World Rep., Aug. 31, 1987, at 39.

305. Gilprin, *supra* note 303, at 39, col. 1. *See Resolving the Debt Crisis*, America, March 22, 1986, at 217.

306. Amuzegar, *Dealing with Debt*, Foreign Policy 140, 151–52 (Fall 1987).

307. *See* N.Y. Times, Aug. 2, 1987, at 12, and Aug. 3, 1987, at A5.

308. Dworkin, *supra* note 6, at 179.

309. G. Fletcher, *Rethinking Criminal Law* 780 (1978).

310. *Id.* at 780–82.

311. Dworkin, *supra* note 6, at 182.

312. See *Agora: The Downing of Iran Air Flight 655* (M. Leigh, H. Maier, A. Lowenfeld, contribs.), 83 Am. J. Int'l L. 318–41 (1989).

313. Resolution adopted by the ICAO Council on 6 Mar. 1984. 23 Int'l L. Mat. 937 (1984).

314. R. S. Baker, *Woodrow Wilson and World Settlement* 109 (1922).

315. S. Wambaugh, *Plebiscites Since the World War* 13 (1933).

316. Baker, *supra* note 314, at 187.

317. *Id.*

318. *Id.* at 188.

319. *Id.*

320. *Id.* at 189.

321. U.S. Dep't of State, Papers Relating to the Foreign Relations of the United States, Vol. IV, The Paris Peace Conference 73 (1943) [hereinafter: FRUS].

322. The premiers and foreign minister of the five Principal Powers, commonly called the "Council of Ten." Wambaugh, *supra* note 315, at 15.

323. H. W. V. Temperley, 2 A *History of the Peace Conference of Paris* 203 (1924).

324. Wambaugh, *supra* note 315, at 14.

325. Temperley, *supra* note 323, at 205.

326. Wambaugh, *supra* note 315, at 31.

327. Temperley, *supra* note 323, Vol. IV, at 303–4, 315.

328. FRUS, *supra* note 321, Vol. V, at 80.

329. C. Seymour, *The Intimate Papers of Colonel House* 438 (1928).

330. FRUS, *supra* note 321, Vol. VI, at 50.

331. *Id. See also* Wambaugh, *supra* note 315, at 33.

332. Temperley, *supra* note 323, Vol. IV, at 327. *See also* Wambaugh, *supra* note 315, at 34.

333. Temperley, *supra* note 323, Vol. IV, at 261.

334. *Id.* at 262. *See also* FRUS, *supra* note 321, Vol. II, The Lansing Papers, at 140, 144–45.

335. *Id.* at 264.

336. Temperley, *supra* note 323, Vol. IV, at 268.

337. Wambaugh, *supra* note 315, at 23.

338. Temperley, *supra* note 323, Vol. IV, at 268.

339. Pomerance, *The United States and Self-Determination: Perspectives on the Wilsonian Conception*, 70 Am. J. Int'l L. 1, 8 (1976).

340. Seymour, *supra* note 329, at 334.

341. *Id.*

342. *Id.* at 335.

343. *Id.* at 345.

344. Temperley, *supra* note 323, Vol. II, at 182.

345. *Id.* at 12. *See also* Wambaugh, *supra* note 315, at 18.

346. Baker, *supra* note 314, at 110–11.

347. *Id.*

348. Wambaugh, *supra* note 315, at 16.

349. M. Pomerance, *Self-Determination in Law and Practice* 4 (1982).

350. FRUS, *supra* note 321, Vol. V, at 88.

351. Wambaugh, *supra note* 315, at 31–32.

352. *Id.*

353. *Id.* at 17.

354. A. Cobban, *National Self-Determination* 26 (1948).

355. Wambaugh, *supra* note 315, at 17.

356. A. J. Mayer, *Politics and Diplomacy of Peacemaking* 397 (1967).

357. Wambaugh, *supra* note 315, at 17. *See also* Cobban, *supra* note 354, at 26.

358. Pomerance, *supra* note 349, at 2.

359. Wambaugh, *supra* note 315, at 17.

360. D. F. Fleming, *The United States and World Organization* 152 (1938).

361. *Id.*

362. *Id.*

363. *Id.* at 152–53.

364. *Id.* at 153.

365. *Id.* at 153–54.

366. *Id.* at 154.

367. Linking the issue of Ireland to self-determination, Balfour wrote, "No one can think that Ulster ought to join the South and West who thinks that the Jugo Slavs should be separated from Austria. No one can think that Ulster should be divorced from Britain who believes in self-determination." Balfour, *The Irish Question*, Nov. 25, 1919, PRO CAB 24/93, *quoted in* T. G. Fraser, *Partition in Ireland, India and Palestine* 27 (1984). For Lloyd George's comments, *see* Fraser, *id.* at 38.

368. Wambaugh, *supra* note 315, at 515.

369. *Id.*

370. J. Barros, *The Aaland Islands Question: Its Settlement by the League of Nations* 116 (1968).

371. Gregory, *The Neutralization of the Aaland Islands*, 17 Am. J. Int'l L. 63, 68 (1922). *See also* Barros, *id.* at 130.

372. Barros, *id.* at 116. *See also* Wambaugh, *supra* note 315, at 516.

373. Gregory, *supra* note 371, at 69.

374. L. C. Buchheit, *Secession: The Legitimacy of Self-Determination* 71 (1978).

375. *Id.*

376. Wambaugh, *supra* note 315, at 517.

377. Barros, *supra* note 370, at 317.

378. U.N. Charter, art. 73.

379. *Id.* at art. 76(b).

380. In conversation with the author, Judge Manfred Lachs, of

the International Court of Justice, formerly legal adviser to the Polish Foreign Office, has observed that "we expected decolonization to take fifty years and disarmament to be achieved in a decade. It happened just the other way around."

381. For a discussion of this system as it operated in Algeria, *see* E. Behr, *The Algerian Problem* 38–40 (1961).

382. N.Y. Times, Jan. 17, 1962, at A5.

383. Saudi Arabia, Syria, Yemen, Yugoslavia, Afghanistan, Burma, Ceylon, Egypt, India, Indonesia, Iraq, Jordan, Libya, and Nepal abstained from voting on a resolution condemning the 1956 Soviet invasion of Hungary. G.A. Res. 1004 (ES-II), U.N. GAOR 2nd Emergency Spec. Sess. (568th plen. mtg.) at 20, U.N. Doc. A/PV.564 (1956). Algeria, India, and Pakistan abstained from voting on a Security Council resolution condemning the 1968 Soviet invasion of Czechoslovakia. 23 U.N. SCOR (1443rd mtg.) at 28–29, U.N. Doc. S/PV.1443 (1968).

384. The parameters of India's independence are set out in India Independence Act, 1947, 10 & 11 Geo. 6, ch. 30. For a discussion of the Kashmir annexation, *see* Franck, *supra* note 237, at 51–53. For the Goa invasion, *see id.* at 53–58.

385. Biafra declared its independence on May 30, 1967.

386. 59 Dept. St. Bull. 353 (1968).

387. G.A. Res. 1514(XV), 15 U.N. GAOR Supp. (No. 16) at 66, U.N. Doc. A/4684 (1960).

388. *Id.* at Preamble.

389. *Id.* at art. 5.

390. *Id.* at art. 3.

391. *Id.* at art. 5.

392. G.A. Res. 3485, 30 U.N. GAOR Supp. (No. 34) at 118, U.N. Doc. A/10426 (1975), calls upon "all States to respect the inalienable right of the people of Portuguese Timor to self-determination, freedom and independence. . . ."

393. G.A. Res. 3458(A), 30 U.N. GAOR Supp. (No. 34) at 116, U.N. Doc. A/10427 (1975).

394. G.A. Res. 3458(B), 30 U.N. GAOR Supp. (No. 34) at 117, U.N. Doc. A/10427 (1975). This resolution appears implicitly to recognize the Moroccan occupation.

395. For a discussion of these events, *see* Franck, *supra* note 237, at 81–82, 169, 228.

396. Behr, *supra* note 381, at 38.

397. The general situation is clouded, however, by events which propelled the Ibos toward secession. In 1966, Ibo army officers had overthrown the elected government of Sir Abubakar Tafawa Balewa.

When these, in turn, were overthrown a pogrom against the Ibos in other (especially Muslim northern) tribal areas caused a million Ibos to flee to their tribal homeland.

398. For the debates in the Security Council on Bangladesh's application for U.N. membership soon after its secession, *see* 27 U.N. SCOR (1658th mtg.) at 4–10, U.N. Doc. S/10759 (1972), in which the opposing Chinese and Soviet positions are set forth. *See also* 27 U.N. SCOR (1659th mtg.) at 1 (1972) and 27 U.N. SCOR (1660th mtg.) at 1 (1972).

399. S.C. Res. S/5002, U.N. SCOR Resolutions (1st-20th yr.) at 3–5, art. 9, U.N. Doc. S/5002 (1961), *reprinted in* F. H. Boland, T. M. Franck, E. A. Gross & O. Schachter, *The Legal Aspects of the United Nations Action in the Congo* 80–81 (The Hammarskjold Forums Working Paper No. 525/62/2, 1962).

400. "A treaty which is a dead letter may be said to be terminated." D. P. O'Connell, *International Law* 266 (1970).

401. Dworkin, *supra* note 6, at 192.

402. *Id.* at 194.

403. *Id.* at 200.

404. *Id.*

405. *Id.* at 201.

406. For a discussion of opposition to the Security Council veto, *see* E. Luard, *A History of the United Nations* 45–49 (1982).

407. See *Basic Documents of the United Nations* 70–72 (L. Sohn ed., 1968).

408. A persuasive case for inequality of voting power was made by the drafters of the U.S. Constitution's provision giving each state, regardless of population, two senators. Oddly, this inequality continues to be regarded quite widely as a legitimate rule, coherent in its logical connection with the underlying concept of the importance of the individual states, as such, in the union. A similar arrangement was adopted with widespread public support by the Soviet Union. Its 1989 elections to choose a new Congress of the People were conducted under rules which allocate one-third of the delegates, each, to the voters at large, to the states equally, and to the party and other professional and social institutions.

409. United States Mission to the United Nations, List of Vetoes Cast in Public Meetings of the Security Council (unpub. mimeo).

410. The United States vetoed a Security Council resolution which called for full compliance with the judgment of the International Court of Justice in the *Nicaragua case*. 41 U.N. Security Council (2704th mtg.), U.N. Doc. S/PV.2704 (prov. ed. 1986), *reprinted in* 25 Int'l Legal Mat. 1353, 1363 (1986). For the text of the resolu-

tion, *see* 41 U.N. Security Council (2703rd mtg.), U.N. Doc. S/18250 (prov. ed. 1986), *reprinted in* 25 Int'l Legal Mat. 1352 (1986).

411. United States Mission to the United Nations, List of Vetoes Cast in Public Meetings of the Security Council (Apr. 14, 1988) (unpub.). Only once did the People's Republic of China cast a solitary veto. *Id.* at 9. France has stood alone only twice since 1946. *Id.* at 10–11. All United Kingdom vetoes during the last fifteen years have been cast alongside the U.S. *Id.* at 12–13.

412. The General Agreement on Tariffs and Trade, 61 Stat. part (5) and (6), T.I.A.S. No. 1700, 4 Bevans 639, 55–61 U.N.T.S. (entered into force for the United States, Jan. 1, 1948).

413. *Id.* at art. 1(1).

414. GATT Contracting Parties, Decision of November 28, 1979, Differential and More Favorable Treatment Reciprocity and Fuller Participation of Developing Countries. GATT, 26th Supp. BISD 203 (1980). *See also* J. Jackson and W. Davey, *Legal Problems of International Economic Relations* 1149 (2d ed., 1986).

415. GATT Contracting Parties, *id.* at para. 1.

416. *Id.* at para. 6.

417. General Agreement on Tariffs and Trade, Oct. 30, 1947, art. XXVIII, T.I.A.S. No. 1700, 55 U.N.T.S. 187, 276–78.

418. Dworkin, *supra* note 6, at 207.

419. Hart, *supra* note 3, at 209.

420. *Id.*

421. *See* I. Sinclair, *The International Law Commission* (1987).

422. J. De Arechaga, *The Work and Jurisprudence of the International Court of Justice*, 1947–1986, 58 Brit. Y.B. Int'l L. 1 (1987).

423. For an enumeration, *see* Vagts, *supra* note 146, at 17.

424. E.g., Statute of the International Court of Justice, art. 38.

425. Hart thought they did give rise to obligation and that the Austinian definition "distorts the role played in all legal thought and discourse of the ideas of obligation and duty. . . . Yet once we free ourselves from the . . . conception of law as essentially an order backed by threats, there seems no good reason for limiting the normative idea of obligation to rules supported by organized sanctions." Hart, *supra* note 3, at 212.

426. *Id.* at 214–15.

427. Libya denied that it had sent soldiers to Chad. N.Y. Times, Feb. 17, 1986, at A3, col. 4; Miller, *Libya Continues to Deny It Fights for the Rebels in Chad*, N.Y. Times, Feb. 21, 1986, at A8, col. 1.

428. Lewis, *France Refuses to Back Chad Offensive*, N.Y. Times, Aug. 11, 1987, at A3, col. 4.

429. While the term "contract" is susceptible of many definitions,

whatever else a contract may entail, it is agreed that it is "a promise, or set of promises, for breach of which the law gives a remedy, or the performance of which the law in some way recognizes as a duty." 1 Williston on Contracts sec. 1 (3d ed. 1957); Restatement (Second) of Contracts sec. 1 (1981). *See also* 1 A. Corbin, Contracts sec. 3 (1963) (which defines a contract to include "a promise enforceable at law directly or indirectly"). In some jurisdictions, courts will routinely mandate specific performance of the promise. *See, for example,* Dawson, *Specific Performance in France and Germany,* 57 Mich. L. Rev. 495 (1959). The Anglo-American legal system, however, prefers to impose damages at least equal to the value of the breached promise. *See, for example,* J. Calamari & J. Perillo, *The Law of Contracts* 580–604 (1977).

430. Hart, *supra* note 3, at 219.

431. Vienna Convention on the Law of Treaties, *supra* note 54, at art. 26.

432. *Id. See* I. Sinclair, *The Vienna Convention on the Law of Treaties* (2d ed., 1984).

433. F. Suarez, *A Treatise on Laws and God the Lawgiver,* Bk. II, 2 Suarez, *Classics of International Law* 349 (1944).

434. G.A. Res. 42/229B of 2 March 1988.

435. The Observer Mission status was created by G.A. Res. 3237(XXIX) of 22 November 1974. The closure of the P.L.O. Mission is required by Title X ("Anti-Terrorism Act of 1987") of the Foreign Relations Authorization Act, 1988 and 1989.

436. Agreement between the United Nations and the United States of America regarding the Headquarters of the United Nations of June 26, 1947. 11 U.N.T.S. 11, T.I.A.S. 1676.

437. Applicability of the Obligation to Arbitrate under Section 21 of the United Nations Headquarters Agreement of June 26, 1947 24 (April 26, 1988) (unofficial advance text).

438. Case concerning *Greco-Bulgarian "Communities,"* P.C.I.J., Ser. B, No. 17, p. 32.

439. Applicability, *supra* note 437, at 1 of sep. op.

440. Military and Paramilitary Activities, *supra* note 74, at 82.

441. T. Meron, *Human Rights and Humanitarian Norms as Customary Law* 80–81 (1989). *See* to the same effect Sohn, *Generally Accepted International Rules,* 61 Wash. L. Rev. 1073, 1077–78 (1986), and Schachter, *International Law Implications of U.S. Human Rights Policies,* 24 N.Y. L. Sch. L. Rev. 63, 68 (1978).

442. According to traditional theory, a state cannot unilaterally revoke a rule of customary international law. *See* Oppenheim, *supra* note 35, at 18. This view, however, does not go unchallenged. Some

publicists believe that a customary norm is only binding upon a state if it is expressly accepted. *See* Tunkin, *Co-existence and International Law*, 95 Recueil des Cours 1, 13–14 (1958). *See also* the "persistent objector" exception, in Sinclair, *supra* note 432, at 258, and Stein, *The Approach of the Different Drummer: The Principle of the Persistent Objector in International Law*, 26 Harv. Int'l L.J. 457, 481 (1985). For the International Law Commission's draft articles on this subject (in its draft on State Responsibility), *see* 2 Y.B. Int'l L. Comm'n 33 (1980). U.N. Doc. A/CN.4/Ser. A/1980/Add. 1, Part 2 (1981).

443. H. Mosler, *The International Society as Legal Community* 19–20 (1980).

444. It is a well-established principle that a new state to the international community is automatically bound by the rules of international conduct existing at the time of admittance. *See* Oppenheim, *supra* note 35, at 17–18. Even Tunkin concedes that "without reservations into official relations with other states," a new state is bound by "principles and norms of existing international law." *See* Tunkin, *Remarks on the Juridical Nature of International Law*, 49 Cal. L. Rev. 419, 428 (1961).

445. There has been wide debate over the rights and obligations a successor state can inherit from its parent. The nineteenth-century doctrine of universal succession maintains that all the rights and duties of the parent pass to the successor. *See* O. Udokang, *Succession of New States to International Treaties* 122–24 (1972). On the other extreme is negativist theory, which holds that a successor inherits no rights and obligations, but begins with a *tabula rasa*. *See* D. O'Connell, *State Succession in Municipal Law and International Law* 14–17 (1967). The truth lies somewhere in between, with certain rights and duties of the parent devolving upon the successor. *See* Oppenheim, *supra* note 35, at 120. Hart further points to evidence that changes in a state's circumstance may automatically accord it new rights and duties, as, for example, when it acquires new territory giving it a coastline. Hart, *supra* note 3, at 221.

446. *The "Tinoco Claims Arbitration": Great Britain v. Costa Rica*, 18 Am. J. Int'l L. 147 (1924); 1 U.N. Rep. Int'l Arb. Awards 369.

447. During Security Council debate on the Falklands war, Mexico rejected Argentina's use of force to settle any conflict. *See* U.N. Doc. S/PV.2362, at 46 (1982). Rio de Janeiro's leading newspaper, echoing the government's sentiments, condemned Argentina "for showing little appreciation for what peace . . . means." *See* N.Y. Times, May

23, 1982, at 1, 14. Moreover, Kenya charged Argentina with "committing naked aggression." U.N. Doc. S/PV.2364, at 23–26 (1982).

448. F. Suarez, *A Treatise on Laws and God the Lawgiver*, Bk. I, 2 Suarez, *Classics of International Law* 74 (1944) [hereinafter: Suarez Treatise I].

449. H. Kelsen, *Principles of International Law* 4, 8 (R. Tucker 2d ed., 1967).

450. *Id.* at 4.

451. Hoffmann, *International Systems and International Law*, 14 World Politics 207 (1961).

452. Hermann, "International Crisis as a Situational Variable," in *International Politics and Foreign Policy: Reader in Research and Theory* 411 (J. N. Rosenau ed., 1969). For a fuller discussion, *see* T. Franck and E. Weisband, *Word Politics: Verbal Strategy Among the Superpowers* 126–29 (1971).

453. *See* Franck and Weisband, *id.* at 129 and, more generally, at 128–31.

454. Gouldner, *The Norm of Reciprocity: A Preliminary Statement*, 25 Am. Soc. Rev. 161 (1960).

455. J. Piaget, *The Moral Judgment of the Child* 161 (1960).

456. The example is a variant on an example presented in Franck and Weisband, *supra* note 452, at 130–31.

457. Sociologists view the community as an arena of social interaction. Therefore, "[a] community is said to exist when interaction between individuals has the purpose of meeting individual needs and obtaining group goals." M. Sussman, *Community Structure and Analysis* 1 (1959). More broadly, the concept of community "expresses our vague yearnings for a commonality of desire, a communion with those around us, an extension of the bonds of kin and friend to all those who share a common fate with us." D. Poplin, *Communities* 5 (1972) (*quoting* W. Minar and S. Greer, *The Concept of Community* ix (1969)).

458. Dworkin, *supra* note 6, at 196.

459. *Id.* at 197.

460. Suarez Treatise I, *supra* note 448, at 176–77.

461. Dworkin, *supra* note 6, at 211.

462. *Id.* at 213.

463. *Id.* at 214.

464. *Id.*

465. F. de Victoria, "De Indis et de Jure Belli Relectiones" (J. Bate trans.), in *Classics of International Law* 153 (1917).

466. H. Grotius, 1 "De Jure Praedae Commentarius" 12 (1604),

in *Classics of International Law* (J. Scott ed., 1950). He also lays down the rule that "Whatever all states have indicated to be their will, that is law in regard to them all." *Id*. at 26.

467. Meron, *supra* note 441, at 42.

468. T. Hobbes, *The Leviathan* (1651), *reprinted in* 3 *The English Works of Thomas Hobbes* (W. Molesworth ed., 1841).

469. J. Locke, *Two Treatises of Government* 1690 (W. Carpenter ed., 1955).

470. J. Rousseau, *On the Social Contract* 1762 (D. Cress trans./ ed., 1983).

471. I. Kant, *The Foundations of the Metaphysics of Morals* 1785 (T. Abbott trans., 1873), *reprinted in The Essential Kant* 295–360 (A. Zweig ed., 1970).

472. Rawls, *supra* note 3, at 11, n.4.

473. Locke describes our natural condition—i.e. our status as free and equal beings—as the state of nature. It is a state of perfect freedom, whereby we order our actions and dispose of our possessions as we see fit. It is a state of equality, "wherein all the power and jurisdiction is reciprocal" and creatures of the same species are "equal one amongst another without subordination or subjection." *See* Locke, *supra* note 469, at 118. The state of nature is only bound by the laws of nature, which proscribe each person from divesting another of the inalienable rights to life, liberty, and property. *Id*. at 119–20.

474. *Id*. at 164.

475. *Id*. at 165.

476. *Id*.

477. *Id*. at 166.

478. Rousseau, *supra* note 470, at 24.

479. Rousseau states that in our corporate capacity "we receive each member as an indivisible part of the whole." *Id*.

480. *Id*.

481. *Id*. at 26.

482. *Id*. at 27.

483. For an explication of the categorical imperative, *see* Kant, *supra* note 471, at 317–24.

484. *Id*. at 324.

485. *Id*. at 329–30.

486. For a discussion of this concept, see *id*. at 334–35.

487. *Id*. at 335.

488. *See generally* I. Kant, *The Philosophy of Law* (2d ed., 1798) (W. Hastie trans./ed., 1887). Kant viewed equality before the law as an a priori principle of a civil state. *See* pt. II of Kant's essay "On the Common Saying: This May be True in Theory, but it does not Apply

in Practice," in *Kant's Political Writings* 74–77, 113–14 (H. Reiss ed., H. Nisbet trans., 1970).

489. For a discussion of the relevance of Rawls's theory to the "society" of states, *see* D'Amato, *International Law and Rawls' Theory of Justice*, 5 Denver J. Int'l L. & Pol'y 525 (1975).

490. Rawls, *supra* note 3, at 11. For an attempt to convert Rawls's test of the parties' subjective preferences into objective mandates of justice, *see* Scanlon, *Preference and Urgency*, 72 J. of Phil. 655 (1975).

491. *Id.*

492. *See id.* at 22, 126–30.

493. *Id.* at 128.

494. *See id.* at 23, 130–36.

495. *Id.* at 131.

496. Rawls explains that generality and universality are distinct. For example, if everyone has to serve the interests of a dictator, there exists the latter but not the former. See *id.* at 132.

497. *Id.* at 135.

498. *Id.*

499. See *id.* at 25, 142–50.

500. *Id.* at 143.

501. *Id.* at 144.

502. *Id.* at 60.

503. *Id.* at 83.

504. *Id.* at 43.

505. *Id.* at 7.

506. *Id.* at 8.

507. *Id.*

508. Parties only reach the question of international justice after having first dealt with the basic structure of social institutions and, second, with natural duties, obligations, and permissions of individuals. The order of progression is supposed to create a coherent set of principles for justice as fairness. And, presumably, by the time the issue of the law of nations is reached, conceptions of international justice are sufficiently circumscribed by the constraints of institutional and individual justice. *See* schematic diagram and discussion, *id.* at 108–11.

509. See *id.* at 58, 377–82. (Rawls considers the situation of a conscientious objector to a war he considers in violation of international law. This leads him to regard the moral basis of the law of nations.)

510. *Id.* at 378.

511. Rawls relies upon J. L. Brierly, *The Law of Nations* chs. IV–V (6th ed., 1963) in stating these basic principles. See *id.* at 378, n. 27. In addition to non-intervention and self-determination, Rawls

also notes the right of collective self-defense, the sanctity of treaties and principles applicable to *jus in bello*. *Id.*

512. Rawls here follows the thoughts of early theorists like Wolff, who wrote in 1749 that "nations are regarded as free persons living in a state of nature." C. Wolff, "Jus gentium methodo scientifica pertractatum" (J. Drake trans.), in 2 *The Classics of International Law* 9 (1934). Upon this view, "states might be conceived as moral beings which are organic wholes with the capacity to realize their nature in the choice and pursuit of ends." *See* C. Beitz, *Political Theory and International Relations* 76 (1979).

513. Rawls, *supra* note 3, at 378.

514. Hobbes, *supra* note 468, at 116–17.

515. *Id.* at 201.

516. For Beitz's analysis of moral skepticism in the international state of nature, *see supra* note 512, at 27–34.

517. Cassese, *supra* note 98, at 144–46. *See also* Halpern, "The Morality and Politics of Intervention," in *Vietnam War and International Law* 39 (R. A. Falk ed., 1968).

518. J. S. Mill, 3 *Dissertations and Discussions: Political, Philosophical and Historical* 238–63 (1873).

519. Hobbes, *supra* note 468, at 115.

520. Charter of the United Nations, *entered into force* Oct. 24, 1945, 59 Stat. 1031, T.S. 993, 3 Bevans 1153.

521. G.A. Res. 2625, 25 U.N. GAOR Supp. (No. 28) at 121, U.N. Doc. A/8028 (1970); G.A. Res. 2131, 20 U.N. GAOR Supp. (No. 14) at 11, U.N. Doc. A/6014 (1965).

522. This is not surprising since "[t]he Assembly has never been able to bring itself to address the extirpation of entire populations— some seven to nine million persons—in Burundi, Kampuchea and Pakistani Bengal." *See* Franck, *Of Gnats and Camels: Is There a Double Standard at the United Nations?*, 78 Am. J. Int'l L. 811, 825 (1984).

523. G.A. Res. 34/22, 34 U.N. GAOR Supp. (No. 46) at 209, U.N. Doc. A/34/36 (1979).

524. The resolution was addressed to both India and Pakistan, but since Pakistani troops were not on Indian soil, it was obviously aimed at New Delhi. G.A. Res. 2793 (XXVI), 26 U.N. GAOR Supp. (No. 29) at 3, U.N. Doc. A/8429 (1971).

525. The Security Council, unable to reach a unanimous consensus among its permanent members, called upon the General Assembly to conduct an emergency special session concerning Soviet intervention in Afghanistan. *See* S.C. Res. 462, 35 U.N. SCOR (Resolutions and Decisions) at 2, U.N. Doc. S/INF/36 (1980). Thereafter,

the General Assembly "strongly deplore[d] the . . . armed intervention in Afghanistan" and "[c]all[ed] for the immediate, unconditional,
and total withdrawal of the foreign troops." G.A. Res. ES-6/2, U.N.
GAOR (6th Emer. Spec. Sess.) Supp. (No. 1) at 2, U.N. Doc.
A/ES-6/L.1 (1980).

526. The World Court ruled that the United States, "by training,
arming, equipping, financing and supplying the *contra* forces or otherwise encouraging, supporting and aiding military and paramilitary activities in and against Nicaragua . . . acted . . . in breach of its
obligation under customary international law not to intervene in the
affairs of another State." *See* Military and Paramilitary Activities, *supra*
note 74, at 146. The General Assembly subsequently passed a resolution calling for "full and immediate compliance" with the judgment.
G.A. Res. 41/31, 41 U.N. GAOR Supp. (No. 53) at 23, U.N. Doc.
A/41/53 (1986).

527. The Security Council failed to act in response to Uganda's
complaint. 31 U.N. SCOR (1939–43rd mtgs.), U.N. Docs. S/PV.
1939–43 (1975).

528. Franck, *supra* note 522, at 811–19.

529. D. Richards, A *Theory of Reasons for Action* 137–38 (1971).

530. Beitz, *supra* note 512, at 92–93. *See also* Cassese, *supra* note
98, at 131–37; Buchheit, *supra* note 374, at 43–137, 216–40, and,
for an early effort to create a legal category of those entitled, *see*
Interpretation of the Convention Between Greece and Bulgaria Respecting Reciprocal Emigration (Question of the "Communities"),
Adv. Op. [1920] PCIJ ser. B, No. 17.

531. Charter of the United Nations, *supra* note 520 at art. 73.

532. Biafra had declared its independence on May 30, 1967.

533. G.A. Res. 1514, 15 U.N. GAOR Supp. (No. 16) at 66–67,
U.N. Doc. A/4684 (1960).

534. *Id.* at arts. 2 and 6.

535. *E.g.*, G.A. Res. 3382, 30 U.N. GAOR Supp. (No. 34) at
84, U.N. Doc. A/10309 (1975).

536. Zimbabwe came into official existence at midnight on April
17, 1980, thus bringing to a close the former white-ruled government
of Rhodesia, which was first established by the United Kingdom under
the Constitution of the Federation of Rhodesia and Nyasaland. *See*
518 H.C. Deb. 996 (1952–53). More generally, *see* Pomerance, *supra*
note 349, and Blay, *Self-Determination versus Territorial Integrity in
Decolonization*, 18 N.Y.U. J. Int'l L. & Pol. 441 (1986).

537. After a new outbreak of killings by anti-government rebels in
late 1982, the Zimbabwean government deployed the army's Fifth
Brigade in Matebeleland North in late January 1983. Amnesty Inter-

national reported allegations of executions, torture, and detention carried out by the Brigade against the Ndebele in its effort to quash the dissidents. *See* Amnesty Int'l, *Country Reports: Africa* 123 (1984). Yet, to Robert Mugabe's credit, his ruling ZANU party has made peace with ZAPU, the opposition party led by the Ndebele leader, Joshua Nkomo. Their alliance, it is hoped, spells the end to ethnic division that has plagued Zimbabwe since independence. *See* N.Y. Times, Dec. 23, 1987, sec. 1, at 3, col. 4. Indeed, a promising sign is seen in the fact that with Mugabe's inauguration as Zimbabwe's first Executive President, Nkomo has also been named Vice President and Second Secretary of Mugabe's party. *See* N.Y. Times, Jan. 1, 1988, sec. 1, at 3, col. 4.

538. For a discussion of U.N. action in Katanga, *see* T. Franck and J. Carey, *The Role of the United Nations in the Congo—A Retrospective Perspective*, in *The Hammarskjold Forums: The Legal Aspects of the United Nations Actions in the Congo* 40–51 (The Ass'n of the Bar of the City of New York Working Paper 525/62/2, 1962). *See also* S.C. Res. 169, 16 U.N. SCOR (Resolutions and Decisions 1961) at 3, U.N. Doc. S/5002 (1961).

539. The separation of the Saar basin or Rhineland from Germany posed a clear conflict with the Wilsonian principle of self-determination, since its four million inhabitants were ethnic Germans. However, the President submitted to geopolitical logic—the creation of a buffer Rhenish Republic would help prevent a German resurgence. The compromise eventually worked out by the powers at the Versailles Peace Conference led to the formation of a Saar territory which was not to be independent but administered through the League of Nations. *See* Seymour, *supra* note 329, at 334–35, 345. *See also* Temperley, *supra* note 323, at 182.

540. Mill, "Considerations on Representative Government," in 19 *Collected Works of John Stuart Mill* 547 (J. Robson ed., 1977).

541. Rawls, *supra* note 3, at 3.

542. R. Keohane, *After Hegemony: Cooperation and Discord in the World Political Economy* 249 (1984). A useful critique of states as subjects of a jurisprudence of justice is found in Skubik, *Two Models for a Rawlsian Theory of International Law and Justice*, 14 Den. J. Int'l L. & Pol'y 231, 236–37, 248–51 (1986).

543. D. Hume, 2 *A Treatise of Human Nature* 277 (A.D. Lindsay intro., 1911) (reprint. 1966).

544. Grotius, *supra* note 466, at 19.

545. Seymour Martin Lipset makes the important point that legitimacy, which is about *process*, has its own morality. It is different, however, from the moral order manifest in justice, because it is a belief in

right *process* rather than in right (substantive) outcomes. Lipset, "Social Conflict, Legitimacy and Democracy," in *Legitimacy and the State* (W. E. Connelly ed., 1984).

546. Convention on the Elimination of All Forms of Discrimination Against Women, U.N.G.A. Res. 34/180 of Dec. 18, 1979, 34 U.N. GAOR Supp. (No. 46) at 193, U.N. Doc. A/Res./34/180; 19 Int'l Legal Mat. 33 (1980). The Convention, as of December 1988 had been ratified by 94 states and signed by 19 more. The reservations permitting discrimination against women in accordance with Muslim religious beliefs are directed at article 9, para. 2, concerning the granting to women of equal rights with men with respect to the nationality of their children; article 16 concerning the equality of women and men in all matters relating to marriage and family relations during marriage and its dissolution "which shall be without prejudice to the rights guaranteed by Islamic Religious Law"; and article 29, para. 2, concerning the right of a State signatory of the Convention to declare its commitment to para. 1 of that article concerning submitting to arbitration any dispute among States regarding the interpretation or application of the Convention. Other reservations apply to articles 2(b) to (f), 5, 6, 10, 11, 13, 15 and 16.

547. N. Machiavelli, *The Discourses* 139 (Walker ed., 1970).

548. *Id.* at 140.

549. E. Pashukanis, *La Théorie générale du droit et la marxisme* 148 (Etudes et Documentation Internationales, 1970 ed.).

550. *E.g.*, Shandro, A *Marxist Theory of Justice?*, 22 Can. J. Pol. Sci. 27 (1989).

551. *Philosophy, Morality and International Affairs* (V. Held, S. Morgenbesser, T. Nagel eds., 1974), at x.

Index

justice, 211–15, 217, 233, 239–40; limitations of the, 9–10; and morality, 214–15; and the national system, 187; and obedience, 8–10, 213–14; and process, 12; and promises, 35; and reciprocity, 199; and right, 11–12; and sovereignty, 9–10; and statehood, 9–10; and symbolic validation, 93
Social conditioning, 13
Social conventions, 37–38
Social regulation, 17
Social scientists, 6–7
Sociological jurisprudence, 7
Sofaer, Abraham D., 69–71, 76, 79
Soft law, 29
Sophist rules: and adherence, 174–75; and coherence, 163, 166, 167, 171–72, 173, 174–75, 178, 180; and determinacy, 74–83, 85–90
South Africa, 112, 122, 126, 133, 135–37, 139–43, 160, 165, 170–71
Sovereign equality, 112–16, 132–33, 138, 176–77
Sovereign immunity, 105–6
Sovereignty: and adherence, 192; and coercion, 21–23, 196; and coherence, 163; and the international system, 9–11, 20, 21–23, 29–30, 39, 48; and law, 29; and legitimacy, 21–22, 39; and the national system, 113–14; and obedience, 21–23, 35–36; and power, 10–11; and the social compact/contract, 9–10; and symbolic validation, 101, 105–6, 112–16; as a teleological concept, 9. *See also* Sovereign equality
Soviet Union: and adherence, 186; and coherence, 176–78; and justice, 224, 241; and self-determination, 162; and symbolic validation, 107–9, 114–15, 120, 124–25, 126, 130–32, 141; and the U.N. veto power, 176–78
Spain, 161
Specificity. *See* Determinacy
Speed limits, 78

Sri Lanka, 172, 173, 229
Stability, 14, 244, 245
State: and the international system, 9–10; and justice, 208–9, 210–11, 222–23, 225–26, 230, 231; and obedience, 8; recognition of a, 8, 123–24; and self-enforcement, 31; and the social compact/contract, 9–10; as a teleological concept, 9; and validation, 8, 112–13, 115. *See also* Recognition
Status, 138–39, 141, 143, 186–93, 196, 200–203, 205
Substantive determinacy, 67
Swan, Donald, 75
Sweden, 159–60
Symbolic validation: and adherence, 97, 106, 107–9; and anachronisms, 106–9; and authority, 123; characteristics of, 92; and coercion, 96; and coherence, 127, 129–30, 134, 136–37, 138–39, 140, 141, 146; and compliance, 92, 96–100, 105–6, 111–12, 127, 128, 129, 133, 138, 141; and consistency, 138–39; and the courts, 129–33; and credentials, 135–37, 138, 141; and determinacy, 123; and diplomacy, 103–5, 109–10, 124; and dissonance, 118, 119–20, 128, 129, 133–34, 136, 137, 139; dual-tier standard for, 140–41, 144; and empirical tests, 117, 119–20, 122; and entitlement, 112–13, 114, 116, 117–18, 122, 127, 134, 135, 136, 139; and equality, 101, 112–16, 119, 132–33, 136, 138; and external/internal references, 139–40; false, 107; and form and function, 116–34; and institutions, 65, 101, 112, 128; and the international system, 100–106; and justice, 96, 232–33, 235; manipulation of, 123–25, 127–28, 135–36, 138; and membership, 135, 141–42; and the national system, 113–14; and obedience, 91–92; and obedience/disobedience, 104–5,